P9-DNJ-227

THE ECONOMIC CHALLENGE OF PERESTROIKA

The Second World

series editor Teodor Shanin
Professor of Sociology, University of Manchester

Forthcoming titles

RURAL RUSSIA UNDER THE NEW REGIME Viktor Danilov
PEOPLES OF THE SOVIET UNION Viktor Kozlov
FIVE DAYS WHICH TRANSFORMED RUSSIA
    Sergei Mstislavskii
IS THERE A FUTURE FOR THE WARSAW PACT?
    Oleg Bogomolov
THE SOCIAL DIMENSION OF THE PERESTROIKA
    Tatiana Zaslavskaya
SEMIOTICS OF CULTURAL HISTORY Yuri Lotman

THE ECONOMIC CHALLENGE OF PERESTROIKA

ABEL AGANBEGYAN

Edited by Michael Barratt Brown
Introduced by Alec Nove
Translated by Pauline M. Tiffen

INDIANA UNIVERSITY PRESS
Bloomington and Indianapolis

U.S. edition published by
Indiana University Press
Tenth and Morton Streets
Bloomington, Indiana 47405

Printed and bound in the United States of America

Library of Congress Cataloging-in-Publication Data

Aganbegian, Abel Gezevich.
  The economic challenge of perestroika

  (Second world series)
  Translated from the Russian.
  1. Soviet Union—Economic policy—1986-
I. Barratt Brown, Michael. II. Title. III. Series.
HC336.26.A42   1988   338.947   88-3000
ISBN 0-253-32093-3

ISBN 0-253-32093-3 cloth

CONTENTS

Map, figures and tables

FOREWORD TO
THE SECOND WORLD

"In the West they simply do not know Russia . . . Russia
in its germination."

Alexander Hertzen

As a publication project *The Second World* pursues an explicit goal,
admits to a bias and proceeds on a number of assumptions. This
should be stated at the outset. The series will aim to let the Soviet
authors and their historical predecessors in tsarist Russia speak with
their own voices about issues of major significance to us and to
them. It will focus particularly on their explorations of their own
society and culture, past and present, but set no rigid boundaries to
these; some of the texts will be more general while others will carry
primary evidence, e.g. memoirs, documents, etc. Many of the texts
have been commissioned to reflect the most recent efforts and the
controversies of Gorbachev's *perestroika*.

To bridge differences of culture and experience each of the books
will carry a substantial introduction by a Western scholar within the
field. Particular care will also be taken to maintain satisfactory
standards of translation and editing.

A word about words. A generation ago the term "Third World"
was coined in its current meaning, to indicate a somewhat imprecise
combination of societal characteristics – the post-colonial experience, under-industrialisation, relative poverty and the effort to
establish an identity separate from the superpowers, the "Bandung
camp".This left implicit yet clear which were the other two
"worlds". It was "us" and "them", those best represented by the
USA and those best represented by the USSR. Much has changed
since, giving the lie to crude categorisations. But in research and the
media, at the UN and on television, the words and the meanings
established in the 1960s are still very much with us. This makes the

title of our project intelligible to all; yet, hopefully, should also make the reader pause for a moment of reflection.

Turning to the invisible rules and boundaries behind our editorial selection, let us stress first the assumption of considerable social continuity between pre-revolutionary and post-revolutionary societies. Present without past is absurd (as is, of course, the treatment of the USSR as simply the Russia of old). Next, to talk of pre-revolutionary Russia/USSR is not simply to talk of the Russians. The country is multi-ethnic, as have been its intellectual achievements and self-evaluations. Yet all the books presented are deeply embedded in Russian language and cultural traditions. Lastly, we shall aim to show Russia/USSR neither as the "goody" nor as the "baddy" but focus attention on the characteristics particular to it.

The Second World is biased insofar as its choice of titles and authors consistently refuses the bureaucratised scholarship and paralytic tongue which has characterised much of the Soviet writing. In other words, it will prefer authors who have shown originality and courage of content and form.

Western perceptions of the Soviet scholarly achievement, especially of its social self-analysis, have been usually negative in the extreme. This was often enough justifiable. Heavy censorship stopped or biased much Soviet research and publications. "Purges" have destroyed many of the best Soviet scholars, with whole disciplines closed on orders from above. The Soviet establishment has excelled in the promotion of safe scholars – the more unimaginative and obedient, the faster many made it to the limelight. However, much of the hostile detachment of the Anglo-Saxon scholarship and the media originated in its own ideological bias, linguistic incompetence and a deeper still layer of mutual miscomprehension. To understand the human experience and thought in a particular social world, one must view it on its own terms – that is, with full awareness of its context – of history, political experience, culture and symbolic meanings. This necessitates the overcoming of stereotypes rooted in one's own experience and a challenge to the most persistent prejudice of them all – the belief that everybody (and everything) is naturally "like us", but somewhat less so (and that the best future mankind can have is to be like us, but even more so).

The bafflement of the mainstream of Western scholarship at the dawn of Gorbachev's reforms has accentuated the collective miscomprehensions of Soviet society. On the one hand stand those who see nothing happening because nothing can happen – "totalitarianism" is not open to any transformation from within. On the other hand stand those to whom the USSR is at long last becoming "like us". Both views miss the most important point, that Soviet society is moving along its own trajectory which can be understood only on its own terms. This makes the need to allow this society, its leaders and its scholars to speak to us in their own voice, an urgent one.

Uniformity and uniformisation are false as perceptions of history and wrong as social goals, but so also is any effort at keeping human worlds apart. This is true for international politics, scholarly endeavour and daily life. Half a century ago a Soviet diplomat, Maxim Litvinov, a survivor of the revolutionary generation which was then going under, addressed the League of Nations to say: "Peace is indivisible." The World War to follow did not falsify this statement, but amended it. Peace proved divisible but only at the heavy price of human peril. The same holds for knowledge.

Teodor Shanin
University of Manchester,
Great Britain

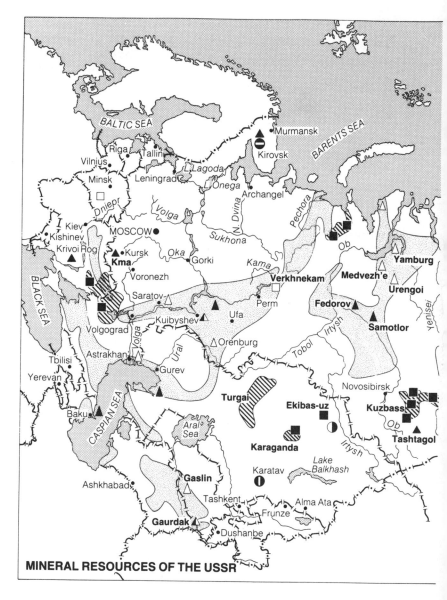

MINERAL RESOURCES OF THE USSR

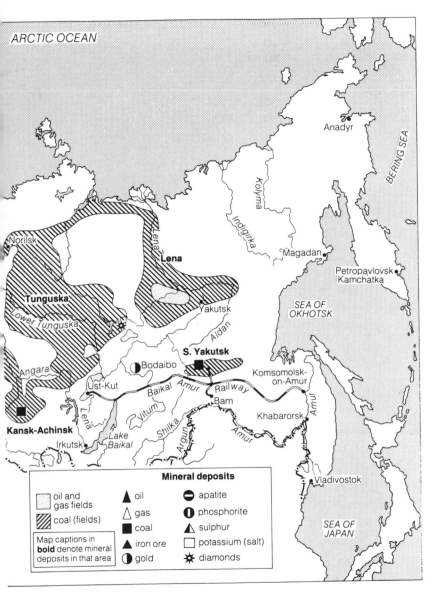

ARCTIC OCEAN

BERING SEA

Anadyr

Kolyma

Indigirka

Lena

Norilsk

Lena

Magadan

Petropavlovsk
Kamchatka

Tunguska

Lower Tunguska

Yakutsk

Aldan

SEA OF
OKHOTSK

Angara

S. Yakutsk

Ust-Kut

Bodaibo

Komsomolsk-
on-Amur

Baikal Amur Railway

Lena

Vitum

Bam

Amur

Khabarorsk

Kansk-Achinsk

Shilka

Argun

Amur

Irkutsk

Lake
Baikal

Vladivostok

SEA OF
JAPAN

Mineral deposits

▦	oil and gas fields	▲ oil	⬤ apatite
▨	coal (fields)	△ gas	◗ phosphorite
		■ coal	◮ sulphur
Map captions in **bold** denote mineral deposits in that area		▲ iron ore	☐ potassium (salt)
		◑ gold	✳ diamonds

INTRODUCTION
Alec Nove

This is an important book. Mikhail Gorbachev, soon after becoming General Secretary, stated that: "the fate of our country, the future of socialism in the world" depends in large measure on how the reform process is tackled. In a world where economic problems worry us all, in east, west and south – a world increasingly interdependent – the efforts of the Soviet leadership to achieve *perestroika* can affect us all. In his capacity as one of the Soviet leadership's principal advisers, Aganbegyan is playing a major role in charting the road that is intended to achieve radical reform, a decisive step towards the modernisation of economy and society. In the pages that follow he puts before us a vivid picture of what has gone wrong, and of the measures required to put things right. His book therefore deserves to be read by anyone interested not only in Soviet affairs, but also in the economics of socialism and in international relations.

Academician Abel Gezevich Aganbegyan was born in Tbilisi, Georgia, in 1932. He graduated in 1955 from the Moscow State Institute of Economics. After a few years' work in the State Committee of Labour and Wages, he was among those who migrated to the new Siberian branch of the Academy of Sciences, in Novosibirsk, in 1961. He played an important part in its Institute of Economics and Industrial Organisation, becoming its director in 1967. Appointed chief editor of its house-journal, known by the acronym EKO, he made of it the brightest and most challenging of the Soviet economic journals. Returning to Moscow in 1985, he became chairman of the Commission for the study of productive forces and resources and the head of the economics section of the Academy of Sciences of the USSR.

He is one of the economists who have been playing a leading role in the preparation of the radical economic reform upon which Gorbachev has launched the Soviet Union. Therefore the present book represents more than the views of its author: this is the kind of voice that the political leadership is hearing, this is the sort of advice they are receiving. Of course, economic advisers are far from being all-powerful; in the Soviet Union or anywhere else there are discordant voices from within the economics profession, and political conservatives may modify substantially the sort of pro-gramme of reform which is here presented. None the less, it is of very real interest to have available both a frank and vivid account of what is wrong with the Soviet economy, and an outline of an alternative model which, the author hopes, is to replace the centralised planning system inherited from Stalin.

Opinions, in and out of the Soviet Union, vary as to the rationality of that system. Was Stalin's despotic rule, with its strict centralisation, the priority of heavy industry, (forcible) collectiviza-tion of agriculture, neglect of elementary human needs – was all this necessary to create the basis of a modern arms industry, which was to save the Soviet Union after the disasters of the German invasion? Or did these brutal methods, and the terror that accompanied them, do more harm than good? Millions of peasants, thousands of army officers, scarce engineers and so many others were done to death. Some Soviet critics now look back at the mixed economy of the New Economic Policy, and criticise Stalin for having eliminated it. Others recall the historic roots of Stalinist methods in Russia's past ("Peter the Great's methods were purely Bolshevik", wrote the philosopher Nikolai Berdyaev). There is no need to enter into these arguments here. Suffice to say that there is widespread agreement about the fact that, whether or not the centralised system conformed to the needs of the USSR fifty years ago, it has become obsolete, a fetter on the forces of production, to borrow a Marxist phrase.

Soviet economists have been pointing out for years that the sheer scale of the decision-making rendered necessary by the very nature of centralised planning was in itself a cause of imbalance, mis-callocation and shortages. And the decisions had to be based on a vast volume of information, which had to be collected, processed and checked. At one time it was thought that computerisation, the development of programming techniques, would or could resolve such problems. Indeed critics of socialism such as Mises and Robbins used to claim that socialist planning could not work because there would be too many simultaneous equations to resolve. In fact Robbins, in a conversation with myself, expressed alarm: he thought that the Soviet system, unlike our own, could generate and define an objective function, a clear aim, a maximand, and then use computers and programming to find an optimal path to the achievement of given objectives.

This proved to be a mistaken view. In the Soviet Union, as in all other countries, a whole number of different objectives are being simultaneously pursued. There was much discussion among Soviet mathematical economists about how to define an objective func-tion, what it is that should be maximised. These was no opera-tionally meaningful result, nor could there be. If the party leadership turns to the economics profession for advice as to what its economic policy should be – and this has been the case – then clearly it cannot be the party's policy that defines the objective, for that is turning in a circle. In any event the simpler and cruder priorities of the first five-year plans have been replaced by much more complex aims. Apart from the continuing themes of energy, metal and arms, much attention has also been focussed on housing, agriculture, consumer goods, trade and many previously neglected services; all this imposed further strain on a planning system originally designed to impose a few key priorities. The demographic consequences of the war underlined the need for labour-saving innovation, higher labour productivity, economy of resources, for what came to be known as "intensive growth".

The reader will find in Aganbegyan's book the many reasons why the centralised systems could not rise to these new challenges. The former director of the Mathematical-Economics Institute, Aca-demician Fedorenko, once quipped that a coherent, fully-checked and disaggregated plan for next year might be ready, with the help of computers, in roughly 30,000 years' time!

The issue of decentralisation was frequently raised, but this could not be the solution so long as plan-fulfilment was the overriding criterion, and the plans were supposed to represent and incorporate the needs of society. A regional or local authority could only be directly informed and concerned with the needs of that locality. The centre then must constantly intervene to prevent other regions from being deprived of resources, as happened after Khrushchev liquidated the central ministries and created the *sovnarkhozy* (regional economic councils), which lasted from 1957 to 1965.

In my own *Economic History of the USSR* the chapter on Brezhnev was headed: "From stability to immobility". Signs were appearing of stagnation, decay; growth declined, remedial action was urgent. The so-called "Kosygin" reforms of 1965 were internally inconsistent and changed little. Further "reforms" announced in 1974 made procedural amendments within the general scheme of centralised planning, without tackling fundamentals. Concerned economists, including Aganbegyan, began sounding the alarm. The need for action was recognised, in words, even by Brezhnev. But the forces of inertia were too strong.

It is not part of my task, in this introduction, to summarize the reform programme which Aganbegyan sets out in his book. Clearly it does represent a truly radical reform, a decisive break with the past. If it is to be implemented, then most economic enterprises in the USSR, most of the time, will be producing for the customers and not for plan-fulfilment statistics. Market forces will play major (though not the sole) role in determining what is to be produced and for whom. The centre will thus be relieved of the intolerable burden of guiding the current operations of enterprise management, of providing the needed material supplies through the bureaucratic system of allocation. Enterprises would stand on their own financial feet. Customers and suppliers will have the right to choose, which implies competition. Competition will also come from an enlarged cooperative sector, and even from some limited private enterprise. At the same time Gorbachev is pressing for growth-acceleration (*uskoreniye*), and the Party congress has adopted an ambitious programme of economic and social transformation through the year 2000, which is outlined in the last chapter of this book. By then the Soviet Union will be a much more modern economy, with massive re-equipment of industry, higher living standards, decent housing for all, and greater freedom too, through *glasnost* and *demokratizatsiya*. All that, of course, on the assumption that the plans will be carried out, and that the radical reform will in fact be implemented.

Are such expectations realistic? How effective would the new economic mechanism be if it were introduced? What are the obstacles to its introduction? No one knows better than Aganbegyan himself that such changes must encounter resistance.

Let us begin by imagining that Aganbegyan's reform plans have been turned into reality. Where might there be problems? Is the scheme as it stands a viable one? In my view there are several question-marks – though I would add at once that I see many virtues in this reform model. The first question concerns the reward of labour. It is to depend directly on the financial performance of the enterprise. However, even if the promised radical reform of prices takes place, many instances are bound to occur where higher productivity can coexist with a financial loss. It is true that the reform model includes the principle of the election of management, and one reason for this (desirable) innovation is precisely the fact that wages would depend on financial results, and so it would be unfair for workers' incomes to suffer from managers whom they do not trust and whom they have had no part in appointing. In a relatively small work-group this could have an effect, but in an enterprise employing several thousands there could be quite serious tensions: those who have worked hard and produced more would surely quite understandably resent it if their wages were cut because, for instance, of some fault in design or inadequate marketing.

A second problem or gap concerns capital investment. As can be seen in Chapter 5, it is envisaged that a large part of investments be financed out of retained profits and bank credits. However, many instances are bound to arise when a firm has considerable profits but has no good reason to invest them in expanding its own productive capacity (for example because it is known that investments have already been made by other firms in the same line of business). A capital market of some kind seems to be needed, permitting such an enterprise to invest (buy bonds in?) another enterprise. In the pre-reform situation the profits would in all probability have been taken away by the ministry, but under the new rules it will not be allowed to do this – in which case there must be some alternative way of finding the mose effective use for the money.

A more general but fundamental issue is the precise dividing line between plan and market. It is still far from clear just what the plan will contain, the range of subjects which would still be within the competence of the central planning organs and ministries. An optimal decision-making structure is by no means easy to define. The level of decision-making must in some degree depend on the sector: thus electricity must surely be much more centralised than, say, clothing or fruit production. There are those, within and outside the Soviet Union, who deny the possibility of an effective mix between plan and market: one recalls the author of an article in *Novyi Mir* who thought it was like being "a little bit pregnant". This is not my view. But there may be much trial and error before the right mix is found.

For the reform to function, it has first to be implemented. Many Soviet economists are frank about the "transitional" difficulties. One of these is intimately linked with the aim of growth-acceleration planned through the year 2000. It could contribute to the persistence of shortages (*defitsit*, of which more in a moment), and also to the preservation of imposed growth-targets (for how does one measure growth-acceleration?). Thus, although gross-output (*val*) is no longer supposed to be a plan indicator, the ministries impose it on their enterprises, "with the object of showing a claimed acceleration" (*pokaznogo uskoreniya*), to cite *Pravda* of 21 July 1987. Similarly, the desirable aim of reducing the wasteful use of energy and metal can easily turn into the imposition of detailed targets for economy, with all the inflexibilities and inconsistencies which such compulsory plan-indicators have caused.

Overcoming shortages is a precondition for the effective implementation of reform. This is required for the normal functioning of the production process; it is a precondition of abandoning material allocation and passing to "trade in means of production". It is also essential for effective labour incentives, since there is little point in earning more if the desired goods and services are not available. There is now a sizeable literature on the causes of shortage (for example Ya. Kornai's *Economics of Shortage*, published in both East and West). Gorbachev himself has noted the dilemma: if the material allocation system is to be abolished only after shortages have been overcome, then it will be necessary to wait for ever since the allocation system itself generates and reproduces shortage. So there is a vicious circle element here, or the Soviet equivalent of "Catch 22".

A similar vicious circle affects labour. Without harder work, better discipline and sobriety, higher living standards are not possible, but some workers do not see why they should work harder until there is more for them to buy, though clearly this cannot happen at once. There is also fear that the reduction in official vodka supplies will be compensated by illegal distillation (*samogon*).

Perhaps more fundament is the problem of stimulating responsibility and enterprise among a management accustomed to obeying orders, of which much is written in the Soviet Union. This is an essential part of the *perestroika* of the human spirit, which is an integral element in the whole reform process, and no one pretends that it is a simple matter. One consequence has been noted, which can adversely affect transition to reform: priority for state orders (known as *goszakazy*) is to be compulsory, at least in the first years, to ensure that top-priority needs are met; while the rest of a given enterprise's productive capacity is to be available for free negotiation with customers. Many managers, reluctant to launch themselves on the unknown sea of freely-negotiated contracts, are seeking as many of these state orders as possible, in the hope of ensuring priority supplies. The effect could well be the preservation of much of the existing system, not because (or not only because) planners and ministries seek to retain their powers, but through pressure from "below".

Then of course a radical reform of the theory and practice of prices is indispensable, if the financial profit-orientated autonomy of enterprises is to have point and meaning. This not only involves grasping the nettle of raising the highly-subsidised prices of basic foodstuffs and also house rents, but equally allowing many millions of prices to be settled by negotiation between the parties to a contract. There is still lack of clarity about what sort of price control there will be, and the amount of flexibility that will be allowed. This also links with the problem of shortage: unless it is overcome, there is a clear danger that free prices would rise sharply.

Much is also being written about bureaucratic habits and resistance to change. Naturally, those party and state officials whose jobs may be rendered redundant by the reform cannot be expected to welcome it. They try to find support in ideology, in the belief that the onward march of socialism is inherently inconsistent with the strengthening of the market mechanism. An example of how such considerations affect reform implementation can be cited from agriculture: the Party leadership has clearly enunciated a policy of encouraging private vegetable- and fruit-growing; yet, according to *Voprosy Ekonomiki* of July 1987, local officials have been arbitrarily limiting the planting of early vegetables, and even going so far as to use bulldozers to destroy private greenhouses! So strong is the belief that private money-making, even if due to legitimate labour, is to be deplored and obstructed. It will take time to change human attitudes, at all levels.

Another contradiction is between reform and democratisation. The reform process is being imposed from above, against considerable passive resistance. Its success depends on willing support from below. To achieve this Gorbachev has been introducing real elections, for local Party and local Soviet institutions, as well as for managerial appointments. But this raises the question of the role of the ruling Party: the *nomenklatura* system gives Party bodies the decisive voice in appointments, including of those nominally elected. How is this form of Party control to be reconciled with the announced democratisation? Is it that the Party will now nominate more than one candidate per electoral district? What possibility will there be for the voters to reject such nominees? Much is still uncertain. Gorbachev had spoken several times of the bad habit of party officials of interfering with the management of factory and farm. Yet if they are to be held responsible should anything go wrong within their sector, how can they refrain from interfering? A new balance needs to be found between political guidance and managerial autonomy. This also affects the implementation of contracts: too often in the past they were regarded as "an empty formality" (as one Soviet source put it), with priority given to obeying orders from above.

Another difficulty arises from the impossibility of making a drastic change in planning methods all at once, and from the contradictions which inevitably occur when change is gradual. For example, enterprises cannot be expected to stand on their own financial feet, and aim at profits, without a radical reform of prices; and they cannot freely exercise their power to choose outputs unless they can choose inputs, i.e. until there is trade in means of production. Price reform, in turn, cannot have the desired effect of balancing demand and supply of materials if profit does not replace plan-fulfilment as the key success indicator, since plans are often expressed in aggregate value terms, and so high-priced inputs can actually be welcomed because they increase these aggregate values (*val*). It must be added that *val* as a target has been repeatedly condemned, and has none the less shown remarkable powers of resurrection; we have seen this in connection with the measurement of growth-acceleration, i.e. of fulfilling growth-targets.

The preceding pages are not meant to be purely negative. This author believes, in agreement with Aganbegyan, that reform is urgent and should proceed along the lines he indicated. In fact I cannot resist citing an article of my own, written ten years ago, entitled "The economic problems of Brezhnev's successors" (*Washington Papers* Vol. 6, 1978, reprinted in my *Socialism, Economics and Development*, London, 1986). In it I imagined a report of a reform committee headed by none other than Aganbegyan himself. Many of his real recommendations are to found there. I certainly hope that the process will be successful. But the task is a formidable one, and it is only right to say so.

However, the readers should peruse the text of the real Aganbegyan and judge for themselves.

AUTHOR'S PREFACE

We live in an interesting period of major transformation in the world.

Soviet society is on the move. In the development of the Soviet economy and other spheres of life a turning point has arrived, a period when there is a reassessment of values which will lay the foundation for the future.

I am an economist and naturally it is hard for me to assess the whole depth and all the dimensions of the *perestroika* – the revolutionary renewal occurring in Soviet society. A fresh wind of change is apparent everywhere. An important change in thinking and in the psychology of the people has led to new approaches to international politics, ideology and economics.

This book is about the *perestroika* of the economy, its problems and the tasks involved. It must be understood that we now find ourselves at the very beginning of a path we have chosen towards the acceleration of the socio-economic development of the country and the transformation of our economic base. Indeed the qualitative changes taking place do not constitute a short-term campaign but a strategic, long-term economic policy.

The *perestroika* of the economy is still proceeding with difficulty and with some pain. There are positive changes for the better, although as yet no major breakthrough. Furthermore, we are interpreting the current situation very critically. Nevertheless, the recognition that there is still much to do, to alter and to transform gives us new energy.

I have tried here to share truthfully and faithfully with the reader my thoughts and reflections on this ongoing *perestroika* of the economy. I like to start from the facts when looking at the tendencies of economic development. As a result, in the book a seemingly somewhat excessive amount of factual material may have been introduced. In doing this I was guided by Lenin's idea that "Science requires facts not dogmas".

Perestroika of the economy is many-faceted. It affects all branches, sectors and spheres of the national economy and touches the whole population. Economic and social processes are, naturally, interwoven. This has made it necessary to discuss the several aspects of *perestroika* in the book and to consider many concepts: the acceleration of socio-economic development, the transition of the national economy to intensive development, the new scientific and technological changes, investment and structural policies; and to examine in detail the various aspects of the radical reform of management and of the whole economic structure, to touch on *glasnost* and democracy as relevant to the economy and on the problems of the country's external economic relations. Particular attention has been focussed on social problems, the standard of living and lifestyle of the Soviet people. Moreover, can the Soviet Union sustain a new spiral of the arms race? I have also tried to answer such questions. The most difficult task for me was to present a picture of the future of our country, a glimpse into the 21st Century, the third millenium. The last chapter has been written in place of a conclusion.

I will state openly that I am a supporter of *perestroika*. Our country, our people, together with its professional economists, have long suffered for this *perestroika* and perhaps to a certain degree have prepared for it and laid its foundations. Before our eyes there is occurring what we dreamed about during the dark period of stagnation, apathy and self-glorification. What is happening in our country now is demanded by the facts of life and desired by the majority of the working people. The whole country is gradually being drawn into the *perestroika*, as democratisation is taking place of all areas of life. In this democratisation above all we see an assured widening and deepening of *perestroika* leading on to its final completion in the future.

I would like to end this preface with the anxious words of our leader, Mikhail Gorbachev, who has said "There is nowhere for us to retreat".

THE ECONOMIC
CHALLENGE OF
PERESTROIKA

1 THE CHALLENGE OF *PERESTROIKA*

The new economic strategy of development for our country proclaimed by M. Gorbachev in April 1985 at the Plenary meeting of the Central Committee of the Communist Party of the Soviet Union (CPSU)[1]. is summed up in the new political concepts of *"uskorenie"* (acceleration), *"perestroika"* (restructuring) and *"glasnost"* (openness).

At the root of this new economic strategy lies the concept of *uskorenie*, the acceleration of social and economic development. This revolutionary strategy is in contrast to the tendency of *zamedlenie*, the slowing down of development of the last 15 years. Figure 1 shows the rate of growth of basic general social and economic indices of development over 15 years to 1985 and projected increase for consumption and accumulation (in figures of percentage growth by five-year period).

---

[1] The Congress of the Communist Party of the Soviet Union (CPSU) elects a Central Committee which meets in Plenary session, and elects a smaller body, the Polit Bureau, and a secretariat to direct the Party's work between Plenary meetings. Mikhail Gorbachev is General Secretary of the Central Committee. Henceforth in this text Plenary refers to the plenary meetings of the Central Committee. (ed.)

Figure 1   Growth rates of national income in the USSR over five-year periods, 1966–2000

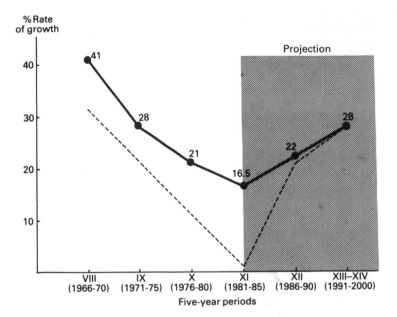

The continuous line signifies indices of growth of national income according to official statistical data. This shows that in three five-year periods from 1971–85 the rate of growth of national income fell nearly 2.5 times. Growth fell both relatively and absolutely. Moreover, it must be taken into account that in the period 1981–85, a part of the growth in national income was obtained through the excess of foreign imports into the USSR over exports. At the same time, to calculate such an index of change in national income in comparable prices (by volume) an index of price increases is used. In my opinion, Soviet price statistics are inadequate and insufficiently account for hidden price increases through changes in the range of products, replacing cheaper with more expensive goods without a corresponding improvement in their consumer quality. If a more realistic index is employed, the rate of growth of the national income and of other indicators of development will be lower than that shown in official statistical publications.

I have therefore tried to show on the graph (dotted line) a more accurate picture of the rate of growth of national income. It is obvious from the graph that in the period 1981–85 there was practically no economic growth. The Unprecedented stagnation and crisis occurred, during the period 1979–82, when production of 40% of all industrial goods actually fell. Agriculture declined (throughout this period it failed to reach the 1978 output levels). The use of productive resources sharply declined and the rate of growth of all indicators of efficiency in social production slowed down: in effect the productivity of labour did not increase and return on capital investment fell, aggravating the fall in the capital-output ratio (*fondootdacha*[2]). Then, towards the end of the 1981–85 period it became possible to improve the situation somewhat. But overall, the 1981–85 plan appeared not to be fulfilled and the country fell into a serious economic situation.

Negative tendencies developed in many sectors, stagnation began and economic imbalances intensified. In these circumstances in March 1985 the Central Committee elected as its General Secretary Mikhail Gorbachev, a young, dynamic leader, university-educated, highly cultured and with a deep professional understanding of the country's economic problems. A new strategy of development by acceleration was worked out in just over a month of intense work, based on previous research.

The quantitative side of this acceleration is evident from the second half of the graph. If one proceeds from the official statistics of 1981–85, the rate of growth of the national income should rise on average by an annual 3% from 1981 to 1985 (16.5% in the five years) up to 4% in the current 1986–90 period (22% in the five years) and to 5% or more in the 1990s (28% in the five years). 3% – 4% – 5% is the quantitative formula of acceleration. If one takes into consideration the actual situation, the stagnation of the economy in 1981–85, then in effect from a zero growth rate we must achieve a radical leap to a 4%–5% rate of growth. The real rate of growth of national income according to the calculations of the author, indicated by the dotted line on the graph, effectively coincides with the projected figures of accelerated growth in the future. This requires explanation.

[2] *Fondootdacha* The indicator of the capital-output ratio characterises the increase in output in relation to each unit of capital added (ICOR). It is expressed by the sum total of production expressed in roubles per one rouble of investment. The rate of growth of this indicator is calculated by the change in volume of products and capital funds, valued in fixed prices.

The methodology of our official statistics calculates national income without incorporating the service sector, while according to UN methodology and that of most countries the service sector is counted in the measurement of national income. Including a calculation for the service sector required no serious amendment to the previous national income growth rate insofar as the share of services in the USSR is very low, and its growth rate in 1981–85 did not exceed the general rate of growth of the national income.

Things are different now, however. According to the current 1986–90 plan the service sector will grow at a higher rate, approximately double that of the total national income, and its weight will therefore also grow significantly. If calculations are made according to western methodology, then all things being equal, the real rate of growth of national income of the USSR will be notably higher than the official indices, although, as already noted above, the low rate of growth of the price indices must be taken into account. Evidently, these contradictory tendencies in the 1986–90 period will balance each other out, especially in the 1990s. Therefore 4%–5% growth of national income according to our plan for the future can be seen to be justified by objective indicators.

So far we have been speaking about the *quantitative* side of the concept of acceleration in the country's development. The term "acceleration" is used precisely in this sense by mathematicians to characterise the rate of growth. But here the meaning of "acceleration" has a different socio-economic sense, which includes not only quantitative but qualitative aspects. Moreover, the qualitative side of the concept of acceleration is more important than the quantitative because it includes the *transition to a new quality of growth* in the Soviet economy. The current structure of the economy of the USSR is backward and conservative. Within it mining and agriculture occupy exaggerated positions, and in contrast manufacturing industry and the processing of raw materials are insufficiently developed. Even worse developed is the so-called tertiary sector, the service sector. In the same way the quality, efficiency, competitiveness of goods produced is universally low. There is a high proportion of obsolete production. The range of goods and services available substantially diverges from effective demand and does not satisfy real social needs. Both the branches providing for consumption and for what one might call welfare services have seriously fallen behind, as has the whole social sector.

It is naturally this obsolete structure of production that in many ways determines the content of growth of the real product. The future is another matter. We intend to make major changes in the structure of the economy, to make it more progressive, efficient and socially oriented by aiming at the satisfaction of social needs and the increased welfare of the people. Therefore the content of the projected growth of social production will be radically changed. We will increase production of high quality competitive products, the share of mining will sharply fall and the extent of processing will increase. The proportion of machine construction will grow especially rapidly and within it the scientific branches, and above all the information industry.

A new quality of growth will appear throughout this process. It will become visible in two main ways. Firstly, in the major change in the factors and sources of this growth. In the past 15 years the economy has primarily developed through extensive factors, through the absorption by industry of more and more new resources. In future it is envisaged that the economy will transfer to intensive development, i.e. development based on increased efficiency and improved quality. Thus the main source of economic growth will be through scientific technical progress.

Secondly, the new quality of growth will be expressed in the accentuation of the social direction of our economic development. Everything connected with the satisfaction of the various needs of the people will receive preferential treatment. A sharp about-turn in the economy will be realised. In the past, the branches of the economy directly connected with the satisfaction of the needs of the people were developed belatedly and their relative importance declined. Their proportion will rise for example in the general volume of capital investment in the national economy.

In speaking here about the renewal of our economic life through accelerated growth, I would note that acceleration of socio-economic development embraces not only the sector of economics, but affects the whole of society. This does not mean a short-term campaign or an acceleration during, let us say, just the next five years. This is a long-term strategy, not just until the end of the century but for at least the next 20–30 years. Thus the programme of the CPSU, the new wording of which was accepted at the 27th Congress is directed at the whole of this era. Running through this programme is the concept of the acceleration of the long-term socio-economic development of the country.

To guarantee advance in our society as a whole, *perestroika* must be realised in the economy. This is a new term in our political and economic practice. Formerly in the Soviet Union, the notion of "perfection" of the economy was current. *Perestroika* is somewhat juxtaposed to this. Perfection implies the improvement of individual aspects and elements of the economy. Here one starts from the premise that the economic mechanism reflects overall the conditions and tasks of development and needs only to be directed, improved and perfected. This is, so to speak, an evolutionary path of change.

Perestroika is different. It signifies profound qualitative changes. *Perestroika* is inevitable when existing economic conditions do not respond to new conditions, formed by the needs of the development of society and the demands of the future. Here it is necessary to change the economic system, to transform and renew it fundamentally. For this transformation restructuring is necessary not just of individual aspects and elements, but of the whole economic system, all aspects and all elements together, in order to achieve a qualitative leap. The essence of the matter is that this is a revolutionary form of change in contrast to an evolutionary form. The term *perestroika* expresses a revolutionary qualitative transformation. This term is many-sided, synonymous in many ways with terms such as radical reform, major reconstruction, radical change, transition to new quality and a breakthrough.

Perestroika in our society affects everything and everyone. It is universal, many-sided and all-embracing. It is not only in the economy that profound reforms are being undertaken. We are also rebuilding our political system, ideology, party work – the whole superstructure rooted in the economic base of society. As an economist I will speak of *perestroika* in the economy. It should be emphasised that it is extraordinarily important that economic reform does not occur in isolation from other sectors of social life but strengthens the transformation of these sectors.

In which directions then is *perestroika* being realised in the economy?

The way I see it there are five major aspects, which I will take one by one.

TRANSITION TO INTENSIVE DEVELOPMENT

We have set ourselves the task of accelerating the socio-economic development of the country in conditions of declining growth of the resources used up in production. In the past, to a considerable degree our economic growth occurred through significant increases in the use of these resources. The Soviet Union is enormous, and rich in resources, and it was natural to develop through extending the involvement in production of the work-force, of fuel and raw materials, of capital investment and funds. If you take a typical post-war five-year period, then usually in these five years the basic application of funds and capital investment increased $1^1/_2$ times, the extraction of fuel and raw materials by 25%–30%, and a further 10–11 million people were recruited into the national economy, a large proportion of whom moved into new branches of production. This was characteristic of the whole period let us say from 1956 to 1975. The last five-year period which involved a large growth in the use of resources was in 1971–75. In that period a composite index for the increase of all resources used in production showed a growth of 21%.

In the following chapters I shall dwell in detail on the method of calculation of this composite index and its component parts. But now it is important for us to present a picture of the overall plan. Thus after 1975, because of a range of mainly objective factors, growth in the use of resources began to decline fairly sharply. The increase of *labour resources* had slowed by 3 to 4 times because the country began to feel the demographic impact of the war. Besides this, there lies ahead a significant redistribution of the numbers of workers from branches of industry into the service sector – education, health etc. If earlier we gained a quarter of all growth in production through quantitative growth, then in the 1986–90 period it is the first time in Soviet history that the increase in production has to be met by growth in the productivity of labour, for the numbers in these branches will not grow. In the 1990s the rate of growth of labour productivity will exceed the growth of production so that some of those involved in branches of production will be freed and transferred to those branches providing services to the population.

Our future plans anticipate that in the 15-year period to the year 2000, with the intended doubling in the national income, the growth of productivity of social labour in the national economy will be of the order of 2.3 to 2.5 times. This means that the number of workers in branches of production will substantially fall. By way of comparison we can introduce the figures of 1981–85. During this period national income increased 1.8 times, the number of workers by 15% and labour productivity 1.6 times. As is evident we must, through accelerated growth of productivity, compensate for the fall in the number of workers and besides this, ensure a rising rate of growth of national income. In this way a trebling of the growth in productivity is anticipated. This would be unprecedented in Soviet history.

Yet more striking are changes in the *extraction of fuel and raw materials*. In the 1971–75 period the volume of output of the mining industry increased by 25% but only by 8% in 1981–85. This decline in growth by a third was mainly connected with the worsening of the geological and economic conditions of mining. With its large-scale mining industry, currently the largest in the world, the Soviet Union is fairly rapidly exhausting the most accessible of its natural resources. To maintain levels of extraction it is necessary to dig deeper, to discover new deposits and to transfer to less favourable fields. The fuel and raw material base in the inhabited regions of the country is already unable to meet our requirements and in many of them the volume of extraction is declining. It is necessary therefore to discover new deposits in the north and eastern regions, to construct transport links, to create new towns and develop territories and attract the population there. All this, naturally, does not come cheap. As a result the cost of fuel and raw materials is growing. The capital investment allocated is growing especially rapidly and the ecological demands in the development of the mining industry are becoming increasingly strict.

Technical progress has been proceeding rapidly in the sphere of more rational use of resources. It became clear that it is cheaper to save one tonne of fuel than to extract it. By maintaining stable levels of extraction of fuel and raw materials, an increasingly large part of the additional need for them must be satisfied through economising and cutting average fuel costs.

In the 1986–90 period two thirds of additional needs are being covered by better use of resources. In the 1990s, in our opinion, this proportion will be up to 75%–80%. Thus the growth in extraction will decline in the future. This is a worldwide tendency that is also characteristic of the Soviet Union. Here too we must transfer from the extensive path of unrestrained increase in the size of fuel and raw material requirements to a more intensive use of resources and more effective economies.

It should also be taken into account that the USSR is perhaps the one country in the world the greater part of whose fuel and raw material requirements is met through domestic production, not imports. Moreover, occupying as it does one sixth of the earth's land surface and being rich in natural resources, the USSR exports, mainly to the socialist countries, oil, gas, timber and many other raw materials. There is neither the opportunity nor the need to behave like the developed capitalist countries in meeting their fuel and raw material supplies. If one of these countries needs additional quantities of coal or non-ferrous metals, it purchases them as a rule from underdeveloped countries, investing capital there when necessary, creating its own companies there or mixed joint-stock companies etc. We cannot behave in this way.

Our approach relates not only to raw materials but, to a certain extent, to labour also. Any shortage of scientists or highly qualified specialists in the USA has been resolved through "recruiting" candidates from other countries through the attraction of higher salaries. Turkish and Yugoslav workers were attracted to West Germany when additional unskilled labour was needed. When this need ended and unemployment began to rise, it is well known that foreign workers were immediately discriminated against. Such a course also is unacceptable to us

In the last decade the rate of growth of *capital investment* has fallen sharply. See Table 1. This also led to a reduction in the growth of the capital stock. Earlier it was increasing by 50% or more every five years, in the 1981–85 period by 37%, and in 1986–90 a growth rate of roughly 30% is planned. Overall by the five-year period 2001–05, calculations indicate that the sum total of capital stock must have doubled roughly in line with the growth of the national income. For comparison we can point to the fact that in the previous 15 years (1971–85) with a 1.8 times increase in the national income, capital stock trebled.

This comparison shows that the capital output ratio has sharply fallen with every five-year period, on average by 14%. In other words for every rouble introduced into the capital stock there has been less and less production, and less and less good use has been made of it. Now this unfavourable tendency must be overcome. In the period 1986–90 the fall in this capital output ratio will slow down, by the mid-1990s this indicator will stabilise and thereafter it is intended the ratio will increase.

Table 1: *Growth of national income, resources and efficiency in the USSR by 5-year periods, 1971–2000* (all figures are of % growth over five years)

Five-year period	Growth rates over the five-year period				
	CAPITAL	RESOURCES	EFFICIENCY	NATIONAL INCOME	AGRICULTURE
ACTUAL					
IX '71-75	41	21	7	28	13
X '76-80	29	13	8	21	9
XI '81-85	17	9	7.5	16.5	6
PLANNED					
XII '86-90	30	7	15	22	14 plus
XIII '91-95 } XIV '96-2000 }	30	5–6	22–24	28	

Thus we must restructure from an extensive to an intensive structure of economy in all sectors. To do this, efficiency in the use of resources is expected almost to double, both to compensate for declining resource growth and to ensure acceleration.

What do concrete calculations reveal? Table 1 and Figure 2 show the rate of growth of national income and the growth of resources (composite index), beginning with 1971–75, the last five-year period in which a large growth in use of resources was recorded.

These figures are based on official data. If my amendments are used again, then the fall up to 1985 was greater still. Even if we take the official indices, the tendency is quite persistent. Efficiency in the use of resources is shown on the graph by the differential between the readings for the rate of growth of the national income and for the growth of resources. This area on the graph is shaded. From the table and graph we can see that a certain inertia occurred in economic development with the predominance of extensive methods and the slowing down of the growth in efficiency.

In the 1971–75 period three quarters of economic development arose from extensive means, in the 1976–80 period two thirds and in the 1981–85 period roughly three fifths. This is the only visible structural improvement, taking into account that with each five-year period the general rate of economic development fell. Overall in the 15-year period we can speak basically of the predominance of extensive over intensive factors of growth: two thirds economic growth occurring through growth of resources and only one third through increased efficiency.

Figure 2   Sources of growth of national income in the USSR – productive resources and efficiency indicators over five-year periods, 1971–2000

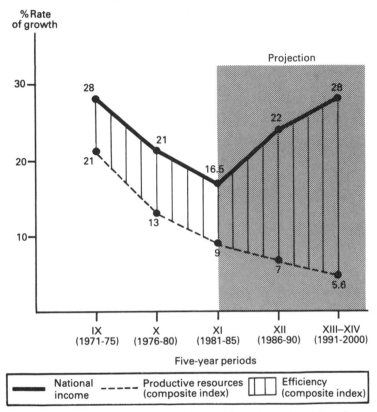

That the situation must change in a profound way is evident from the graph. In 1986–95 we envisage the acceleration of the rate of growth of the national income with a continuing reduction in the growth in the input of resources. The divergence of the two lines on the graph therefore will grow sharply and we must guarantee faster increases in efficiency than in the rate of growth of national income. The details of the changes that are envisaged are shown in Table 1, which has an additional column for growth in agricultural output.

The achievement of these faster rates of growth in efficiency will undoubtedly be extremely difficult. How then do we intend to overcome such gigantic negative tendencies in the rate of growth of efficiency and to attain a qualitative change for the better?

One possibility is the *mobilisation of organisational, economic and social reserves and potential* through better use of existing resources and equipment; the reinforcing of discipline and order and the increase of responsibility; the strengthening of people's interest in the results of their work, their qualifications and education. Through better attitudes to work, enthusiasm and creativity, better organisation and management and appropriate technology, it will be possible to achieve a rise in productivity, economies of fuel and raw materials, better use of equipment and at the same time to raise the quality of goods.

Use of these resources and of this potential is a very immediate issue. The experience of many work collectives and the practice of implementing economic reforms in the past in the Soviet Union and in other socialist countries points to these areas of potential growth. A basic instrument for mobilising this potential is the *perestroika* of management, strengthening interest in the final results of labour and raising the quality of organisation and management. In this the emphasis on the needs of people is of great significance. The more care that is taken over the conditions of work and lifestyle of working people, the better they work. Mobilisation of these organisational economic reserves is especially important in the first stages of acceleration, so that growth of cost effectiveness and quality can be reached in the short-term, whereas *perestroika* of the structure of production needs time. Other things should however be considered. The potential for raising future efficiency given the existing productive technical base and qualifications of workers will decline as these reserves are increasingly mobilised. Possibilities are also limited by existing technical levels of production.

Here is a typical example: the ZIL-130 150 hp 5-tonne lorry requires 29 litres of fuel per 100km according to the planned rate of consumption, but in fact it often needs 35–40 litres. The engine is labour-intensive to maintain, has many lubricating points, is not very powerful and the weight-bearing capacity of the trailer is limited. Of course, with a better attitude to work it could function better and more efficiently: for example, by making the routes used more economic to lower fuel consumption, being more careful with the engine and extending its operational life before capital repairs are required etc. But all these reserves and possibilities are limited by the technical design of the vehicle itself. The limits of organisational, economic and social reserves are clear.

Another issue is *scientific technological progress*. If we modify this vehicle from use of petrol to diesel, the consumption of fuel, even for a more powerful engine, could be halved. Additionally, the weight-bearing capacity of the trailer could be increased and the lorry could run two to three times longer prior to service, through having less lubricating points. The potential for such scientific technological progress in the future is unlimited. Cost effectiveness can be increased not just by percentages but several times over, so that by more intensive production growth can be accelerated. We place great weight on this. But to modify old technology it is necessary to convert to mass production, and to implement technical reconstruction throughout industry and its branches. We recognise the high cost effectiveness of a diesel ZIL, but in order to achieve this, the Moscow Vehicle Factory must be restructured, and the old machinery replaced. This requires time and large capital investment.

Therefore it is very important not to contrast these two means of raising efficiency – the organisational changes and scientific technological progress – but organically to combine them. We can expect initial acceleration, stimulus and development of the economy in the near future mostly through organisational, economic and social factors. We must begin technical reconstruction, raise the level of Soviet machine-building and adapt to mass production the new, more cost effective technology and begin to spread it to an increasing number of branches. Having started acceleration through organisational and economic factors, efficiency will be further developed and extended by scientific technological progress.

Besides this, the mobilisation of organisational, economic and social reserves is very important for obtaining efficiency in the use of the new technology. Indeed the new technology requires that people take greater interest in its use and at higher levels of organisation and management . Often this technology is more expensive and can give results only when it is fully and intensively used by qualified personnel.

Technological progress is many-sided. It includes an evolutionary process in the perfection of technology as well as revolutionary, generational changes in technology i.e. in the transition to totally new technological systems. In the last fifteen to twenty years in the Soviet Union the evolutionary way of technological progress has prevailed. Progress was sluggish and poorly reflected in the growth of efficiency in the economy. Existing technology was being renewed slowly, old systems were retained, equipment became obsolete and as a consequence, efficiency and growth rates declined. The renewal of machinery and equipment and of the whole capital stock of actual enterprises was only taking place at a rate of 2% to 3% per year.

The idea of acceleration of the socio-economic development of the country requires a qualitatively different approach. Therefore we have fundamentally altered our scientific technological policy, laying great emphasis on revolutionary forms of progress, on major technological reconstruction of machine building and on a high rate of planned renewal of machinery and the rapid dismantling of obsolete departments and their replacement by new, appropriate science and technology. As an example, in the Soviet machine building sector in the 1981–85 period only 9% of all equipment was renewed, while in the 1986–90 period 40% will be changed. This will mean a rise in the annual rate of planned renewal of the range of machinery produced from 3.1% in 1985 to 13% in 1990. If, moreover, in 1985 only 29% of machine building production has been up to best international standards, in 1990, with this high rate of planned renewal and with the introduction of a whole new generation of technology, we hope to have arrived at a figure of 80%–90% being up to worldwide standards.

This will require, of course, a major redistribution of capital investment and other resources into machine building and the guarantee of the priority development of this branch. Whereas in the 1981–85 period the volume of capital invested in machine building grew by a total of 24%, now in the 1986–90 period the plan is to ensure a growth of 80%. These new approaches are being realised through the new structure of investment proposed. The proportion of capital investment directed at the technical reconstruction and renewal of existing capacity has been raised sharply and the share for the construction of new enterprises reduced. Earlier on, a little over one third of capital investment went on technical reconstruction. In the 1986–90 period more than half of all capital investment is earmarked for this. Correspondingly, the structure of capital investment in production is changing, and the proportion accounted for by equipment and machines within it is substantially rising. The volume of construction work is falling.

STRENGTHENING SOCIAL PROVISION

In the Soviet Union an unjustifiable gap has opened up between industrial power, science, culture and the educational level of the population on the one hand, and the level of satisfaction of the material and social needs of the population on the other. In the beginning this situation was associated primarily with our difficult history and the destruction wrought during the First World War and the Civil War. It was necessary to rebuild the economy. The country was backward, agrarian, and without advanced heavy and armament industries. In conditions of imperialist encirclement and of political pressure we had, in the shortest time possible, to undertake the country's industrialisation and create a modern industry. Events showed that the course towards industrialisation was the correct one.

In the Second World War, 20 million lives and one third of the nation's capital stock were lost. It was followed by years of rebuilding. Simultaneously, the expensive problems of unravelling the secrets of the atomic bomb, and the creation of a rocket defence shield had to be undertaken to guarantee the peaceful labour of the Soviet people from the growing threat, above all from the USA. In these conditions energies and resources were concentrated on the development of heavy industry and armaments, and what was allocated to the development of welfare services and to raising the standard of living of the people was insufficient. Even in these difficult conditions working people were guaranteed the social gains of the socialist revolution. Unemployment was abolished, free health care and education were provided, much housing was built by the state and pensions came wholly from the state budget. A 40-hour working week was established in the country. The material welfare of the population increased. But all this was done within certain limitations.

In the last fifteen years, as an aspect of the negative processes mentioned above, the fall in the rate of growth and in economic efficiency has been especially painfully reflected in our inability to resolve our social problems. Resources were allocated to the social sector according to the so-called "residual principle", whereby capital investment was firstly directed towards industrial goals, while housing, the raising of living standards and other improvements in people's lives only received what remained.

As a result, for example, the proportion of capital investment in the economy allocated to housing construction was reduced from 23% in 1960 to 14%–15% in the last five-year period. The expenditure on education as a share of the national income reached 10% in 1950 (the highest rate then in the world) but this has fallen in recent years to 7%. The health system has also been neglected, with less than 4% of the national income allocated to its development when other countries allocate 8%–12%.

The development of agriculture, food and light industry has seriously fallen behind and the service sector has not developed. Provision of housing has been poor. Pensions, introduced in 1956, were progressive for their time, but through 30 years they have hardly changed, becoming an acute problem. Insofar as old equipment has basically been retained, industrial renewal has proceeded at a slow rate and has not been comprehensive. Working conditions have barely changed, and the numbers of manual workers remains almost static. Half of all workers, including collective farm workers, must still be classified as manual workers, and there is still a significant proportion of unskilled labourers. The ageing economic system of administrative commands from above aggravated this unbalanced development, neglecting the social sector, and exacerbating the gap between consumer demand and supply. The market has not been supplied with necessities and the demands for meat, dairy products, fruit, high quality goods and various services are not being met.

The stagnation of the economy in the 1981–85 period and the economic crisis implicit were accompanied by a growth in such anti-social processes as speculation, bribery, and the use of one's position for personal ends. The phenomena of stagnation and apathy, consequences of the negative tendencies of development, led to the loss of interest in their work among part of the population and reinforced negative attitudes to public property. Even worse, a tendency to hoard and be greedy developed. Social justice was systematically violated. Plans to boost welfare were not fulfilled while hidden price increases occurred. The tendency towards levelling out of wages differentials and arbitrariness in establishing their scale together with privileges for certain categories of workers did enormous harm. Widespread drunkenness undermined the healthy population and this is one of the reasons that life expectancy in the USSR has failed to rise in the last 20 years and that the death rate for males of active age has actually worsened.

The new economic and social policy of the party has given top priority to overcoming these unfavourable social phenomena. The whole social sector and the welfare of the people have to be brought into line with the industrial achievements of the country and the actual needs of society. From our enumeration of negative processes and phenomena it is evident that a great deal remains to be done. Above all, priorities must be changed and more resources accorded to the development of the whole social sector.

In order to solve the housing problem, the worst social problem of the country, it is intended to increase construction by one and a half times and to complete 40 million well-built flats and houses by the year 2000, i.e. doubling the existing housing stock. Calculations show that with the current rate of population growth (on the threshold of the year 2000 it will exceed the 300 million mark, as against the current total figure of 283 million) this will be sufficient housing given an equitable distribution system to provide every family with a separate, well-built flat. We shall be maintaining our country's preference for very low rents. Indeed currently, people's expenditure on rent and public utilities totals only 3% of their income.

In the near future it will be necessary to resolve the *food supply problem*, to supply the market with a full variety of food products and, above all, to meet fully consumers' demand for meat and dairy products. To achieve this, in the 1986–90 period it is intended to raise the growth of production of food by two and a half times. In the 1981–86 period the volume of production rose by a total of only 6% against a population growth of 4%. To cope with this the Soviet Union was obliged to purchase some 40 million or more tonnes of grain and about a million tonnes of meat from abroad. Initial successes in the development of agriculture in 1986 enabled imports of foodstuffs to be cut by a half – the result of improvements in the supply system. In the 1986–90 period it is intended to increase the volume of agricultural production by 14.4% overall. Anticipated annual demand for meat will grow from 62kg per head in 1985 to 70kg in 1990, and for milk and dairy products (expressed in terms of milk) from 325kg to 340kg.

To satisfy consumer demand fully it is intended to reform retail prices, sharply reducing the state subsidies on the sale of meat and dairy products. This raising of prices is to be realised in a democratic way after consultation with working people and with full compensation through additional payments to the population from state funds. Yet greater efforts will be required to supply the market with widely sought after goods and to bring an end to the chronic gap between demand and supply. For this it is intended to raise one and a half times the rate of growth of the production of consumer goods and, most importantly, to improve substantially the quality of products and restructure the range of products available in the light of consumer demand. It is also intended to raise two to three-fold the growth rate of the service sector.

A fundamental change for the better is planned in conditions of work and, above all, the reduction of unskilled manual labour. Currently almost half the working population are engaged in manual work, but by the year 2000 the proportion of manual labourers should have fallen to between 15% and 20%. Widespread technical reconstruction and re-equipment of production, the spread of automation and complex mechanisation will substantially change the nature of work, and make it more attractive, creative and interesting. Collective forms of organisation of work are being strengthened, giving additional impetus to creative initiative.

In order to improve the lives of pensioners a new pension law has been prepared envisaging a significant increase in the size of pensions while the existing pensionable ages of 55 for women, 60 for men are to be kept. (People working in heavy industry and also in the far north become pensionable respectively 5 and 10 years earlier.)

A fundamental improvement of the health system in the country is crucial. The construction of health centres has sharply increased, the personnel of the Ministry of Health has been reorganised, and its leadership replaced. An increase in salary for doctors and medical workers by an average of 40% has been announced. A major legislative programme for the strengthening of health care is being prepared. The resolutions on the struggle against drunkenness in the Soviet Union, taken in May 1985, have enormous social significance. During their implementation sales of alcohol have fallen over a two year period by 40%. This was immediately reflected in a fall in the death rate especially of men of active age. In 1986 for the first time in the last 20 years life expectancy of the population grew by one year. It continued to grow in 1987.

The education system is being reformed. 11-year compulsory education is planned for children from the age of 6, the material resources of schools are to be stepped up, teaching is to be combined with vocational education, teachers' salaries raised by 30%. The teaching of many subjects is being restructured. The teaching of information and computer technology, for which schools are now being equipped, has been made compulsory.

Putting the social policy into effect goes hand in hand with the principle of social justice in modifying the former unjustifiable levelling out of salaries. Now salary levels are more closely linked to the quality and quantity of work, following the basic socialist principle of distribution[3]. Wages now depend on a working collective's final output. There are wider opportunities for more productive and efficient labour. In the 1986–90 period new rates and scales of pay up to 20%–30% higher are being introduced, based on qualifications, quality of products and conditions of work. These increased basic rates are being introduced through mobilisation of enterprises' and economic organisations' own resources and through additional increases in efficiency. Collective forms of organisation are spreading and these will stimulate the work ethic and justify wage differentials. For it is the collective itself that determines the salary of its members based on the importance and results of the job.

The aim to advance social justice underlies all other aspects of this effort as well: the improvement of living conditions, the allocation of housing, the organisation of leisure, the granting of various privileges and advantages. Control over the observance of the principles of social justice is invested in workers' collectives and their unions. The rights of workers' collectives and unions are being greatly expanded.

A developed socialist way of life is envisaged and the consolidation of the advantages of a socialist society in the qualitative renewal of people's lives. All measures will start from the fact that in the

[3] "From each according to his ability; to each according to his work" is the principle referred to. (ed.).

Soviet Union there will as before be no unemployment. At the same time we have in mind greater freedom of choice of occupation. Organisations concerned with work and social questions are to be encouraged to develop a training system and refresher courses paid for by the state. All the rights to leisure, housing and other benefits will increasingly be realised as the material base of society grows stronger.

RADICAL REFORM OF MANAGEMENT

This element of *perestroika* in economic life is the determining one. The existing system of economic management does not correspond to new conditions, to the goal of the acceleration of socio-economic development. Indeed the existing system of management is out of date and acts as a brake on the development of the economy.

All other efforts to transform the economy are now coming up against the absence of solutions to the problems of management in the working of the economic mechanism. At present this mechanism encourages extensive and impedes intensive development. It further complicates the problem by making scientific and technological progress unprofitable and failing to guarantee advantage to those who raise the quality of production. It encourages new construction but makes work on technical reconstruction unprofitable. This system hoards the depreciation funds, perpetuates the output of old products, and does not push enterprises to renew their funds and products. It hinders *perestroika*.

The existing system of economic management, based on the command system, represses democracy, initiative and the creativity of workers and does not encourage the potential for work or social activity. It does not make workers interested in the final product of their labour. The unjustifiable levelling of wages, the shortages, the gap between supply and demand for individuals and society, the residual principle in the allocation of resources for the development of the social sector – these are all products of the old economic system.

A chief characteristic of the existing system of management is the predominance of administrative methods, with economic methods having only secondary significance. This system has been formed over a long period of Soviet history. In the ups and downs of history the state used its administrative power to achieve its priorities. With the transition of the country to industrialisation at the end of the 1920s and early 1930s it became a priority to distribute resources away from agriculture and consumer goods and into heavy industry.

Indeed, on the eve of industrialisation our country was predominantly agrarian, with the proportion of agriculture in the total national product around 60% and with the remainder coming mainly from food and light industry. During these years in the Soviet Union neither metallurgy, nor the chemical industry, nor hydro-electricity, machine building or arms industry were well-developed. Later, the situation in the world became critical when the fascists had come to power in Germany and several capitalist states undertook an economic blockade of the Soviet Union, then the only socialist country in the world. It was clear that a war against the Soviet Union could flare up. Industrialisation was a matter of life or death.

It was necessary to end the backwardness in an unprecedentedly short period, to create a powerful heavy industry and strengthen defence. This required enormous resources. The planned rate of accumulation in the national income had to double, raising it to a third of the whole national income, with almost all these resources allocated to the creation of heavy industry. At the beginning of the 1930s millions of people were recruited into the construction of the giants of Soviet heavy industry: Magnitogorsk and Kuznetz metallurgical plants, Chelyabinsk and Stalingrad tractor factories, the Gorky Car factory all came into being at that time. Several aviation factories were built; aluminium, ballbearing and machine tool construction industries were created as well as many others. The Dnieper hydroelectric power station and a great number of thermal electric power stations were built. In a word, the Soviet Union became visibly industrialised.

This fundamental transformation of the economy occurred with the help of central planning by directives. Five-year plans were aimed at this, the first of which began from 1927–8. (At this time the economic year did not coincide with the calendar year.) In the three pre-war five-year periods, uncompleted because of wartime pressures, a gigantic step forward was made in the Soviet Union in the development of industry, and above all in heavy industry.

From the beginning of the 1930s economic methods of management were curtailed. Trade between production units was replaced by centralised allocation of resources and the market contracted.

The primacy of production was established along with the secondary role of the consumer. Financial reforms at the beginning of the 1930s ended commercial credit and erased the differences between direct finance and credit financing. Rather than self-financing, the external budget control method of financing prevailed. The work done by enterprises was determined by directives, which year after year became more detailed. Financial accountabililty became a formality; prices were virtually irrelevant and many branches were unprofitable. Losses were hidden in the form of subsidies from the state budget.

Administrative methods were extended to official employment policy. All managers were appointed from the top down. Assessment of work was made according to the degree to which the plan had been fulfilled. Army-like disciplinary methods were propagated. These administrative methods of management became more brutal during the Second World War (1941–1945), when a large part of industry was evacuated to the Urals and Siberia from the western and central regions of the country occupied by the fascists. It was necessary fundamentally to restructure industry, subordinating the development of the economy as a whole to the task of "Everything for the front, everything for victory!". Fighting took place on the territories of the most developed and densely populated regions of the country, where a large part of industry and other branches of industrial enterprises were concentrated. The roads and towns over a large part of the territory of the European part of the country were destroyed during the war.

In the most difficult post-war circumstances development had to be re-established, and resources redistributed from the east of the country to the west. Only in the 1950s did the country heal the wounds of war and exceed the pre-war level of economic and social indicators. From this moment the administrative system of management, created in these extreme conditions, began to impede the country's development. To a certain extent this was recognised, particularly in sectors such as agriculture. Here the administrative methods were especially intolerable and ruinous, because of the very nature of agriculture, the need to consider local conditions, and the importance of the knowledge, experience and skills of rural workers.

Secondly, in the period 1953–57 after Stalin's death, and also during the economic reforms of 1964–65, attempts were made to introduce economic methods of management more widely. But these attempts were not all-embracing and touched only individual branches and sectors of the economy. Despite isolated positive results, there were few successes at that time. Ultimately, a relapse occurred back to administrative management and command systems.

With the development of productive forces, the unfolding of the scientific and technological revolution, the strengthening of socio-economic factors in economic development, the administrative system of management began to stand in ever greater contradiction to the growing needs of the development of society and finally came into sharp and protracted conflict with them. The situation worsened at the beginning of the 1970s, when the potential of extensive development through growth of resources began to decline, when a new stage of the scientific and technological revolution began and the needs of the population grew significantly. In this period the system of management of the economy began to act as a serious brake on development. As a result, towards the end of the 1970s and beginning of the 1980s crisis arose. Stagnation had occurred in the economy. The standard of living had stopped rising.

It became clear that this could not continue, that fundamental change was needed. A major element of *perestroika* in the economic sector is the radical reform of management of the whole economic system. It has necessitated two long years to work out the direction of this reform, conducting numerous economic experiments to test the elements of the new economic system. This period is now behind us. The June 1987 Plenary completed the working out of a new integrated management system. An expanded programme of *perestroika* of the economic system was accepted. The essence of this *perestroika* lies in the transition from administrative to economic methods of management. For this the basic element in production is the transfer of associations and enterprises to full economic accountability, self-financing and self-management. The dynamic development is economic democracy, the workers being widely involved in management, and now able to elect their own economic managers.

Transition to economic methods greatly increases the role of prices, finance and credit and enhances motivation and incentives to work. Therefore, the immediate task of *perestroika* of management is the fundamental reform of the pricing system and the financial credit system. This will create the preconditions for a broad and universal transition from centralised allocation of funds for the supply of goods to numerous options for trade between units of production. Simultaneously, a direct relation is established between the size of the enterprise wage fund together with its material incentive fund and the end results of the workers' labour. Changes in the structure of rates and wages are taking place. A broad transition is occurring towards collective forms of organisation and work incentives. Work collectives have received the right to determine wages.

All this requires radical changes in the central system of planning and management. Instead of detailed directives of tasks, planning is being concentrated on the establishment of norms of economic proportions[4] with economic incentives, while a system is being developed for consumers to order products from producers. Among these consumers will be state organisations, placing state orders.

The activity of the various ministries and regional authorities will also change fundamentally. The ministries will refrain from detailed regulation and trivial involvement in the activities of enterprises, to become the planning, economic and scientific and technological headquarters of industry. The role of regions in management will be greatly strengthened. The formation of local budgets will be changed to a system of economic proportions. Regional management bodies concerned with economic activity are being created as departments of local authorities.

All these ideas and measures for radical reform characterise a universal, fundamental transformation of the system of management, a *perestroika* of all component parts of the economic system. This *perestroika* will be undertaken mainly in the forthcoming two to three years, so that by the 1991–95 period the country will have entered a new and interlocking system of management. This management system must become the agency for accelerating socio-economic development. It must motivate and intensify development through the application of scientific and technological progress, plant renewal, high quality control, and through the

---

[4] These norms are called "normatives" in Russian and relate to the financial proportions established in the accounts of an enterprise that regulate the wages fund, taxation, depreciation, new investment etc. (ed.)

mobilisation of both public opinion and economic reserves of productive capacity.

MORE COOPERATIVES AND SELF-EMPLOYMENT[5]

In the preceding period of administrative management, the development of cooperatives in the Soviet Union was curtailed. Industrial cooperatives which were quite widespread in industry, and above all in the production of consumer goods, were abolished by decree in the 1950s, and cooperatives were not tolerated in commerce, foodstuffs, services and many other branches, where all organisations and establishments were state-run. Simultaneously in the 1950s and especially at the beginning of the 1960s, collective farms were reorganised. Some collective farms (*kolkhozy*) were changed into state farms (*sovkhozy*). Remaining collective farms were amalgamated and enlarged. Thus, the cooperative sector in the Soviet economy was reduced to a minimum. The remaining collective farms and fisheries were run as state enterprises under an administrative system of management.

At that time the view was widely held that it was necessary to merge state property and property that was collectively or cooperatively owned, and that state ownership was a higher form than that of a collective farm or a cooperative. Self-employed workers were subjected to severe restrictions under the administrative system of management. Whereas in earlier times the typical artisan producer worked on a small scale, gradually the number of individual craftsmen declined because of the harsh tax and administrative system. In other sectors, notably consumer services and commerce, self-employment was not permitted at all.

Authorised self-employment was permitted only within the private plots in the rural economy, mainly among citizens in villages, small towns and settlements. Sale of products from the private plots was permitted in collective farm markets. But even here, under the pretext that the private plot economy distracts workers from the state economy, various limitations were introduced, mostly at the hands of local officials. This led to a fall in the

[5] Self-employment in Soviet conditions includes family employment, while neither use wage labour. (ed.)

role of the private plot economy in the supply of goods. The development of horticultural associations was also checked. Not all those wanting to receive a piece of land for horticulture and market gardening received one under the pretext of shortage of land. The official waiting list for such land allocations exceeded six million.

All these measures to curtail cooperatives and self-employment conflicted with the interests of working people. Horticultural and market gardening cooperatives sprang up spontaneously wherever the state permitted, voluntary building brigades became widespread on a semi-legal basis, that is 'moonlighters' (*shabashniks*), who undertook agricultural and other building contracts and received money on completion of the job. Hundreds of thousands of people took part in such unplanned construction, widespread in many collective and state farms and in northern regions, where state construction organisations could not manage the volume of work. Self-employment, involving hundreds of thousands of people, became widespread on a clandestine level, usually as a second job in addition to work in a state organisation. Individual car repairs, private taxis and production of many goods in strong demand have become particularly widespread. All this has become a significant part of the so-called "submerged" or "unofficial" economy and a supplement to the main state economy. Even black markets sprang up with a turnover of many billion roubles.

Since state organisations in commerce and the service sector have not met the demands of consumers, the practice of offering services illicitly using state property has become common. As an example, state drivers often work as private taxi drivers in their free time. Sales assistants with access to goods of which there is a shortage sell them under the counter for extra money. Private cars are repaired for fees paid directly to mechanics in state garages and the garages receive nothing. The administrative system of management has unsuccessfully fought this black economy, and been able to do nothing about it. With increased shortages and the gap between the population's needs and state organisations' ability to satisfy them, this black economy has spread.

Now with *perestroika* and the transition to economic methods of management, conditions for the development of cooperatives and self-employment have fundamentally changed. Their development is now considered as an important way to democratise economic life. What has concretely been done to advance it? Above all, industrial cooperatives have been revived in the food, service and other sectors. More than three thousand were formed within months of the new laws being passed. Of course, this is a very modest beginning closely linked to the fact that the organisation of cooperatives started during the summer when most of the population is on holiday. It also reflects the hesitancy of many citizens who, being previously brought up to have a negative attitude to such types of work, have become alienated from it, and are now waiting and watching to see the results of the first cooperatives. There are also serious difficulties facing the first cooperatives, given the existing centralised system of supply of material and technical means through the allocation of resources. Thus it is difficult for cooperatives legally to obtain the materials they need for production. There is no free market and few workshops, and so the fate of the cooperatives often depends on whether they can find premises or not.

These economic limitations are to be ended as soon as the material and technical supply system is replaced by a wholesale trade system. By 1990 60% of all products are to be sold on a wholesale basis. After the retail price reforms at the end of this five-year period, the limitations now placed on cooperatives obtaining many of the goods they need will be lifted. (The cooperatives have now to obtain many goods, primarily, state-subsidised meat and milk, exclusively from the collective farm market and not from state shops. This limits their activity.) With the transition of enterprises to full self-accounting as profit centres with financial independence they can themselves decide questions like the renting of premises. Thus in this respect also the organisation of cooperatives will be made easier.

The continued survival of the administrative system of management, bureaucracy, and all the delays in decision-making etc. are reflected in the slow organisation of cooperatives. Not all the problems of cooperative work are resolved and in the final analysis there is still notably no direct authorisation of intellectual workers' cooperatives. Without this the Moscow Council cannot organise, for example, the "Polyglot", which combines foreign language specialists and teachers who are prepared to teach foreign languages, give coaching, translate and interpret at conferences etc. It is expected that in the near future the question of intellectual cooperatives will be resolved.

In what sectors are cooperatives most widespread now? Many cooperatives have concentrated their efforts on the fuller use of secondary supplies, industrial by-products and the manufacture of various articles from them. The authorities responsible for material and technical supply who are also responsible for the utilisation of secondary resources do give assistance in organising these cooperatives, finding premises, providing equipment and ensuring delivery of raw materials. Cooperative cafes are proliferating. In Moscow, for example, 118 have started up in a matter of months. The main problem here is in obtaining premises. A total of 118 cafes for Moscow is not many. At the end of the 1920s there were about 3,000, when Moscow was inhabited by one quarter of the present population. So, there is great potential.

Increasing numbers of cooperatives are starting up in the service sector, providing a whole range of services: car repairs, childminding, cleaning and many others. The Kishnevsk cooperative "The Volga", for example, attracts many students into its ranks and offers 20 types of services. Currently 300 people work in the cooperative, but they wish to make a major increase in its activity. Such services are offered both to private individuals and to state enterprises and organisations. Car repair cooperatives, for which there is a particular need, could be greatly speeded up if the Ministry of Transport would give assistance, renting out the necessary equipment, providing spare parts and tools. This is not yet forthcoming. Ministries, associations and enterprises have not yet turned their attention to cooperatives and the self-employed.

Taking the example of socialist countries which have started before the USSR with developing cooperatives and expanding self-employment, one can say that cooperatives and individual work could meet up to a half of the needs in services, one third of catering and produce up to a quarter of all consumer goods.

Self-employment must be developed alongside cooperatives. More than 200,000 individual work permits have been granted. There is one factor hindering the development of self-employment: in the USSR people are not usually permitted to be self-employed if this work is their main job (an exception is made for artisans). Pensioners, students, and a few others can do so. Wage labour is forbidden in the USSR and citizens working on a self-employed basis may not take on others, with the exception of some categories of trainees. In the Soviet Union a worker cannot employ others for a wage. We consider this exploitation and it is illegal. If several workers are required for production, they may, however, organise a cooperative, where the rights of each member are equal and there are no employer/employee divisions. The whole collective chooses the chairperson and can vote him or her out if necessary. All profit belongs to the cooperative members and not to the chair, and they jointly decide what to do with the profit.

As distinct from the laws concerning cooperatives, a special law was passed governing self-employment, which came into effect on May 1 1987. This authorised all kinds of self-employment. The numbers of self-employed doctors, teachers and tutors and members of other such professions, especially private taxi drivers, are all now increasing. This rise is especially marked in the Baltic cities. Local organisations and councils have broad powers to organise and stimulate such self-employment, but where the authorities have made excessive demands, the self-employed sector has developed poorly. In Moscow, local authorities made more demands on private taxis than on state-owned ones, and as a result very few commenced operation. This local authority was obliged to review its rules and we can expect to see the authorisation of private taxis in Moscow in the same way as has happened in other cities.

The rights of local authorities (the councils of people's deputies and their executive committees) are undergoing a process of democratisation and broadening. In particular, their budget is being increased. It will be established by a set proportion of the resources of every enterprise in the region. With the extension of their rights, local authorities' responsibility increases for meeting the population's needs. *Glasnost*, criticism, control from below, regular reports by the representatives to the electors will become the practice. In these conditions the population can exert pressure on the management of local authorities, demanding of them greater efforts to improve living standards. This pressure from the population will increase because in the future a transition is to occur to a system of nomination for elections of several candidates for every vacant position. In these circumstances local authorities, as I see it, will increasingly seek to encourage cooperative and self-employed activity as an important means to meet more fully the needs of the population, giving cooperatives and self-employed workers an assured future.

The development of cooperatives and self-employment is not a departure from socialist principles of economic management. In Soviet conditions a cooperative is a socialist form of economic management, foreseen by Lenin in one of his last articles "On Cooperatives". As is well known, Lenin's last articles were dictated by him. He was extremely ill and sensed his imminent death; these articles are rightly seen as his last will. It is symbolic that among the various questions to which Lenin wished to draw society's attention, was the question of cooperatives as an important form of socialist economic management. Lenin fully understood that a socialist society could not be developed solely on enthusiasm and on the application of administrative measures. He wrote about the need to employ the principles of material self-interest, self-financing, financial accountability (*khozraschet*)[6] and material responsibility. The cooperative form of economic management is indeed a form which ensures greater material incentive in work, more responsibility and the ability to pay one's way. At the same time it is a democratic form since it is voluntary. Lenin attached fundamental importance to the voluntary nature of the cooperative. Cooperatives are self-managing organisations, where the collective itself decides everything and things are not fixed from above by an official. Thus the potential advantages of cooperatives within our society are far from exhausted. And we know from economic history, no economic form will disappear if it contains within it potential for self-development. The development of self-employment has also to be approached as a way of strengthening the material interest of individuals in creative labour.

The aim of socialist development in the final analysis lies in meeting the needs of all members of society more fully. Cooperatives and self-employment contribute to this end and therefore reinforce our socialist principles. They completely correspond to Gorbachev's slogan for *perestroika*, "Give us more socialism!"

---

[6] Financial accountability (literally cost accounting) is described in detail in later chapters. Basically it implies that the enterprise is allocated funds by the state for which it is responsible to produce goods and services in a certain sector, paying its way and making a profit. It may use this income as it wishes subject to fixed guidelines (called 'normatives' and described later) on the economic proportions assignable to basic wages, capital amortisation, contributions to the state budget. (ed).

GLASNOST, DEMOCRACY AND
SELF-MANAGEMENT

Democratisation of the whole of our society including the development of *glasnost* is an important aspect of *perestroika*. As it applies
to the economy, debate is proceeding on an increased role for
workers' collectives in the resolution of economic questions, and in
the transition to self-management. In the Law on Socialist Enterprises, workers' collectives have been granted extensive rights in
framing the plans of economic development for their enterprise,
deciding on the way incentives should be offered, on work
conditions and salaries, and the social development of their
collective.

Of particular significance is the right of workers' collectives to
choose their economic leaders, at brigade, enterprise and association level. Earlier, under the administrative system, directives on
the conduct of the plan, even the smallest details, were handed
down from above. Now, with full economic independence and self-
accounting, the welfare of the collective depends above all on work
organisation and levels of productivity. Its leader, as head of the
working collective, must take the lead in striving for higher
efficiency and productivity.

Perestroika is a difficult and painful process. Its success is
determined by the socio-political climate of the society in which it
occurs. The most complex question concerns the *perestroika* of
people's thinking and consciousness. For, the consequence of
perestroika in thinking and consciousness defines the way they work
towards the transformation of society. Karl Marx wrote: "An idea
becomes a material force when it takes hold of society." The idea of
perestroika must come to grip society for *perestroika* to move into
gear. But how can this transition to a new way of thinking and an
understanding of new tasks be assured? Here the media of mass
information are of inestimable help. *Glasnost*, truth, criticism and
self-criticism are the instruments that will effectively prepare for the
new consciousness. Change in the sphere of ideology is thus the
inspiration for *perestroika* of the economy and of other parts of
society.

This is what is happening in our country now. Enormous changes
are apparent in publishing, television programmes, the activities of
writers, film makers and theatre directors. Freedom of expression
has been expanded. Ongoing changes are being analysed critically

and past experiences are being assessed. All this is directed at working people. Everyone feels that it has become easier to breathe, and that the socio-psychological climate in the country is receptive to *perestroika*. Thus *glasnost* is working and encouraging reform of the economy.

THE FIRST STEPS

Such are the main directions of *perestroika* of the economy. But what stage have we reached? We have virtually only just begun the *perestroika*. Most attention in this first stage has been directed towards the social factors affecting acceleration. It was necessary to convince working people of the need for *perestroika*. A great job has been done here and its results lie in the psychological preparedness of broad masses of the workers for *perestroika*. On the other hand, the challenge of discipline and order, accountability and initiative, the improvement of economic management and the chance to experiment, to work with greater independence, have all positively affected our development. In the preceding six to seven years up to 1985, the growth of industrial production in the country was on average between 3% and 4% a year. After the April Plenary it reached about 5%. This additional growth of industrial production was achieved thanks to the acceleration in the growth of productivity, the previous rate of 2%–3% having risen roughly to 4.5%. In the most recent period, for the first time, the whole growth of industrial production has been achieved through growth in productivity without an increase in the number of workers.

We have managed to overcome past difficulties. So while a pronounced shortage of fuel and energy resources was experienced in the previous two years the situation has corrected itself. The fall in oil extraction has also been stopped (extraction fell from 616 million tonnes in 1983 to 595 million tonnes in 1985). The oil industry recently began to increase extraction and for the first time in many years fulfilled the plan: in 1986 615 million tonnes were exracted. Steady growth has continued in 1987. From 1978 the coal industry also stagnated and failed to fulfil the plan. A turning point has been reached here and the volume of mined coal is now rising steadily. Despite the Chernobyl accident the supply of electricity to the economy has remained constant.

Problems with metallurgy have also been corrected. Technical reconstruction work has begun to be carried out more intensively.

The volume of production has grown, above all of highly cost-effective rolled steel and pipes. Machine building is being restructured. In 1986 alone the volume of capital investment in the reconstruction of the machine industry increased by 30% i.e. by more than in the preceding five-year period, even though this has still not been reflected in the renewal of products of the machine-building industry. The annual rate of renewal of the whole range of products increased from 3.1% in 1985 to 4% in 1986 and to 4.3% in the first half of 1987. This is still not enough. Generally, *perestroika* in machine building is proceeding with difficulty. The changes in policy and the extension of state quality control have disturbed parts of the machine building industry, and their work has slowed down. I hope that these are temporary difficulties connected with reorganisation.

As to the remaining branches of industry, those of light industry still work unsatisfactorily. In 1986 their rate of growth was only 2% overall. It did not improve much in 1987. It should be taken into consideration, however, that light industry has transferred to a new system of planning, whereby the enterprises' plans are now wholly determined by commercial orders. Many enterprises have had to change their range of products in response to consumer demand. This has resulted in trade stocks not merely remaining constant, but actually declining. Overall, such a low rate of growth in this sector negatively affected the growth of commodity circulation.

Agriculture has developed better than other branches in the past two years, mainly as a consequence of changes in scientific, technological and investment policy in the villages, and of fundamental changes in the management system and economic organisation. In 1986 the volume of agricultural production grew by more than 5% including a 1% increase in the private plot economy, and 7% in the state economy. The figures are shown in Table 2.

All this made a 5% increase in the volume of production in the food industry possible, including an increase of meat and dairy products by 6.3% in 1986 compared with 1985. This enabled us to cut by half the imports of grain and meat from the West.

Other branches of the economy have also started to work more successfully. Overall there has been a certain acceleration, but a turning point has not yet been reached. The fact is that there is as yet no firm base for it in scientific and technological advance. Stop-gap measures alone are being undertaken in this field. And while there is no firm base, development is not permanent. Hard frosts in January and February 1987 immediately affected the growth rates. Growth came to a halt during these months, and although agriculture increased production in the following months by between 4% and5%, overall for the first half of this year the volume of production has increased by only 3.5%.

Table 2: *Increases in agricultural production in the USSR 1986–87, compared with previous five-year period averages and 1985 (all figures in million tonnes)*

Product	Increases		Output 1986–7
	Over previous five-year average	Over 1985 level	
Grain	+30	+20	210
Meat	+ 1.5	+ 0.7	18.7
Milk	+ 5.5	+ 2.5	1

Note: 1 Dairy products as a whole were up by 10m tonnes in 1986–87 over 1985 to a total of 105m tonnes.

As before it is proving difficult to satisfy consumer demand to meet the sums of money available for purchases. The retail trade finds it difficult to guarantee a supply of goods. It has not been possible to improve the financial indicators of internal trade significantly either. Additional difficulties have arisen because in 1986, due to the fall in the prices in the West of fuel and other goods that we export, the USSR's external current trade balance fell by 7.9%. In the first six months of 1987 exports fell by a further 4%. These are temporary difficulties, although it demonstrates in what difficult circumstances *perestroika* is being undertaken.

Against all these difficulties and setbacks, *perestroika* is gathering force and now the USSR is entering a new and crucial stage during which, on the basis of the resolution of the June Plenary Meeting, the large scale transition is being implemented in all branches of the economy to new economic conditions.

The social *perestroika* is also gathering force. The residual principle for the allocation of resources to social needs has been ended. This is particularly noticeable in housing construction. In 1986 for the first time in a number of years 118.2 million square metres of living space were completed, 5.2 million more than in the previous year. Measures for the improvement of education and healthcare are being taken. The death rate fell from 10.6 to 9.7 per 1,000 people. Death by accident, poisoning and trauma fell especially sharply (by 22%). Persistent efforts by society to combat drunkenness have had some effect. In a word, work on *perestroika* continues, and there are changes for the better, but there has still not been a breakthrough.

It is clear that *perestroika* is revolutionary in character and that its full realisation will alter and renew our whole society. The economy will be qualitatively different. Where are we headed, what final goals are we pursuing and how will *perestroika* be realised? Above all, *a transition is envisaged from an economy of shortages, with power in the hands of producers rather than consumers, to an economy of social production, oriented to the satisfaction of social needs, working to the demands of the consumers and ending all shortages*. We cannot have an economy of shortages if from a socialist perspective efficiency is defined as the full satisfaction of social needs. Also the excessive power of the producer in conditions of shortage – in conditions, that is, where the consumer has no choice – leads to deformation of the structure of the economy and to the development of production by producers pursuing their own interests. As a result the economy of shortages produces many goods in excessive quantities.

The Soviet Union now produces four and a half times more tractors than the USA, despite a lower volume of cultivation. At the same time, for every tractor we produce almost half as many trailers and attachments, on which their effectiveness depends. It is obvious that such a quantity of tractors is not necessary, but they are produced and thrust upon the collective farms and state farms which purchase them as a rule not out of their own resources, but through loans or grants from the state. Similarly more combines, agricultural machinery and work stations, four to five tonne vehicles and many other types of machinery are produced than necessary. As soon as an enterprise transfers to a system of full financial accountability and economic independence and comes to purchase its means of production at its own expense, the demand for these inflated runs of production will be substantially reduced. In 1988, for example, collective and state farms have ordered 30% fewer combines than were previously distributed to them each year.

The agro-industrial association "Kuban", which transferred to full economic autonomy earlier, has for some years ordered roughly half as much agricultural machinery as before. When there is a transition in a collective or state farm to working in contract teams, and when land and agricultural technology is rented out to teams then up to 40%–50% of the tractors, combines and other machinery will not be required any longer.

If the structure of production is considered from the point of view of social need, then the superfluous production of many metal goods becomes evident, and one begins to understand why there are shortages of metal. Indeed, the USSR smelts 156 million tonnes of steel, more than twice the USA, and yet there is a much smaller volume of end products. To the locally produced metal we must also add several million tonnes of rolled steel purchased from other countries and costing up to two and a half billion roubles of hard currency. A significant part of this metal went into the production of superfluous machinery. And this is one of the reasons for the hypertrophied development of metallurgy in the USSR, where the volume of production exceeds the total metal production for the whole of Western Europe.

The same picture appears not only in relation to the means of production but also with consumer goods. In 1987 the USSR may exceed the 800 million mark in shoe production, 3.2 pairs per person per year. In Czechoslovakia 1.7 pairs per person suffices. In the USA, where the population is but a little greater than the USSR, only 300 million pairs of shoes are produced and that has been sufficient. But in the USSR 800 million pairs were not enough, and we still purchased a large quantity of footware from Czechoslovakia, Yugoslavia, Finland, Italy and many other countries. All this footware is being produced, but the quality is poor and having bought these shoes people are not satisfied and seek new ones. As soon as modern, fashionable shoes come into the shops queues form, while poor quality shoes sit on the shelves swelling stocks. This applies to many other products.

The problem is, however, not only one of excess production. Much more important is the fact that in circumstances of shortage the demand for quality falls. Producers who barely give a thought to consumer demand have articles turned out to suit their own convenience. Purchasers of machinery and other goods are often obliged to undertake additional work to adapt them to their needs, and a great deal of energy and resources are directed to this. Shortages are the outcome of an inappropriate economic system and not of any lack of resources or other means. Indeed our country has resources of all types at its disposal, yet demand is not satisfied. One of the important tasks for the radical reform of management of the whole economic system consists in ensuring the subordination of production to consumer demands. This will lead to the most fundamental changes in the structure of production and the quality of products. It will be necessary to cut down production of certain types of goods and, in contrast, to increase the production of others. Overall this will lead to a considerable increase in efficiency, and to a fuller satisfaction of social needs.

Among social needs, the satisfaction of people's consumer demands is of special importance. Until recently the economy was oriented towards production. Everything connected to the development of production was accorded priority status. Resources for the social sector were allocated in such a way as to protect the development of production. This also distorted the structure of the economy. A gap formed between the level of industrial development in the country and the degree of satisfaction of people's social needs. Today this gap is being closed. We need to transfer from a resource-producing economy towards a social economy, to an economy for the individual with priority development of the whole welfare service and social sector.

Finally, another task, closely related to the first, is the *transition from a predominantly extensive economy to a highly intensive economy in which the main factors of economic development are increased efficiency and quality*. For this a breakthrough has to be achieved in the use of resources and in the transition from a wasteful economy to a resource-saving economy. The main path of intensive development is via *scientific technological progress*. Here a transition is required from evolutionary scientific technological progress to the carrying through of a scientific technological revolution. Thanks to the intensive development of technology, the economy will gain flexibility and adaptability to changing conditions.

A very important goal is the effective inclusion of the Soviet Union into the international division of labour. The USSR's share in international trade does not correspond to its economic might. The structure of its exports appears undeveloped, it is dominated by fuel and raw materials. There is an irrational import structure where a large share is made up of foodstuffs and metals, while the major share consists of machines and equipment. However, many of the machines purchased are serial products, which could be produced internally. It is envisaged that the Soviet Union should move from this position to a more open economy. The development of international exchanges should accelerate faster than the growth of production. Especially important is the preferential development of external economic ties within the framework of the CMEA* of the allied socialist countries. Of key significance here is the implementation of programmes of scientific technological progress with these countries.

We are against autarky and for equality and mutual benefit in the development of international economic exchanges. Two goals relate to this. First of all, external economic exchange can be used as an additional lever to increase efficiency in Soviet economic development. And secondly the development of economic cooperation between countries strengthens mutual trust and facilitates the efforts for peace. To implement fully the enormous plans of acceleration of socio-economic development in the USSR, involving the wholesale renewal of the Soviet economy, we naturally need peace. Disarmament, if it occurs, will free additional resources to accelerate domestic change and, above all, ensure growth in the living standards of the Soviet people. At the same time, Soviet leaders have insisted that part of the economic resources released by disarmament are to be used for assistance to underdeveloped countries.

In the end we have to move from a command economy with mainly administrative methods of management, towards a democratic, independent, self-managing economy, to an economy in whose management the broad masses of working people are actively participating. All this will fundamentally change the look of our economic system. The advantages of socialism within our economy will become apparent. We want a highly efficient economy, to reach the highest productivity levels in the world, to be at the forefront in technology and quality of production and at the same time to avoid unemployment, preserve the short working day and strengthen the social achievements of working people all on a broad democratic foundation.

* For definition see footnote 15, page 148.

It is towards the achievement of these goals that the CPSU Programme, adopted at the XXVII Party Congress, is orienting our society. Its goals cannot be achieved in the short term. The largest leap is to be made in the period up to the year 2000. By this time the material technical base of our society will be renewed. The scientific technological revolution will have unfolded widely in the country and, using its achievements, we should advance to the foremost position in the world. But our backwardness compared to the most developed countries in the world is too great to be overcome before the end of the century. Thus in terms of productivity we are two and a half to three times behind the USA and two to two and half times behind other developed Western countries.

To a certain extent such backwardness has occurred because of the low labour productivity in Soviet agriculture, which is five times inferior to the USA. Evidently to a certain extent such a large difference in productivity between agriculture in the USSR and USA is connected with the less favourable natural climate and conditions for development of agriculture in the USSR, where a considerable part of arable land is situated in arid zones having overall temperatures lower than in the USA. Allowing for agriculture, then the level of development in the Soviet Union is two to two and a half times below that of the USA and one and a half to two times below that of other developed Western countries.

During the last 20 years productivity in the USA and in European countries has grown at an annual average rate of 2.5%–3% per year, although higher rates can be expected in the forthcoming period. We plan now to increase productivity by an average of 6% per year up to the year 2000. By then at such a rate we should outstrip the productivity levels of many European countries and closely approach those in the USA. This also applies to other indicators of efficiency. By the year 2000, we intend to lower national consumption of metals 1.9 times, energy consumption 1.4 times. In so doing we will have reached the level of material resource consumption of the most developed countries.

As has already been stated, major efforts will be made to improve the quality of products and their competitiveness. By the year 2000 differences between the USSR and other countries should be largely eliminated. Increases in labour productivity and other indicators of effectiveness and quality of products will create a material basis for an end to the wide differences which currently exist in the USSR in levels of real income, food and consumer goods, housing, health provision and many other aspects of the standard of living. I do not think that in 15 years it is possible for the USSR to reach the highest standards of living in the world. This will be especially difficult to achieve in the service sector, which is extremely underdeveloped, and also in the housing sector of the economy. But it is clear that with the high rates of growth planned (two to three times faster than those in Western countries) the gap will rapidly close and we will come near to the indicators of the most advanced countries. All this will secure a higher standard of living, together with the social achievements of socialism.

A certain period of time beyond the year 2000 will be required therefore to draw up to, and then possibly to overtake, the USA and other countries in productivity, efficiency and quality in the various aspects of the standard of living of the population. In any case we look with confidence to the future and hope that the 100th Anniversary of the Great October Socialist Revolution in 2017 can be celebrated with the fulfilment of the prophecies of Lenin of higher levels of productivity under socialism than under capitalism.

WILL IT HAPPEN?

Talking of *perestroika* and mentioning its difficulties and especially its inspiration, begs the following obvious questions: Where are the guarantees that all this will happen? Is *perestroika* real and lasting? In raising these questions many critics refer to our previous efforts to restructure the economy in the mid-1950s and to undertake economic reforms in the mid-1960s, which ultimately failed and were abandoned. Will this *perestroika* not end in the same way? These questions are reasonable and the answers are difficult. It is not easy to see into the future and to be absolutely certain. But it seems to me that this *perestroika* will be successfully completed. I see serious arguments for it. Above all, one can undertake to complete an important task when that task has become a necessity, much overdue, like this *perestroika*. It is not an invention of the leadership, nor a subjective wish of a group of individuals, but a real need for our development. This *perestroika* has been prepared by the whole course of our previous history.

But such an answer is of course too general and will satisfy no one. Therefore I will try to introduce other arguments for my optimistic viewpoint.

First Argument

A litmus test of real efforts towards *perestroika* lies in our attitudes to the past. If one really wishes to undertake a restructuring, then one must critically assess the past and extract lessons for the future from it. This is never easy. Indeed we all hold collective responsibility for the past. Criticising the past we are, in effect, being critical of ourselves. On the other hand, when one makes criticisms of the past, feelings inevitably arise that all the failures are the responsibility of one's predecessors and this is not really in order. For in the past not only bad but good things happened, and when one criticises the past a sense of inner protest arises in some people.

Yet one cannot help it, one can only move confidently into the future taking one's past into account. In this respect this is a very special period in the Soviet Union. The past 10–15 years have been characterised by serious negative tendencies and it is not easy to face up to this. Of prime importance is the fact that for the first time in the CPSU Programme reasons have been shown for the negative tendencies of the 1970s. It might seem out of place in a Party Programme, a document that looks to the future – many voices have claimed as much during its discussion. But the criticisms were included in order to clear the way forward. Criticism of the past, extracting both positive and negative lessons, are signs of a desire to leave behind the failures of the past, to avoid repetitions of past mistakes and to complete *perestroika*.

Second Argument

As to the pace – is *perestroika* slowing down as the process broadens and deepens? Let us recall the major turning points so far. At the April 1985 Plenary Meeting of the Central Committee the idea of acceleration of Soviet socio-economic development was voiced for the first time and the need for *perestroika* discussed. At the June 1985 meeting on the question of accelerating scientific technological progress, positions taken in the April meeting were considerably developed. Here a new scientific, technological, investment-directed and structural policy for the current stage was established, as a starting point for a reworking of the 1986–90 period. Suggestions for the *perestroika* of management were made in greater detail.

The most important next landmark was the XXVII Party Congress which developed and approved the broad ideas of *perestroika*. For the first time questions of *perestroika* in the social sector were specifically posed; the analysis of *perestroika*'s direction and route and the methods to implement it were further considered. All this was recorded in both the new CPSU Party Programme and in a document titled "Main Directions of the Economic and Social Development of the USSR in the period 1986–90 and the Prospects up to the year 2000".

Next, the January 1987 plan introduced at the Central Committee Plenary Meeting was of great significance. It worked out in detail questions on the development of democracy in our society. Fundamental reasons for the failure of past attempts at *perestroika* were uncovered. It was concluded that these attempts were not undertaken on a genuinely democratic basis and did not establish democracy as necessarily the most important phenomenon in the transition to self-management. Resolutions on changes in the policy of recruitment, placement of personnel and training, were also then accepted as crucial.

In June 1987 the Central Committee adopted a programme for the implementation of radical reforms in the whole system of management of the economy. It was declared that at one of the forthcoming Plenary Meetings of the Central Committee the ideas for the period 1991–95 would be considered. This will be the first five-year period when the new economic system is in place, and therefore the plan must be innovative. On it will fall the burden of relating the structure of production directly to social needs. This will also be a five-year period of major acceleration in scientific technological progress, of broadening the intensive methods of production and securing the production of high-quality goods. Work for this began in the period 1986–90. The 1991–95 period will see the deepening and development of the general effort towards *perestroika* and the acceleration that goes with it.

A most important future step will be the convocation of an All-Union Party Conference at the end of June 1988. Such an All-Union Party Conference has not taken place for almost fifty years, and a return to this democratic form of Party forum is in itself significant. But even more important are the two key issues on the agenda, consideration of which must give a powerful impulse to the basic direction of *perestroika*. One concerns the route of *perestroika* and the tasks involved in its development. The second concerns the democratisation of society and of the Party.

Perestroika thus continues step by step and the guiding force of the Communist Party is appearing as its inspiration and organiser.

Third argument

Critical analysis of previous reforms in our economy shows that they were not successful because they were not all-embracing. On the one hand the reform of the economy did not coincide with reforms in society, nor in the party. On the other hand in the economy itself, these reforms embraced only individual branches or sectors. The overall system of economic management was based on the old principles. Therefore ultimately a relapse occurred with the old ways preserved. These crushed the new methods and gave them no chance to develop.

What is important in this *perestroika* is that it has an all-round character, it embraces the whole of social life, not just the economy. We have already mentioned that *perestroika* is inspiring new economic thinking, and creating a new socio-pyschological climate of change in society, which in itself assists economic reform. The *perestroika* of economic life has an all-embracing, many-faceted character and affects all elements, branches and sectors of the economy. It is very important that the *perestroika* of management, for example, goes hand in hand with the introduction of new investment and a new structural policy, with the acceleration of scientific technological progress, and with a new approach to the selection and deployment of personnel. Old elements cannot suppress the new since *perestroika* is occurring on many fronts. Everywhere old methods are being replaced by new. *Perestroika* in one area reinforces *perestroika* in another, mutually enriching each other. Only a general *perestroika* will mean movement forward without having to stop because the rearguard is lagging behind.

Fourth and Most Important Argument

This concerns the drawing of the broad masses of working people into *perestroika* . "Secret" attempts at *perestroika* – reforms from the top, in which the working people themselves are not involved and which touch only individual sectors of the economy – are doomed to failure. Such reforms from the top are easily rescinded and undone. Things are quite different with a powerful popular movement. A strong desire for change, if it captures the masses, is very hard to arrest. Thus the development of democracy and the direct involvement in *perestroika* of the whole population and the working people are the best guarantors of the irrevocable renewal of society. We believe in *perestroika* and are optimistic. And although it is proceeding slowly, with difficulty, and many mistakes have already been made along the way, with more probably yet to come; nonetheless, as Gorbachev has said, there is nowhere for us to retreat. We must move forward, increasing speed as we go.

2 ON THE EVE: THE LESSONS OF HISTORY

Perestroika of the Soviet economy is not being implemented in a vacuum. *As a result of previous development, the Soviet Union has achieved a highly industrialised economy, has developed science and an educated population.* Here are some statistics characterising the national economy of the country.

The Soviet Union occupies one sixth of the earth's land, more than 22 million square kilometers. On this territory in 1987 there lived 283.1 million people. Of these 140 million are employed in the economy. The country has enormous natural resources of all types. Thanks to this, the Soviet Union is perhaps the only country in the world which satisfies its own fuel and raw material needs through its own production and exports significant quantities of fuel, raw materials, timber and other resources to other, mainly socialist countries. The 1913 pre-revolutionary Russia had only a little more than 4% of the world's industrial production. The Soviet Union today accounts for roughly one fifth of world industrial production. More is produced in the Soviet Union today than in the whole world in 1950.

Of all the countries of the world the Soviet Union produces the most oil, gas, ferrous metals, minerals, tractors, reinforced concrete, woollen materials and shoes, lumber, sugar beet, potatoes, milk, eggs and many other products. In hydro-electricity and chemical products, machinery, cement and cotton Soviet production occupies second place after the USA, and in coal mining and grain production third place after the USA and China.

For every 1,000 persons employed, about 900 have secondary education (eight to ten years) including 125 with higher education. After ten years at school, a further four to five years is required in the Soviet Union to achieve higher education.

Every people prides itself on its historical achievements. Our people also has something to be proud of. After the October Revolution in 1917, the country transformed its economy along socialist lines. Russia, as is well known, was a predominantly agrarian country and exceptionally backward. Its industrial production placed it fifth in the world and fourth in Europe, but in relation to its 143 million population, Russia was larger than both America and the countries of Europe. After seventy years of Soviet rule the USSR has become a strong industrial power. A socialist society has been constructed that ensures the population not only freedom, but a real right to work, leisure, education, living accomodation and a guaranteed old-age all funded by the state. Therefore each Soviet citizen is *socially protected* and is not threatened by unemployment and poverty and can look to the future with confidence.

At the same time it must be recalled that the development of the Soviet Union has occurred in unbelievably difficult circumstances. After the October Revolution a civil war and imperialist war was unleashed on the country which did great damage to the economy. Production declined five times compared with 1913 levels. From this initial level we began peaceful development through the New Economic Policy (NEP)[7] at the beginning of the 1920s. It took

[7] The New Economic Policy was introduced by Lenin in 1921 to replace the war-time economy, total centralisation and restriction of the money economy (war communism), of the previous period. NEP was designed to encourage exchanges of products between town and country. Private enterprise was permitted not only in agriculture but in small-scale industrial production and in retailing. State enterprises were switched from a system of administrative commands to one of self finance and cost accounting, and were often expected to compete on the open market with the private entrepeneur. NEP was expected to operate for a transitional but fairly extended period as a stage towards the transformation to a socialist society. (ed.)

seven to eight years to reach 1913 levels again. By then a whole decade had passed after the October Revolution. There followed an extremely hard thirteen-year period of industrialisation and the overcoming of backwardness. By 1941 the Soviet Union was already producing 10% of the world's industrial ouput and had caught up with the developed European countries. Compared with the pre-revolutionary period the social product had increased five times, comprising an eight-fold increase in industry (thirteen-fold in heavy industry), 1.4 times increase in agriculture, six-fold in capital investment and seven-fold in turnover of consumer goods. Illiteracy was overcome, and unemployment ended. The population reached 194 million on the eve of the Second World War.

There followed once more the hardest of experiences; the war against the German fascists (1941–45) and the subsequent excruciating period of rebuilding an economy destroyed by war. It was only by the end of the 1940s and the beginning of the 1950s that the wounds of war had been substantially healed and economic indices reached pre-war levels. Ten years had once again been lost. Moreover, an irreplaceable loss during the war was the death of 20 million Soviet people. Many tens of millions of people were wounded and became invalids, millions of families were without food and tens of millions of children were orphaned.

The transition to peacetime life was not simple. In 1945 the USA first acquired atomic weapons and dropped atomic bombs on Hiroshima and Nagasaki. One reason for this was to frighten the USSR and force it to make concessions in the post-war organisation of the world. For the third time, the Soviet people faced a life and death dilemma arising from imperialism. It was necessary to strain all its energies and resources to acquire its own atomic weapons and to create from scratch first atomic, and then hydrogen bombs, and the means to convey these atomic weapons, long-range strategic aircraft, nuclear submarines and ballistic missiles. And all this deprived us of opportunities, as it still does today, of undertaking social development and achieving real growth in the living standards of the Soviet people.

The arms race, emanating from the USA, continued in ever widening spirals encompassing newer and newer areas, and becoming more and more costly. And now, despite all the efforts which the Soviet leaders exercise on behalf of the people, the arms race threatens to spread into space, and this may be the most dangerous of all developments so far. Not only the Soviet people, but all mankind would become hostage to space-based nuclear weapons and stand together on the verge of death.

The Soviet Union's suggestion of giving up nuclear, chemical and biological weapons, and military stations in space, and the implementation of general disarmament by the year 2000, including the destruction of strategic and other armaments, could open up a new peaceful era in the development of all countries. We are convinced that in peaceful conditions the socialist economic system would gradually reveal its advantages and ensure to the Soviet people high living standards and the conditions in which all members of society can develop freely.

Reviewing our achievements during the seventieth anniversary jubilee of the Great October Socialist Revolution, one is bound to experience not only some feelings of legitimate pride in the historical successes, but also a certain bitter feeling of loss and waste, of tragic mistakes and fundamental omissions during our difficult past. I will not stir up old, pre-war memories here when, against the background of a substantially correct course in industrialisation and in the cooperative organisation of the peasants, tragic mistakes occurred. The repression of some parts of the peasantry during the over-hasty collectivisation of agriculture at the beginning of the 1930s, caused hunger and deprivation for the working population during 1931–35, when food rationing had to be reintroduced. The mass arrests and the elimination of political and military leaders, representatives of the intelligentsia and other strata in our society, especially in the events of 1937, make up black pages in our history. Repression also returned in the post-war years, especially in the years of struggle against so-called cosmopolitanism in 1948.

After the death of Stalin the Party exposed his cult of personality at the XX Congress and condemned these tragic events. It would be incorrect, however, to see the whole development of socialist society only through the prism of these massive criminal activities, without noticing the overall forward movement of socialist society.

The post-war developments are of particular significance for the matter in hand, and we shall expand on them accordingly. When the wounds of war were healed and the Soviet Union passed to a new stage of its development, the one-sidedness of the structure of the economy became clear, in particular the neglect of agriculture and of the production of goods demanded in the social sphere, the development of which was subordinated to the growth of heavy industry.

The retarding effect of command methods of management, developed during the process of industrialisation and in the rebuilding of the war-damaged economy, became all too apparent. Rigidly administrative, regulatory, centralised methods of leadership did not correspond with peaceful economic development any longer. The need for an about-turn was becoming more and more evident, i.e. for a turn to economic and social policies geared to production for the satisfaction of social needs. The economy had to be converted to tackling the tasks involved in raising the people's standard of living. If such a turn-around had been achieved in time and in an appropriate way, we would have had much more success in the post-war period.

Twice attempts were made to achieve a breakthrough in changing the structure of the economy and introducing a new economic mechanism. These attempts did speed up economic growth and brought significant improvements in the standard of living of the population. But in the end the administrative methods of management and the process of extensive development still held sway and a period of rising rates of growth was succeeded by periods of declining growth and of stagnation. The contradictions which became apparent in the 1950s, between the development of the production forces and the growing needs of society on the one hand, and the increasingly obsolete productive relations of the old system of economic management on the other hand, became sharper with every year. The conservative structure of the economy and the tendencies for extensive investment, together with the backward system of economic management gradually, turned into a brake and and an obstacle to the economic and social development of the country.

All this has been especially noticeable in the last ten to fifteen years, when new circumstances – the slower growth of resources, the transition to a new stage of the scientific technological revolution and the developing needs of the population – have all tended to exacerbate the contradictions we have mentioned. A situation approaching crisis has arisen in the Soviet Union. The new economic strategy of the Party, *perestroika*, has come to define the way out of this situation. In carrying out this new economic policy, announced by the April 1985 Plenary meeting of the Central Committee, we should not repeat the mistakes of past reforms. Negative and positive lessons have to be extracted from the experience of the past, so that knowledge of the past can equip us to strengthen and deepen the *perestroika*.

Let us then consider the experiences, albeit ultimately unsuccessful ones, of implementing the major economic and social reforms in the Soviet Union: the first in the 1950s after the death of Stalin and the second in the mid-1960s after the dismissal of Khrushchev.

The first about-turn in economic and social policy began in 1953, when after the death of Stalin a new political leadership under N.S. Krushchev advanced a programme of accelerated development of agriculture and of consumer goods production. The main object of the about-turn in economic policy was agriculture and this was natural. In the composition of the national income at that time about 70% was generated from products originating in agriculture. Thus the welfare of the people was determined by the development of agriculture. The situation in this crucially important sector was extremely difficult. The level of agricultural output had not reached pre-war indices. Exchanges between the towns and villages were unequal. A large part of the national income, generated in agriculture, was confiscated for state purposes. Collective farm workers lacked the basic rights of citizens. A detailed administrative system of management controlled agriculture. Part of production was compulsorily procured for derisory prices, not even covering the cost of production. Other ways of obtaining rural production by the state involved purchases at higher prices, but these also did not guarantee the real viability of collective and state farms.

The vast majority of collective farms were economically weak. Payment in kind predominated: grain and other agricultural products being handed out for a day's work. The size of the payments in many cases did not ensure the reproduction of human power. The greater part of collective farm workers lived off the products grown on their own family plots, where a small amount of the collective farms' land was left in the hands of its members' families for their use. Collective farm workers were legally tied to one collective farm and could not transfer freely to the towns or to another collective farm. To do so required a special administrative authorisation. Collective farms did not have the necessary resources for the proper conduct of agriculture. Tractors, combines, agricultural tools were on the whole concentrated in Machinery and Tractor Stations (MTS) belonging to the state which undertook the mechanised work for collective farms and received payment in kind – a share of the harvest. Besides this taxes were levied on collective farms and on their workers, making it disadvantageous to increase production and to earn higher incomes. The standard of living in the villages was primitively low. Most villages did not have electricity, let alone running water and central heating.

I recall that when I married in 1953 and temporarily worked in a textile factory in a small town of Sobinka in Vladimir Region, I decided to call on my wife's relatives in the village of Zhokhovo in the same region. This village was situated 80 kilometres from the railway and there was absolutely no means of transport available to it. In actual fact there was no road in our understanding of the term either. There was a cart-track impassable in autumn and spring and covered with snow in the winter. I walked almost 20km on foot. Zhokhovo, which is situated 150 km from Moscow, did not at this time have electricity. The economy was predominantly based on exchange of goods in kind and on self-sufficient consumption, with the shop open only twice a week and in a neighbouring village at that. In this shop, there was virtually nothing besides sugar and salt, so that in the village the people baked their own bread, drank their own milk and ate their own eggs etc. all produced on their family plots. For a "day's work" (a unit of labour in the Kolkhoz) they received only several hundred grammes of rye or another grain. Working on the collective land brought no benefits other than receiving the plot of land for the family's use. I recall that a major event for the inhabitants of the village was the permission to plant grass in small clearings in the wood, giving up a large part of the hay to the collective farm but with the right to keep a part of it for themselves. The collective farm workers called this form of receiving fodder for their own animals "the percentage".

The collective farm workers had no guaranteed income, no pension and no sickness benefit. Their lives depended mainly on their family plots. Evidently the situation was similar in many other collectives and state farms, although in the wealthier regions of the Caucasus, Kuban, the Ukraine, Uzbekistan and the Baltic, the level of development of agriculture and of the villages themselves was much higher.

In September 1953 an important Plenary meeting of the Central Committee took place at which Khrushchev made an address. A new agrarian policy was declared. Prices were significantly raised. Taxes were cut, and monetary payment for goods was gradually introduced into agriculture. A guaranteed wage was to be paid to collective farm workers and state assistance to the villages increased. Greater economic independence was granted to the collective farm workers, their interest in the results of their work being strengthened. Simultaneously a decision was taken to develop the virgin lands, in the Altai province, Kazakhstan and several other regions. Previously untouched lands saw the establishment of tens of new state farms with roads and electric cables laid etc. The virgin lands were used largely for the production of grain. Thousands of mainly young people moved to these regions. New life began in the uninhabited expanses of Siberia and Northern Kazakhstan.

In 1956 measures were taken towards the improvement of the land for agriculture, primarily through irrigation. Basic resources for carrying out this work were provided by the government. Attempts were also made to extend the production of tractors, combines and other agricultural machinery for the villages. Production of fertilizer was also increased. All these and other measures helped greatly to speed up agricultural growth. In the period 1954–59 the volume of agricultural output increased on average by more than 7% a year. Of this growth roughly one half resulted from extensive factors of inputs – through the expansion of arable land which grew by 42 million hectares and through increasing the numbers of livestock. But half of the growth was achieved through intensive factors – the increase in yields and labour productivity. The rapid development of agriculture helped the food industry and the related branches of light industry using agricultural raw materials. As a result the supply of foodstuffs and of light industrial products from this source increased sharply.

During the six years 1954–59 per capita income grew by 37%. If in the post-war period there were quite a few destitute people, beggars, and impoverished families, by the end of the 1950s these had practically disappeared and the diet including that of poor families had improved greatly. Simultaneously important measures were taken to develop the production of consumer goods in industry. Mass production of consumer durables was undertaken:

television sets and fridges were being produced, and one could buy a private car for the first time. The sale of electrical goods, crockery, and furniture speeded up. Industrial branches were formed for the production of widely sought-after consumer goods, in which enterprises of both heavy industry and the arms industries became involved. Great efforts were made to develop commercial activity and public catering. Self-service shops appeared and a network of restaurants and cafes was developed.

Growth of production and trade in consumer goods made possible rapid real rises in wages and other incomes of the population. From 1956 measures to increase and regulate wages were initiated. The minimum wage which was established by the state began to be raised. From the mid-1950s to the present day the minimum wage has trebled, against a rise of 1.3 times in the index of prices calculated by the Soviet Central Statistical Board .

In 1956 a pension law was passed, one of the most progressive laws in the world at that time. A low pensionable age and sharp increases in the pension were laid down. In the second half of the 1950s the length of the working day was reduced: firstly to 7 hours per day, and later a 40-hour working week was introduced. For some categories of workers engaged on the land or in heavier work a 35-hour working week was then established.

At the end of the 1950s mass construction of accommodation was begun on an industrial scale using preformed concrete panels. The volume of housing construction was one and a half times greater than in the preceeding period. Life expectancy in the Soviet Union approached the levels of the most developed countries. The country was making great progress. The first "Sputnik" was launched into space, sparking off a feeling of great enthusiasm and legitimate pride in the country. Grandiose plans were being made. It was declared that two decades were sufficient to obtain an abundance of food and consumer goods and to solve the accommodation problem. In the 1950s the Soviet Union was developing at twice the rate of advanced capitalist countries, with the exception perhaps of Japan. The gap in the level of economic and social development between the Soviet Union and the USA was rapidly closing.

In the debate taking place about the closing of the economic gap, it was above all the indices of industrial production (metal, electro-energy, cars, work stations, textiles, meat products etc.) and of national income which were taken into account. The qualitative aspects of change had not been sufficiently considered. In the relation between the individual worker's productivity and the quantity of production, sufficient attention had not been given to indices of cost-effectiveness such as use of raw materials, employment of capital investment, and construction time.

Extrapolations were made from which it seemed evident that within fifteen to twenty years the Soviet Union would lead the world in total output, productivity and the standard of living. These extrapolated indices were based on faster rates of growth than in the West and were at the root of the new Party programme accepted at the XXI Congress of the CPSU. Alas these grandiose plans have not been realised. They were often unrealistic, calculated on a continuing tendency of extensive development and did not take into consideration any decline in the growth of resources. But also, these plans were not successful because of the errors and failings permitted in the following period of development.

Already by the late 1950s the voluntaristic and ungrounded nature of the economic policy became more apparent. To a certain extent this was related to some dizziness with success. But evidently a deeper reason lay in the preservation of the administrative system of management, the lack of development of democratic principles in the direction of the country. One after the other hasty and unthought-out measures were implemented for reorganising the national economy.

The general reorganisation of management of the economy was not well founded in the total transfer of authority from the branch to the region. Sovnarkhozy [8] were organised locally and underwent constant transformations: in the beginning each Sovnarkhoz was rather large – one for several regions – and they encompassed not only branches of industry but also construction. Then the Sovnarkhozy were broken up into smaller units, construction units becoming part of a different structure. At the same time the system of central planning was reorganised several times, including the Central Planning Office (Gosplan)[9] which was replaced by the

[8] Sovnarkhoz (Soviet Narodnogo Khoziastva) i.e. Soviet (Council) of the National Economy, were authorities set up for the management of the economy, organised on a more regional basis in contrast to the central ministries which were organised by branches of production. (ed.)

Government Scientific Council and the State Economic Commission. Then the Central Planning Office was reconstituted as a long-
term planning agency while the annual plans rested with the State
Economic Commission. Finally they were all united in the Central
Planning Office. Branch planning agencies were initially abolished,
but then partially re-formed as state committees for groups of
branches. These committees, however, had no management rights
over their branches, since this was the role of the Sovnarkhozy.
Alongside the central planning agencies an All-Union Council of
National Economy (VSNKh) was set up. With these numerous
shifts, continuity in branch management was lost. For example, all
branches of industry within Moscow were made responsible to the
Moscow City Sovnarkhoz. Formerly, under the ministerial system
these branches of industry and corresponding enterprises all over
the country had come under the supervision of the several
ministries.

As a result of all these changes the rate of growth of production
began to fall. The rate of capital return in industry, which up to this
point had grown continuously, also declined. Reserves began to
grow faster than production, numerous imbalances in the development of the national economy arose and difficulties grew in ensuring
inputs for enterprises. In this transition to regional management,
the command–administrative style of management was not
changed. Only the agencies which implemented the administrative
management were changed. There was no progress whatever in the
use of economic methods of management, which would take
account of the interests of basic units of production.

In agriculture, after five to six years of rapid development, mainly
associated with the strengthening of economic methods of management and the direct benefits derived by agricultural workers from
the results of their work, a return to administrative methods of
management took place. Republics, regions and collective farms
began to have unreal obligations thrust upon them to increase the
sale of meat, milk and other products to the state. Simultaneously
various obstacles were put in the way of the development of family

---

[9] Gosplan is the government agency that has for long been in charge of both
short-term and long-term planning of Soviet social and economic development and of controlling plan fulfilment. In this book it will be referred to
henceforth as the Central Planning Office. (ed.)

plots, where there was a decline in numbers of livestock and of many agricultural products. A significant proportion of workers in small settlements and villages who had previously met their own needs became themselves consumers of foodstuffs, buying these products in the shops or in the market.

Administrative pressure from higher authorities managing the collective and state farms also increased. The subdivision of regional party committees into industrial and agricultural was not thought through either, and led to trivial interference by specialised agencies of the Party into the affairs of the collective and state farms. At the end of the 1950s steps were needed to reorganise the Machine and Tractor Stations (MTCs). Their abolition was decreed and their machinery was sold off to the collective farms and state farms. Accordingly machine operators who were previously working for the MTCs transferred to the collective farms. In itself the measure was effective in uniting the village workers with their means of production. But this major action was implemented without sufficient preparation of machine maintenance services by the collective and state farms and without providing sufficiently long terms for the purchase of this machinery. As a result the machinery was handed over and was set to work without the means for its proper maintainance. Its value sharply deteriorated and the length of break-down periods grew. The state's demand that the machinery be purchased from the MTCs by payments made over a very short period, took almost all the collective and state farms' savings, leaving them immediately in a difficult financial situation.

With the transfer of machinery to the collective and state farms prices were raised for fuel and spare parts, and this worsened still further the financial situation of the collective farms and state farms, many of which began trading at a loss. The issue was aggravated by a slight fall in agricultural state purchase prices, resulting from the assumption that with good harvests production costs would be lower.

The insufficiently thought out and hasty decisions on agriculture resulted in the slowing down of its development. The growth of agricultural production came up against an invisible barrier. The loss of pace in the growth of agricultural output was also due to the decline in the growth of land under crops, which occurred in the period prior to the development of the virgin lands. While in the 1954–59 period the annual growth of agricultural production was more than 7%, in 1960–64 it fell to 1.5%–2% and per capita agricultural output did not increase at all.At the same time increases in monetary income and in the wages of the population continued. A contradiction therefore arose between demand and supply. There was a particularly acute shortage in the production of meat and dairy products. To improve the situation, in 1962 the government initiated a significant price rise for these products without sufficient compensation being offered to the general population.

Thus it was that the negative tendencies clearly visible in the development of industry and agriculture in the late 1950s and up to the mid-1960s led to a sharp fall in the rate of growth of the Soviet national income. An annual growth rate of 12% in 1958 fell to 4% in 1963 (a year with a very bad harvest), and to 6% in 1964. If one takes into consideration that in these years there were also some hidden price rises, which did not appear in the official retail price index, then it can be reckoned that in the 1962–64 period there was actual stagnation in the national economy. Something had to be done.

Thus from the end of 1964 after the October meeting of the Central Committee, when Khrushchev was removed from his position as General Secretary and Chairman of the Council of Ministers, *a new turning point in the economic policy of the country was reached*. Immediately single regional party committees were recreated (instead of the dualistic industry and agriculture division), and a single State Planning Office was organised to undertake branch administration via the ministries. The Sovnarkhozy were abolished. All this created a new economic structure for the conduct of an economic reform.

The first step of this reform was to take place in agriculture. At the March 1965 Plenary meeting of the Central Committee a new form of agricultural planning was agreed. Once again purchase prices were raised, taxes were reduced and measures were taken to broaden the development of farming on family plots. Collective and state farms were partially freed from detailed administrative interference. Henceforth purchase prices for planned output were established for five years and for many products they remained unchanged throughout the whole of this period. Agricultural products delivered in excess of the plan were sold for one and a half times the ordinary price. Simultaneously other important measures

777

777

were taken by the government to assist the countryside. All this helped to double the rate of growth of agricultural production. In the period from 1966 to 1970 the volume of agricultural output increased at a rate 21% above that of the previous five-year period.

The accelerated growth of agricultural production allowed the rate of production to increase in branches of light industry based on agricultural raw materials. As a result the production of consumer goods grew faster in 1966–70 than the production of the means of production. All this significantly affected the growth of the national income, since a large share of it was still made from foodstuffs and products manufactured from agricultural raw materials. A major event of this period was also the carrying through of economic reforms in industry approved at the September 1965 Plenary meeting of the Central Committee. The conceptual preparation of these reforms was made by academics. Discussions were held in the newspapers and journals in the preceding period. Academics argued through the necessity for a transition to economic methods of management, for stimulation of market relations, and an increase in the role of profit in economic development. Prof. E. Lieberman, a well-known economist among Western specialists interested in the Soviet economy, then came forward with a number of interesting articles and suggestions. In the Academy of Sciences at that time a commission composed of such well-known specialists as V.S. Nemchinov, L.V. Kantorovich, L.M. Gatovskii, K.H. Plotnikov, V.P. D'yachenko, was working on the preparation of the reforms.

I was a member of this commission and well remember the sharp debates out of which the new economic system evolved. We were aiming at a major reform of wholesale prices and at the introduction of payment for resources (this was then introduced but only for direct inputs), at strengthening the role of profit and at the transfer to wholesale purchase of the centralised supply of materials and machinery. This was an interesting period in the development of economics, when the discussion involved deep questions as to the nature of value and price. There was even a special commission of the Academy of Sciences working on this problem. Commodity production was also discussed, the relation between use value and exchange value in socialist conditions, the question of single level pricing and the principles applied in determining price (whether it is necessary to involve in prices the capital consumed in the process of production, etc.).

The September 1965 Central Committee meeting on the whole met the expectations of the advanced economists. For that time its resolutions were fairly radical. It did not remove the system of planning by directive, although it limited it to only a few indicators, and gave unprecedented freedom to the enterprises to plan independently their rates of growth of productivity, ways to cut production costs, the setting of average wages (departing from the centralised planned wages' fund and the fixed system of differentials, tax rates, etc.). On the basis of norms governing economic proportions and profit margins, each enterprise created funds for generating the development of production, for new housing and for material incentives. All this created a stake for the enterprise and its collective, in the viability of its work and the improvement of economic performance indicators. Results were not slow in appearing. Growth in productivity substantially accelerated, the rate of growth of profit doubled, capital output ratio in industry began to improve again, enterprises' stocks began to fall and the proportion of unused capacity sharply declined.

Among enterprise collectives and their leaders a taste for economic work appeared, and a certain re-evaluation of ways and means took place. Indicators of the volume of output of actual products, viability, rate of growth of wages and material incentives came into force. The major reform of wholesale prices introduced in industry in 1967 also played a role here. But unfortunately not everything prepared as part of the plan for economic reform was implemented. In particular uniform economic norms of profit were not established for the formation of funds for the various incentives in different branches or groups of enterprises. In fact these profit norms came to be reassessed each year depending on the results achieved and were different for each enterprise. This greatly weakened the economic stimuli, for efficient work led to higher norms being imposed the following year and the best enterprises came under greater pressure from the ministries and planning authorities than the worst ones.

Similarly the profit norms introduced for the formation of wage funds did not take account of the true proportions between growth of output and growth of wages. The system retained many weaknesses which led to a rise in wages without a corresponding increase in output. Wage rises over the five-year period appeared excessive as there was no corresponding increase in production of consumer goods. In some years the average increase in industrial wages even outstripped the growth in productivity. When all this became apparent additional measures were needed. There were two options: the first was to improve the economic indicators for the setting of wages, i.e. to make it disadvantageous for an enterprise to overdraw money from the wage fund. This road was taken in Hungary; reforms had been introduced there for setting wage funds which, when they were first implemented, appeared to be even stricter than the administrative regulators of direct planning adopted in the USSR. A second option was to return to an administrative method of management and to introduce the planning of productivity by directive, relating growth of productivity to wages. Unfortunately, it was the administrative methods that were adopted. This was the familiar way and although the hold of administrative methods was slightly loosened during the economic reforms, nevertheless their position had not really been undermined and they prevailed once again over economic methods. After the determination of labour productivity had been returned to a system of direct planning, costs of production followed likewise. When each year a shortage of a particular product occurred, as a result of being omitted from the plan, it was included in the next plan and increasing numbers of directives from above covering specific products were established for each enterprise. As a result of all this, a total relapse to administrative methods of management took place which destroyed the main achievement of the new style of management, and particularly its effect in reducing the number of directives and strengthening the economic methods of management.

At the September 1965 meeting of the Central Committee the question was also posed of effecting a major transfer to a system of wholesale trading between production units. But no concrete timescale or form for this transition was decided upon. General directives were given that the transition to wholesale trading would be implemented as the rate of growth of production increased and shortages ended. But what was not taken into account was the fact that the shortages themselves were a consequence of an imperfect economic system; and with the persistence of centralised supply of materials, these shortages would never disappear. Thus there was no transfer to wholesale trading, although individual experiments were undertaken with most surprising results. In particular, in five regions the rigid rationing system for fuel and lubricants was cancelled and they began to be sold freely. At the beginning their consumption rose slightly since organisations which were not used to free trade stored them. But once they were convinced of the fact of wholesale trading in petrol and other oil-based products, the level of consumption began to fall, and the final demand for fuel and lubricants appeared lower than it had been under the central supply system. Thus the shortage was evidently fictitious. But this experiment was unfortunately not continued.

Of no small importance has been the requirement of a legal and organisational guarantee of the transition of enterprises to the new conditions of economic management. In the period of economic reform (1965) the "Law on socialist enterprises" was passed in which enterprises were given fairly wide-ranging rights. Thereafter different decrees were passed on the various questions of planning, finances and material supply etc. Each of these decrees contained clauses cutting down the enterprises' role, making the "Law on socialist enterprises" unworkable. The fact is that this document was endorsed by the USSR Council of Ministers, but as other proposals were also accepted by the same government body it was these latter that were put into effect. At this time in the work of the Central Planning office, the Ministry of Finance, the Labour Committee and other central economic departments responsible for issuing instructions, the range of guidelines and regulations was expanded widely. The rights of enterprises were usurped by the ministries and institutions and to all intents the "Law on socialist enterprises" came to a *de facto* halt. The administrative approach prevailed. This became possible because no measures to defend the rights of enterprises were envisaged.

The organisation of the economic reform had likewise not been fully thought out. After the acceptance of the main reform proposals by the Central Committee and the Council of Ministers, the matter of its execution, the interpretation of the relevant clauses and the issuing of instructions were transferred to an Inter-Institutional Commission, set up by the Central Planning Council. This Council approved the Commission and included in its members representatives from the Ministry of Finance, from the State Supplies Board, from the Price Committee, Labour Committee and other institutions. This commission could then decide issues only through compromise, since each commission member had to receive approval for his moves from his own institutional chief. These compromises always leaned towards administrative methods of management since all the institutions attempted to strengthen their influence over the enterprises, while there was nobody on the Commission to represent the interests of the enterprises. As a result the Commission which was set up to promote reform actually caused it to fail.

When the economic reform was being considered it was intended that it should spread to all branches of the economy. One of the best experiments associated with the reform took place not in industry but in the transport enterprise *Glavmostoautotrans*. But in fact when the reform was introduced it was applied only to manufacturing industry. An attempt to transfer construction to new economic management was in the end turned into the old, predominantly administrative management method. When we speak of the retreat from the economic reform of 1965, it is particularly important to mention that this reform of industry and agriculture did not coincide with the transformation of other sectors of society. Economic reform was to be reflected in changes in the conditions of management in the main enterprises, collective and state farms. The activities of the ministries of planning and the financial authorities were not included in the economic reform. These worked as before using predominantly administrative methods. The administrative form of management even intensified among the central economic institutions and branch ministries. The machinery of state grew, new sections and departments were created and the central economic institutions expanded. Thus reform of the main production units was not reinforced by reform of the central structure. Nor, on the other hand, was this reform reinforced by changes in the structure of wages. The system of wages remained the same: with the same norms, rates and the predominance of piece-work over payment by the hour. Now things are different – a transition is occurring towards collective forms of organisation, with an extension of working collectives' rights to choose their own forms of incentives. This did not exist previously.

Finally there was no real advance in investment and restructuring or in the acceleration of scientific technological progress. It is true that economic reform mobilised reserves of economic capacity, but such reserves have limits and as they are used up, each further step in development requires increasing effort. Therefore, it is very important to undertake simultaneous measures to increase the effectiveness of capital investment and the acceleration of scientific technological progress, if one wishes to prolong the rate of acceleration of growth after organisational and economic reserves are exhausted. This did not then occur, and when, after the 1965 economic reform, the rate of economic growth doubled, this growth was not taken up and expanded by further measures of economic policy. Organisational reserves and economic potential were used up and the rate of growth started to fall. In fact this fall was steeper still because of the relapse into administrative methods.

Economic reform in the 1960s also failed because reform in the economy was not reinforced by corresponding measures in social life. Little changed, for example, in the activity of the Communist Party organisations, which continued to work in the old way. No additional measures were taken to democratise management, nor to draw new recruits into management from the broad masses of working people, not to mention the broader aspect of democracy in society at large. Therefore this reform only touched workers and collective farmers in its initial stages when they noticed how their wages were affected by new management methods. These workers and farmers played no role in working out the plans of their enterprises or the ways that funds for incentives were to be used, so that their interest in the change in economic policy was that much less. It should be noted that the mass media at that time did not come out in favour of the reform. They more often wrote of the shortcomings of economic methods and many articles called for the return to fixed indicators of productive work and costs. Articles also appeared saying that under socialism it was not financial costs but real indicators which were important. Therefore it transpired that the economic reform in agriculture and industry became, as it were, a foreign body in the existing system of economic and social relations. And this foreign body was ultimately suppressed by the environment and assimilated by prevailing attitudes.

After the failure of the 1965 economic reform and of the acceleration of growth following this reform, the reverse process began which we have already noted. A sharp fall in the rates of socio-economic development occurred in the 1971–75 period, as Table 3 shows.

Table 3:   *Rates of growth of USSR national income and efficiency in two five-year periods, 1966–70 and 1971-75* (all figures are of % growth over five years)

Plan period	Industrial output	Agricultural output	National income	Composite efficiency index
VIII 1966–70	50	21	41	18
IX 1971–75	32	13	28	5

Note: These are the official indices, which still somewhat overstate the real growth rates.

It was characteristic of the 1971–75 period that there was a significant increase in all types of resource inputs. This increase was even slightly larger than in the 1966–70 period. A fall in the general rate of growth was associated therefore with a sharp decline in productivity and other indicators of efficiency, as we can see from the last column in the table. Growth in productivity fell one and a half times. The capital output ratio and return on capital investment declined sharply. In the two periods between 1976 and 1985 that followed, further falls came which resulted primarily from the reduction in the growth of available resources. Efficiency of social production continued to grow as slowly as in the 1971–75 period.

What *lessons* can be learned for the implementation of the current *perestroika* from the unsuccessful reforms of the 1950s and 1960s? The first lesson is that *major* perestroika *can succeed only if it is all-embracing and includes the whole of society and all sectors of the economy*. Precisely such an all-embracing approach is being used for the current *perestroika* of Soviet society. In contrast with past reforms today's *perestroika* includes both base and superstructure, both the economic system and economic policies, both organisational economic measures and measures for scientific technological progress. All sectors, branches and elements are being included within the framework of economic *perestroika*. Success depends on such a broad approach.

At the same time major efforts are being made to achieve a radical reform of management. In contrast to previous efforts, this system will be completely reformed, and major changes will be made to the central state machinery as well as in the activity of the main units of production. The changes will affect all sectors of the economy, planning, the finance and credit system, material supply, wages etc. New methods of economic management are being introduced. This is central. In order to avoid the mistakes made during the 1960s reforms, a "Law on socialist enterprises" has been passed by supreme judicial decision. Proceeding from this law, proposals have been made and adopted for the transformation of all institutions of central management. So that the proposals and administrative steps are not altered, they will not this time be implemented by an inter-institutional commission, composed of institutional respresentatives, but by a government commission for management, headed by N.V. Talyzin, Vice-Chairman of the Council of Ministers, and President of the Central Planning Council. It is made up of top leaders of central economic institutions plus, for the first time, senior academics.

The most important lesson to be drawn from an analysis of the past concerns *the need for democratisation of society* as the indispensable element in a successful *perestroika*. Only through democratisation can the majority of working people be brought into the management process. The way forward lies in self-management. The development of democracy has been widely reflected in the mass media, whose role has markedly increased so that it has become, as it were, the popular monitor of the progress of *perestroika* in society.

3 EFFICIENCY AS THE DRIVING FORCE OF *PERESTROIKA*

One of the hardest problems to solve in the acceleration of the socio-economic development of the country, is that this must be achieved in circumstances of a falling growth of natural productive resources. This process started in the 1971–75 plan period. Let us consider the tendencies of Soviet economic development since the 1970s (see Table 4 below).

This shows that the 1971–75 period was the last in which there was a significant growth in productive resources. In this respect it was a five-year period that was typical of the whole post-war period of Soviet economic development. In the three five-year periods between 1956 and 1970, productive resources increased in roughly the same degree as in the 1971–75 period. Projections for the future show that 1971–75 was the last period in our generation with high growth in productive resources. More recently the growth rate of productive resources has greatly decreased. Above all, beginning in the 1981–85 period the growth of labour resources was falling and thereby the number of workers in the branches of production. Normally over a five-year period the population of working age (in the Soviet Union this is from 16–55 years for women and up to 60 for men) increased by ten and eleven million. In the past five-year period the growth in the labour force even exceeded this figure, because of higher participation rates in the labour market. (While in the 1960s for every 100 people of working age roughly 18 were not employed, the proportion is now 8 to 9 per 100.) Out of the additional labour force in the 1961–70 period four and a half million workers went into manufacturing industry, approximately one million into construction, one million into transport, up to two million into trade and supply, two million into state farms (there was actual decline in the membership of collective farms), roughly two to three million into the health service, education, culture and science, and up to one million into housing and services.

Table 4: *Development of the USSR economy, resources and efficiency, 1971–85: percentage change over five-year periods*   (official figures)

	Five-year plan periods		
Indicators	IX 1971–75	X 1976–80	XI 1981–85
Global indicators			
National income	28	21	16.5
Real per capita income	24	18	11
Productive resources			
Basic productive funds	52	43	37
Productive capital investment	44	23	17
Production of mining industry	25	10	8
Number of workers in all branches of production	6	6	2
Efficiency of national production[1]			
Capital output ratio	−16	−15	−15
Efficiency of capital investment	−11	−2	−0.5
Efficiency of use of industrial material inputs[1]	2	10	8
Productivity of labour	21	14	14

Note: [1] Index of efficiency calculated in relation to index of national income according to official statistics.

From 1981 to 1985 the Soviet Union entered a demographic slump directly reflecting the consequences of World War Two. In the 1980s the children of parents born during the war are coming of working age. The birth rate fell during the war and the number of adult parents, and thus their children, is consequently smaller than for other generations. Also from the mid-1980s the numbers of persons reaching pensionable age was rising sharply. Up to now the proportion of men who fought in the war and had become pensioners was relatively small as many of this generation perished. The post-war generations – correspondingly two, three and even five times larger – are now reaching pensionable age. These two trends are coinciding. Therefore the growth in numbers of persons of working age in the population is falling sharply. Instead of the former normal increase of ten to eleven million workers, in the 1981–85 period it was three and a half million only and in the current period, 1986–90 – the demographically most acute years – it was about two and a half million.

It should also be noted that the rates of growth of the working population in the periods 1981–90 are mainly occurring because of an increase in the size of populations in Central Asia and Azerbaidzhan. These are regions far from the territories occupied during the war and where the traditionally high birth rate was maintained. In Russia, the Ukraine, Belorussia and the Baltic republics the size of the working population in the 1980s will not increase at all and in certain regions it will fall.

All this is leading to a decline in the number of workers employed in branches of production. This fall is occurring at an even greater pace because of the redeployment of the population into the service sectors. Therefore in the 1981–85 period the number of workers employed in industry rose overall by one million and in agriculture by less than half a million. In construction the figure hardly grew, in transport it rose by only half a million, in commerce by half a million but in health and education by more than a million. The falling growth in the number of workers requires increases in labour productivity. If earlier 20%–25% of all growth in social production was achieved through increased numbers of workers, and 75%–80% through higher productivity then in the 1981–85 period the element of productivity growth was 90% and the impact of the number of workers fell to 10%.

Simultaneously growth in productive capital investment has declined more than two and a half times and growth of overall productive resources has slowed down. This is connected with the reduction in the proportion of capital accumulation in the national income as a consequence of the increased share of resources going to consumption. This share has increased from 71% in 1970 to 75% in 1985; the accumulation fund declined correspondingly from 29% to 25%. This redistribution within the national income was connected with the wish to find additional resources for raising the standard of living. It was necessary to raise the efficency of productive capital investment and therefore to improve the capital output ratio since only this would sustain the required rate of growth of the national income in conditions of declining productive resources. But it is obvious from the indicators shown that this has only been partially achieved, through stabilising the efficiency of capital investment. At the same time the capital output ratio continued to worsen against the slow growth of resource inputs.

The growth in the extraction of fuel and raw materials has fallen even more, by three times. This fall is mainly the result of worsening geological and economic conditions in the mining industries. The quantities of fuel and raw materials extracted in the USSR are immense. In 1985 for example, 615 million tonnes of oil, 686 billion cubic metres of gas, 751 million tonnes of coal, 112 million tonnes of iron ore were extracted in the USSR and 295 million cubic metres of timber prepared. With such rates of extraction, good deposits and favourable fields are rapidly becoming exhausted, and to maintain these rates of extraction it is necessary to transfer to new more difficult deposits, deeper fields and worse conditions. Thus the yield of oil and the extraction of iron ore are falling and mining for coal and precious metals has to be done at greater and greater depths.

In the Soviet Union the centres of production are not evenly distributed. More than 70% of production and the corresponding population are situated in the European part of the USSR and in the Urals. It is here that most resources are consumed. Yet these regions make up less than a quarter of the territory of the USSR with only one tenth of the reserves of fuel, only one quarter of the forests, a fifth of water resources etc. A large proportion of resources are concentrated in Siberia and the Soviet Far East – more than four fifths of the fuel reserves, three quarters of the timber and, if one takes into account the flow of rivers, three quarters of all fresh water. (This excludes Lake Baikal which represents 80% of Soviet resources and 20% of the world's supply of fresh water.) At the same time Siberia and the Far East account for only one tenth of production and population. Kazakhstan and Central Asia occupy as much as one third of the land area of the country. They are rich in mineral resources, have large populations (one sixth of the total USSR population), and a high proportion of Soviet agricultural production. But these regions have only 5% of the river waters and practically no timber.

When the level of development of the economy was still relatively low, the intensive processing of fuel and raw materials in the inhabited European part of the country ensured the development of the economy in these regions. Coal came mostly from the Don region, oil from the Volga and Baku, timber from the northern regions of the European part of the country and the Urals, precious minerals were mined in the Kola Peninsula, the Urals and the Caucasus etc*. But the needs of the growing economy increased the demand for fuel and raw materials. By the mid-1970s the flow of fuel and raw materials extracted in the European part of the USSR could not grow any further. Additional requirements were met primarily by the rapid development of the extraction industry in Siberia. In the 1976–85 period, despite the fact that capital investment increased, oil extraction in the Volga region began to fall, coal from the Don Coal fields fell, as did the preparation of timber in the northern regions and the Urals. Nickel extraction on the Kola Peninsula stopped completely, nickel being brought to the Kola enterprises from Norilsk by the northern sea route.

All this required the transfer of mining to the uninhabited regions of the east and north. In Western Siberia, mainly the Tyumen Region, in the mid-1960s an oil and gas complex was created as the main fuel and energy base of the USSR. Timber production increasingly moved to Eastern Siberia and the Far East. The extraction of precious metal ores was significantly expanded there also; for example in Norilsk, situated further north than the Arctic circle in Krasnoyarsk Province. The establishment of new fuel and mineral bases necessitated the development of these regions, the construction of transport and communication systems, the creation of towns and the transfer of hundreds of thousands of people. Suffice it to say that more than one and a half million people moved to West Siberia from other parts of the country. In the 1981–85 period on average about ten billion roubles of capital investment was made there each year, as much as the whole costs of the 3,000km Baikal–Amur link. With such resources three enormous Volga-type car factories could be built, with an annual production of more than 700,000 vehicles.

All this led to serious increases in the prices of fuel and raw materials, particularly as the result of the high capital investment

* A map outlining the mineral resources of the USSR can be found on pages xii–xiii.

incurred. While 20–25 years ago one rouble of production in the extraction industry required two roubles of capital investment, by 10 years ago this figure had grown to three to four roubles of capital investment and in the 1981–85 period it exceeded seven roubles. Production costs grew for many types of raw materials as did the labour intensity needed for their extraction. A further price increase occurred through the tightening up of ecological and safety requirements in mining. In these conditions it is more advantageous to concentrate on measures designed to economise in the use of raw materials than on additional extraction. It requires two to two and a half times less resources to save one tonne of fuel in the USSR by economising than it does to mine an extra tonne.

Here it should be noted that the previous low prices of fuel and raw materials and their abundance in the USSR led on many occasions to the most extravagant use. This is still the case now because of the low prices for fuel and raw materials, which are usually two to three times lower than the world price. Therefore the Soviet Union has a large potential for economies in the use of fuel and raw materials as a part of a resource conservation policy.

As is evident major *perestroika* was necessary in many directions, and especially a change from extensive to intensive development. This has not yet occurred, although there have been some successes in this area. If one compares the three recent five-year periods then it is obvious that in the 1971–75 period efficiency of production was increased mainly through higher productivity. However, this result suffered to a considerable extent by the worsening of the capital output ratio and the efficiency of capital investment, the more so since the rates of consumption of materials in production hardly fell.

In the 1976–80 and 1981–85 periods better use of industrial raw materials was achieved and a slight decline occurred in the consumption of materials in production. At the same time the indicator of efficiency of capital investment was static. The rates of growth of productivity in the past could not be maintained, indeed they fell substantially. Thus the rate of growth of productivity in industry fell from 34% in the 1971–75 period to 17% in the 1976–80 period and the same low rate was repeated in 1981–85. Over the same period, there was a decline in the growth of productivity in all other sectors – construction, transport and agriculture.

We will try to present in a general way the ongoing tendencies of development. For this let us recall that labour lies at the base of all productive resources. At any time the basic fund of capital investment which is created by labour is being used up in the extraction of fuel and raw materials and the production of equipment, in construction and assembly work. Since at the basis of any productive resource there is in the end only labour , it is possible to conflate indicators of these various resources into one measure, which we can call an index of efficiency in the use of resources (see Table 5).

Table 5: *Indices of efficiency in the USSR economy, 1971–85: percentage growth per five-year period* (official figures except where indicated)

	Five-year periods		
	IX	X	XI
Indicators	1971–75	1976–80	1981–85 (forecast)
National income	28	21	16.5
Productive resources*	21	13	9
Efficiency of productions*	6	7	7
Contribution of factors of economic growth in the rise in national income			
extensive %	75	67	60
intensive %	25	33	40

* Our estimate

A small advance was achieved in the 1976–85 periods with a larger contribution to growth through intensive factors. However these could not compensate for a still larger decline in the use of productive resources, leading to a consequent fall in the speed of economic development.

In the 1986–90 period and in the following years the growth of productive resources will fall further and the average index will hardly grow more than 7% in the period 1986–1990 (compared with 10% in 1981–85, 13% in 1976–80 and 21% in 1971–75). In the following five-year period after 1990 growth will fall to 5%–6% for the following reasons:

1) The 1986–90 period coincides with the least favourable post-war

demographic period mentioned above and no growth is expected in the number of workers in production. For the first time in the history of the Soviet Union all growth in production must be realised through increased labour productivity.

As early as 1986, the first year of the current five year period, the number of workers in all branches of production has only increased by a total of 0.3%. In manufacturing it also increased by 0.3%. At the same time in agriculture and railway transport the growth in productivity has outstripped growth of production and the number of workers has substantially fallen.

In the first few months of 1987 growth in the number of workers in production came to an end and all growth of production in industry and in other branches is occurring through increased productivity. In the future, considering the need to redeploy large numbers of people into health, education, housing and other branches of the service sector, the number of workers in industry, agriculture, construction and transport will have to fall; and this can only come about as a result of more rapid growth of productivity than in the volume of production in these branches.

2) Because of the existing structure of the economy and the shortfall in investment in certain branches (machine building, construction, metallurgy) capital investment will barely grow beyond 25% in the five years. This planned growth of capital investment in the 1986–90 period seems greater than it was in the 1981–85 period (17%), although it is less than in all the preceding five-year periods (28% in 1976–80, 43% in 1971–75). A slight increase in the growth of capital investment in the 1986–90 period compared with the 1981–85 period derives primarily from the necessity for considerable investment in the reconstruction of existing enterprises to create conditions for the acceleration of scientific technological progress.

At the same time capital investment is increasing in fuel and energy where there was a shortfall in the past and in branches of the production infrastructure. As has been mentioned, the proportion for the social sector is also rising in the total volume of capital investment in the economy.

How will this accelerated increase of capital investment be ensured? One of the main sources is the higher growth of final ouput in the 1986–90 period compared with the 1981–85 period resulting from the acceleration of the country's socio-economic development. On the other hand in the 1986–90 period, no decline is envisaged in the proportion of accumulation in the national income. It is possible that it will even grow slightly.

3) With the worsening of geological and economic conditions the tendency towards limited growth in the extraction of fuel and raw materials will persist, although in the 1986–90 period the mobilisation of reserves will mean an improvement in the rate of growth in some branches of the mining industry. We have managed to overcome a decline in the development of the oil industry. Having achieved a maximum extraction in 1983 of 616 million tonnes, extraction then fell to 595 million tonnes in 1985. The growth rate of extraction fell even in Western Siberia, where it was until recently rising rapidly, making up for the shortfall from older deposits. After the 1985 Party Management Conference, serious measures were taken in the city of Tyumen to open up new deposits, to intensify oil extraction, to mechanise the industry and to increase drilling etc. In the intervening two years an additional thirty-six oil wells were sunk in Western Siberia, more than in the whole previous period. All this made it possible to overcome the unfavourable tendencies in Western Siberia. In one year, 1986, the increase in the extraction of oil in the Soviet Union was 20 million tonnes and in 1987 growth in oil extraction was continuing.

The same negative tendency in the coal industry has been overcome. While in the whole of the 1981–85 period the volume of coal extracted grew by only 10 million tonnes, in 1986 alone it rose by 25 million. Natural gas extraction is being stepped up. The volume of extraction is growing at an unprecedented rate. Gas is replacing fuel oil and in large towns also replacing coal with a view to improving the environment. This is helping to intensify technological progress in industry, to improve the environment and to switch to gas for a large part of the fuel and energy balance of the Soviet Union. Thanks to the enormous gas pipeline construction a nationwide gas network is gradually being laid down.

It has also been possible to overcome the decline in the timber industry. In the preceding five-year period the volume of output was static, but has been rising since 1986. But these successes in additional extraction of certain raw materials do not make it possible to stave off the general tendency to falling growth rates in the extractive industries. This tendency will appear even more clearly in the 1990s.

The limited increases in extensive factors in economic growth cannot be relied upon to achieve acceleration of the socio-economic development of the country. The economy must move decisively and rapidly to intensive development and to the acceleration of efficiency through better use of resources. The situation which has arisen during the 1981–85 period and projections for the future are shown in Table 6 below.

To accelerate the annual rate of growth of the national income from 3% to 4% the rate of growth in efficiency needs to be doubled, ensuring that the five-year growth rate rises from 7% to 14%. Such an increase in efficiency can only be achieved if the rate of growth of productivity is increased one and a half times, if the rate of use of material resources in production is halved and the capital output ratio is improved two and a half times compared with the indicators of the 1981–85 period.

Table 6:   *National income and resources of the USSR: 11th five-year period (1981–85) and future projections for the 12th, 13th and 14th periods up to the year 2000: percentage growth per five-year period* (official figures except where indicated)

Indicator	XI 1981–85	XII 1986–90 (forecast)	XIII & XIV 1991–2000 (average 5-year projection)
National income	16.5	22	28
Productive resources*	9	7	5–6
Efficiency of production*	7	14	10
Impact of categories of economic growth on the rise in the national income			
extensive %	60	33	25
intensive %	40	67	75

* Our estimate

In the last 15 years the efficiency indicator of the economy in each five-year period rose by roughly 7%. The economy continued, through inertia, to develop extensively. In the new conditions, these tendencies in economic development are to be overcome and the whole of the economy is to be steered onto the path of intensive methods so as to achieve a marked acceleration in socio-economic development. The most important reserve for increasing economic and social efficiency in the whole economy and the means also to accelerate socio-economic development lies in improving the quality of production. At the XXVII Party Congress the importance was clearly recognised of placing the improvement of quality in production at the centre of all economic policy. "Quality and again quality" is our slogan for today. Only having solved the problem of quality, can the problem of quantity be resolved? Although questions of raising the quality of production were repeatedly posed earlier, it is especially important now to turn attention to this key problem for our economic management. It should be noted that quality is a good general index of efficiency. Material resources and social labour which are used up in low quality production and even in defective production are resources wasted as the products fail to meet social needs. Improving the quality is therefore the only possible way to end the shortages in the economy.

The problem of quality is particularly obvious if one considers a product's life cycle. Take for example machines and tools. The matter does not end with the investment of energy, material and labour in the making of the machine. After this, during the use of the machine further expenditure is needed. In the case of a tractor or a car, the investment during the production process may make up 3%–4% of the aggregate cost borne by society during its working life. The rest consists of maintenance costs, running costs, spare parts and many other things. Cost depends directly on the quality of production. Spending an extra 50 roubles on a new tractor model to improve its reliability can mean an annual saving of about 500 roubles. This is a fairly typical example. High quality is a decisive factor in increasing efficiency in production.

Indivisibly linked to the problem of quality is the question of the breadth of re-equipment, especially in relation to machinery and tools. Machines cannot be operated without tools and jigs and if, having bought the machine itself, a factory does not obtain the equipment to go with it the machine will stand idle. To an even greater extent this is true in the case of computer technology, when it is set up without all the necessary additional hardware and full software. Machinery can produce high quality results only if it is set up properly and is put immediately to work. There is a great potential in the country for improvement of quality, but to make a radical improvement, it is necessary to work hard in perfecting production and the related technology, to increase the qualifications of the personnel, and to adapt the planning, management and incentive systems to achieve all this.

To achieve high efficiency and quality there lies ahead for us the implementation of a whole system of crucial economic management measures, aimed at the acceleration of socio-economic development. These measures can be divided into two groups.

Firstly, there are measures for mobilising organisational, economic and social reserves and the potential for better use of available resources. To have an impact, these measures, as a rule, do not require capital investment and can be achieved in the short-term. But such reserves and their potential are limited.

Secondly, the more significant and more profound potential lies in scientific and technological progress and therefore this represents a major strategic element in the acceleration of socio-economic development.

The resolution of both requirements depends to a certain extent on the creation of new economic and organisational conditions during a major *perestroika* of the planning and management of the whole economic system.

The hardest period will be that running from 1986 to 1990, when we face two tasks. The first is to accelerate the current rate of socio-economic development. The second is to prepare conditions for large scale acceleration in the following five-year periods (1991–2000). Thus in the 1986–90 period we will not yet be able to use scientific and technological factors to the full in order to raise efficiency because time is needed to renew capital and to change the structure of production for introducing new machinery and new technology.

Here is an example. For about 20 years petrol-driven goods vans with not very powerful engines have been produced at the Gorky Car Factory. A new model, the GAZ-6308, has been prepared: with a more powerful diesel engine and a fuel consumption of 14 litres per 100km (compared with 19 litres for the current model) as well as a trailer of 8.5mt (instead of 4.5mt). Expected mileage was raised from 250 to 350 thousand km before capital repairs are needed, and maintenance costs reduced by one and a half times. The productivity of drivers is set to rise on average 1.7 times. The state commission, when approving the new model, noted that the new vehicles represent an annual saving to the national economy of 393 million roubles i.e. a colossal saving. When can this be expected? Mass production lines have to be converted, i.e. a diesel factory costing 800 million roubles built and a further 500 million roubles spent on refitting and resconstruction. Recovering this outlay will take only about three years. From 1988 production of these machines should begin (the first stage of reconstruction) but the real effect will be felt only when old vehicles are replaced on a large scale by the new, i.e. in the 1991–95 period, and the greatest effect will be felt in the period up to the year 2000 (the second stage of reconstruction).

Are there sufficient reserves to increase the efficiency of the existing productive base through better attitudes to work and higher productivity, through higher quality production, economies in use of materials and resources etc.? That is the question. There are numerous examples testifying to the enormous potential offered in the short term by raising productivity, economising in fuel and raw materials, improving the indicators of the capital-output ratio and efficiency of capital investment. Every economic organisation has such reserves, and significant progress can be made if each can be involved and the interests of working collectives harnessed.

According to economists' estimates it is possible to raise the rate of growth of the national income by these means in the order of 1.3 to 1.5 times and to accelerate the growth of productivity and other indices of efficiency one and a half to two times. This is shown by the current experience of the other socialist countries where a decision to use existing resources better by perfecting the economic system has been consistently pursued. The Soviet experience of economic reform in 1965 showed the same.

Let us recall that in the 1966–70 period the rate of socio-economic growth fell substantially and negative tendencies arose because of errors that were made. Thus the official rate of growth of national income fell: in 1960 it was 8%, in 1961 7%, in 1962 6% and in 1963 4%. The capital-output ratio, and efficiency of capital investment also worsened. Use of fuel and raw materials increased. The rate of growth of productivity sharply declined. In consequence the rate of growth of real income slowed down and the supply of foodstuffs and industrial products deteriorated.

The October 1964 Plenary of the Central Committee renewed the leadership and made major changes to the system of planning, management and incentives. The ministries and related management structures were re-established, and the role of centralised planning and of the Central Planning Office was increased. The March 1965 meeting of the Central Committee introduced a new form of planning and a new economic system for agriculture, upgrading this crucially important sector of the economy. The September 1965 meeting of the Central Committee took steps to implement reforms in industry, oriented towards its transition from administrative to economic methods of management, and increased independence for enterprises. All these measures were reinforced by Party work to provide for the well-being of the people and the expansion of opportunities for working people's initiatives. As a result the rate of socio-economic development rose sharply in the period 1966–70 compared with the previous period, as is shown in the data in Table 7.

Table 7: *Basic socio-economic indicators for the USSR for the five-year periods 1961–63 and 1966–70: percentage growth (official figures)*

	1961–65	1966–70
Overall indicators		
National income	32	41
Per capita income	19	33
Productive resources (total)	22	20
Basic productive funds	59	48
Mining industry production	32	28
Number of workers employed in branches of industry	6.5	6
*Efficiency of social production (total)**	8	18
Capital output ratio	−17	−5
Efficiency of capital investment	−16	−10
Efficiency of use of industrial raw materials	0	10
Productivity of social labour	24	33

* Indices of efficiency are calculated in relation to indices of national income.

It should be noted that in fact the turn in 1966–70 was sharper than is evident from the indicators above, because the table compares five-year periods and the upgrading of the economy had already begun in 1965. Moreover, the conditions for the upgrading in 1963 and the beginning of 1964 were much worse than the average indicators for the whole 1961–65 period. Nevertheless it is quite clear that the rate of socio-economic development rose sharply. This was mostly the result of the doubling of the rate of growth in agriculture, the total growth of which in the 1966–70 period was 21% compared with 11% in the preceding five-year period.

Because the growth of productive resources in the 1966–70 period was even lower than in the 1961–65 period, all the acceleration of socio-economic development was achieved through the rise in efficiency of production, the growth rate of which more than doubled. The capital output ratio trebled and the efficiency of capital investment grew one and a half times, while significant economies were made in fuel and raw materials (in the previous period there had been none). The rate of growth of the national income rose almost one and a half times.

We have dwelt in some detail on this interesting experience of significant acceleration of the country's socio-economic development since similar tasks face us now – both to overcome existing negative tendencies, and to achieve a major breakthrough in the 1986–90 period, by doubling the rate of growth of efficiency of social production. Of course the circumstances now are different. Scientific, technological and economic potential have greatly increased and there are opportunities to activate not only new organisational and economic reserves but also the potential of science and technology in upgrading the economy.

4 THE CHALLENGE OF TECHNOLOGICAL BREAKTHROUGH

The Soviet Union faces major tasks, which the continuing *evolutionary path* of scientific and technological progress cannnot alone resolve. The evolutionary path applies above all to the perfection of existing machinery and technology, for example, creating more powerful tractors without major changes in agro-technology and the whole technological system applied to agriculture, or in industry the speeding up of rotary mills with no new techniques of metal working. Usually this assumes the growth of labour productivity with sometimes slightly reduced material inputs.

If the whole production process is not being transformed through such an approach, the number of workers as a rule does not fall. There has also been that paradoxical occurrence, when even with a significant increase in productivity the number of manual workers not only has not fallen, but has even risen. Improvements of existing machinery and technology are related to additional capital investment. Usually each further improvement requires a corresponding increase in inputs. Therefore the evolutionary form of scientific and technological progress usually coincides with an increase in the use of the resources necessary for production.

Until recently an evolutionary form of scientific and technological progress predominated in the Soviet economy, and thanks to this, efficiency of production has advanced very slowly, by less than one and a half per cent per year. The composite index is made up of the growth of productivity in the economy by roughly 3% a year and economies of fuel and raw materials of roughly 2% a year. But these results are partly lost by the simultaneous increase of 3% in the resources made available for production.

Since we must overcome the current trends and achieve a qualitative breakthrough in the development of the forces of production, we can no longer rely only on the evolutionary form of scientific and technological progress. It cannot guarantee radical increases in economic efficiency. Such radical increase can only be assured by *revolutionary changes* in scientific and technological progress, with the transition from the old generation of technology, to fundamentally new technological systems. In that case productivity and other indices of efficiency can improve many times over and not only by percentages as with the evolutionary method.

We will illustrate this point with a few examples. Through inertia and through using old technology an electric steel smelting plant was built not long ago at the Kuznetsk Metallurgical Kombinat. All steel processing involves electric furnaces and is therefore time-consuming. A 100mt electric furnace here should produce 200 thousand tonnes of steel. The new technology for this process differs fundamentally. The electric furnace is used only for the melting of the metal, which is then processed in a special crucible, using plant for vacuuming steel and synthetic sinter etc. This guarantees both higher quality metal and an increase in the volume of steel produced from a 100 tonne furnace of up to 400–500 thousand tonnes i.e. an increase of two to two and a half times. To do this the whole technology must be renewed. Different building construction is needed, more powerful transformers, larger capacity design, etc. Productivity however rises sharply, electricity is economised and the capital-output ratio improves with simultaneous improvement in the quality of the output.

Another example can be taken from coal mining. Adding machinery to the mining of coal while retaining the traditional technology cannot improve productivity. Productivity was indeed falling year after year. This was not only because of the worsening geological conditions but because of the piecemeal approach to technological development of mines and the retention of many old production methods. If radically new technology is applied then two, three or four times the current productivity can be achieved. Yet, work on integrated technology in the extraction of coal for the "mining of the future" to replace the traditional methods has come to a halt.

A new techonological revolution in mining coal has appeared with hydroextraction. When the development of hydro-extraction was under the indirect guidance of the All-Union Institute of Hydro-Coal (in Novokuznetsk), with its own experimental factory, phenomenal results were achieved. Average monthly output per man for example in the Northern Baidaev No. 2 mine exceeded 300 tonnes, double that of other mines working in similar geological conditions. Productivity levels of two and a half to three times were reached in these hydro-mines, working narrow and steeply dipping coal beds. The construction of hydro-mines has worked out 30% cheaper with much less metal and timber required, and with much improved working conditions and safety levels. It is not accidental that licences have been acquired for this new technology, which is now spreading to Canada, India, China and elsewhere.

One last example can be taken from the thermal energy sector. To increase the output of power stations there are two options: increasing the aggregate boiler volume or transferring to fundamentally new types of furnace. The Central Turbine Institute in its investigations took the second option and proposed the construction of a small vortical furnace. The boiler construction department of the Institute undertook a trial at several power stations (Rostov, Novosibirsk, etc.) and proved that the new furnace was reliable and efficient. It needs a smaller boiler and for this 25% less metal is required, the buildings can be much smaller and the amount of loading work is reduced; while the time needed for construction is halved because of the smaller volumes, the simplicity of the design of the buildings, making serial installation possible. Simultaneously consumption of fuel falls slightly and because of its fuller combustion harmful substances emitted into the atmosphere are reduced. But boiler construction factories, in pursuit of plan fulfillment indicators which are based on the metal input, continue to produce the old models. The matter has reached the point of the farcical. An old model large boiler was made for the Beresovsk HEP station 117m high, weighing 26mt to be suspended from a beam with a diameter of 6m. The height of the building is 132m. Even if this gigantic boiler proves workable and as powerful as is projected, it will nevertheless be extremely difficult to repair and maintain. The important thing is that it requires enormous quantities of additional metal and construction materials. If the smaller boiler with the same power were adopted, the height of the building could be cut to 50m, the capital-output ratio would improve significantly and the construction time would be sharply abridged.

It is evident from these and many other examples, that the revolutionary approach to scientific and technological progress assures both significant growth of productivity and reduced material consumption, plus as a rule an improvement in the capital-output ratio. Scientific and technological progress must be targeted precisely at economic efficiency and the avoidance of all types of waste.

From an economic point of view technological renewal can be considered as progress only when it assures a rise in economic efficiency. I do not refer here to the cases where new technology is used only for improving the conditions of labour, health, and safety and the conservation of the environment. In these circumstances not only economic but social efficiency must be considered. If by renewal the economy is rid of one type of waste, for example the reduction of labour inputs, but simultaneously creates additional and still greater labour costs involved in increasing the capital stock, then this would not be progress but regress. Thus the economic evaluation of new technology must in our view be undertaken quite rigorously.

Not all of the planned initiatives of scientific and technological progress are currently proving to be effective. Thus, the proposed robotisation of production in several enterprises by self-adjusting robots has become extremely expensive to undertake with five to ten times less reliability than the best forecasts. One fairly large robot, for loading and stamping, usually frees one worker, but is less reliable in operation and requires more expenditure on repair and maintenance. The average cost of such a robot as shown by research in several machine-building enterprises, is 40 to 50 thousand roubles and at the most it replaces 4 thousand roubles a year in wages. Obviously this robot is ruinous from an economic point of view. It is quite different with the introduction of complex automated technology, where robots can undertake welding, soldering and painting and do the jobs better than they could be done by hand, and can be used without interruption for two to three shifts. For here new technology both increases productivity and improves the quality of the product without greatly enlarging capital costs.

I have touched on the example of robots not only because it is a contemporary technological problem, but mainly because this is a very typical case. With increasing regularity one comes across the introduction of poor quality robots in factories of more than twenty ministries, where the conditions are just not appropriate for them. Instead of one robot taking the place of one stamp operator, for the same resources one could have several modern 5-tonne unloaders, each of which would release up to ten workers from heavy manual work. The ministries have the resources to develop all sorts of inefficient work methods, and yet over ten years the limited resources have just not been found to complete the reconstruction of the Lvov factory for auto-loading equipment, the only factory in the Soviet Union producing these machines.

In order effectively to turn scientific and technological progress towards the acceleration of the socio-economic development of the country, preference must be given to revolutionary forms of science and technology, and these must be aimed at a decisive increase in economic efficiency. In a word, a scientific and technological revolution is needed. To achieve such a revolution and ensure that its achievements are put at the service of the socialist economy, the form of this revolution must be considered together with the specific characteristics of its current stage of development. We see above all that a scientific and technological revolution is a complex socio-economic phenomenon. It involves not only a process of integration of science and production, when production increasingly becomes the technological application of science, but also requires *perestroika* of the economy and a quite new investment policy.

A revolution in education and the training of the labour force is an organic part of such a technological revolution. A new type of worker is needed for the new machinery and technology, not purely in terms of general education and professional training, but with a more responsible attitude to work and with higher organisational ability combined with discipline, creativity and initiative. The next basic requirement of a scientific and technological revolution is a fundamental improvement in organisation and management. New machinery and technology must coincide with better organisation of production and management. The process of management itself is greatly influenced by scientific and technological progress. The whole range of scientific methods and approaches is being applied not only to contemporary technological equipment but, in the use of information technology through computers etc., to the communication system of modern organisations.

From such a broad understanding of the new science and technology the need arises to introduce a wide and integrated system of measures to accelerate its progress in the economy. Precisely such an approach was evident in Gorbachev's report to the Central Committee at its June 1985 meeting to discuss questions of accelerating scientific and technological progress. It included a whole range of current and future economic, organisational and social problems, the development of education, the role of the higher echelons of management in each link of the national economy.

In the recent period the rate of scientific and technological development in the world has substantially speeded up. A new stage in the scientific and technological revolution has begun. Particularly characteristic of this stage, in our view, is the design of highly efficient integrated technological and economic systems appropriate for all types of production, based on the the latest generation of technology. Thus each production process is gradually taken over by advanced integrated technology, which runs through the whole of the productive process from beginning to end, transforming not only its basic tasks but also those that are ancillary to it. This process is achieved by the linking of a series of machines and attachments. New integrated technological systems require a new organisation of production and management and therefore we may consider it a technological–economic system. Such systems are very efficient, with three to five times greater productivity, reducing by one and a half or more times the consumption of energy and materials. This as a rule improves the capital-output ratio and radically improves the quality of production.

Good examples of these revolutionary technological systems in addition to those already mentioned, are: converter production with continuous casting in metallurgy, mass produced rotors and rotor conveyor-belts, industrial systems of mass cultivation and livestock production and new continuous processes in the petrochemical and chemical industries, in biotechnology etc. Before our very eyes flexible production systems for machine construction are being established, based on computerised information technology. There are great differences among these new technologies yet all show some generic characteristics.

Firstly, they are based on a small number of operational stages. The new technology is often based on the uniting of many operations into one process. Metal cutting can be replaced by using plastic materials. Transport and processing functions are being combined on production lines. Thanks to new catalysts the stages in chemical processes are being reduced. The condensed nature of these usually results in a highly intensive flow of production and the volume of output of products is greatly increased. Higher temperatures and pressures can be used. There is a further consequence: the rise in the reliability of the whole productive process, among its other characteristics, is often the deciding factor in ensuring efficiency. Indeed, reliability is a specific quality of automation and ensures a sharp reduction in running costs.

Secondly, the new technological systems leave less industrial scrap. Besides having large economic advantages they prevent pollution of the environment. In current conditions, with massive production volumes, this aspect gains greatly in significance.

Thirdly, current production systems are characterised by a combination of new technology with micro-electronics, and as a result a new degree of quality is achieved when the systems are automated. Through fusing the new technology for metal processing with micro-electronics, processing centres have been established using flexible production modules for integrated automated production. Another example is in automated rolling mills, the construction of which allows for feedback from computers in managing the process. The broad introduction of micro-electronics into production is a most important feature of the current stage of the scientific technological revolution.

Fourthly, an increasing number of new technologies are based on new ideas about the micro-structures of matter. These technologies include atomic energy, laser technology, bio-technology and its sub-divisions such as genetic and cellular engineering etc.

It is sometimes thought that technological progress is inevitably linked to a worsening in the capital-output ratio, for the reason that the new electronic machinery and equipment is very expensive. For example, a processing centre with a capacity of twenty or more simultaneous metal-processing operations costs 100,000–200,000 roubles. A traditional machine capable of doing one operation costs only a few thousand roubles, i.e. 100 times less. But two rows of processing centres (each made up of four to six units) with a flexible production system can, in terms of productivity, replace a whole factory floor of existing machines. If these processing centres are used for only one or two shifts, the capital-output ratio actually worsens slightly compared with the old technology. But if one of the centres is used without interruption, then the capital-output ratio improves one and a half times, even without calculating the economies of capital investment on buildings and equipment. To achieve this result, however, processing centres must be very reliable, and with a high level of automation, operating on the night shift without human intervention. Repair and maintenance work and computer programming can be undertaken during the first shift or more probably on the second. The capital-output ratio can be improved to an even greater extent by transition to the new generation of plants in the chemical industry, in metallurgy, and in transportation especially if capital investment savings on reduced fuel consumption are taken into account.

Obviously we have not mentioned all the special properties of current technological systems. But what has been said is sufficient to show the need for an all-embracing approach to the technological transformation of production and the introduction of new high-level technology. Technological progress will stem from science. Therefore one of the most important tasks for accelerating technological progress is the further development of the scientific potential of the country. The USSR has always devoted much attention to the development of science. There are in the country about a million and a half people employed in this sector, one quarter of all the scientists in the world. More than 30 billion roubles per year is spent on the development of science, and this represents about 5% of the Soviet national income. Roughly the same percentage is spent in the USA, while the figure for other developed countries is substantially lower.

The achievements of Soviet scientists in various fields of science are well known – in nuclear energy, space exploration, in mathematics, physics, chemistry, microbiology and other specialisms. The present aim of achieving a major acceleration of scientific and technological progress will mean increased demands on scientific work. Higher priority is to be attached to development in the fundamental sciences, and to the role of academic institutions in the creation of a theoretical basis for radically new types of machinery and technology.

In the last two years a new method has been developed for integrating science and production through inter-branch scientific technological complexes, following the experience of the E.O. Paton Electro-Welding Institute. This institute is a major scientific technological complex incorporating a large research collective and construction department and several enterprises. This enables the institute to undertake not only research and development, but also to prepare prototypes, and introduce them into enterprises. The institute has an agreement with hundreds of enterprises which it supplies with new electronic welding technology and robotics. It also coordinates research and technological work on the development of welding methods across the whole country. Other such inter-branch complexes for laser, chemical catalysts, personal computers, biotechnological and corrosion treatment in industry etc. have been organised along similar lines.

A further important initiative for integrating science and production is the creation of networks between large scientific bodies and production-oriented associations along the lines of the Kriogenmash and Svetlana associations. The Nikolaevsk association may well come to the forefront of scientific technological progress through its production of lubricating equipment. We think that complexes of scientific technological associations should be created capable of developing and introducing integrated technological systems. To do this effectively research departments must be included in these associations, together with construction and project departments, testing and prototype factories and training centres for personnel. These organisations should be capable of introducing new technology and re-equipping the production lines of whole branches of production.

I gave the example of electro-welding above, although in fact at the Kuznetsk metallurgical plant no new technology has been introduced. Strictly speaking there has been nobody to introduce it. Currently the metallurgy industry works in such a way that one organisation does the designing, but is completely divorced from research, construction and production. Attention is rather given to the traditional and often obsolete old technology. On the other hand, the electronic furnace manufacturers from the Novosibirsk

Thermal Electricity Association in Siberia do not have a research department. Its construction department specialises only in the construction of electronic furnaces and does not consider the whole technological process of electric steel production. Therefore this association builds only electronic furnaces, while the metallurgy factory orders from elsewhere its loading apparatus, cranes etc. In a word, no one will take responsibility for making a change. Yet, the share of electro-steel in Soviet production following the example of other countries should in future rise significantly since modern technical progress requires much higher quality steel. Furthermore in the Soviet Union, especially in Siberia, very cheap electricity is produced and therefore the cost of electro-steel should be lower than elsewhere.

To reach world levels in this crucial area, which is a current aim, it should be possible to create a major scientific productive complex along the lines of the Siberian Thermal Electricity Association. It will aim at introducing new thermal electric technology, particularly in electric smelting production. Such an association would have to design its own technology and prepare and supply its own equipment and, in cooperation with other enterprises, to install it and take responsibility for the results. To do this within these associations there must be a research department, designers working on the production not only of electric furnaces but of vessels, vacuum machines and other units. The organisation must also have the right to place orders for steel production with enterprises and organisations from other ministries. Thus a metallurgical factory which wants to develop its own electro-steel production will not have to deal with numerous design and construction organisations for the development of a piece of equipment but with one general contractor. Currently this all-round approach to the introduction of integrated technology is wanting not only in the field of metallurgy but in many other industries; because of this the Soviet Union has been incurring great losses.

Here is a fairly typical example. In the Don coal fields increasing quantities of coal are being mined from beds less than 1.3 metres thick. (We mention 1.3 metres as a limit because with the shearers used to mine large quantities of coal, this is the minimum size of face that is workable.) If the bed is 1 metre thick, which actually happens at many Donbass mines, then with the smallest shearer available, along with the coal a further 30cm of waste rock will be cut. For this reason along with the coal some 25 million tonnes of rock are brought to the surface. This rock then has to be separated from the coal. The losses incurred in extraction, transport and separation of these 25 million tonnes and the wastage of coal during this process, are estimated at an annual 600 million roubles. This loss results in fact from the lack of a shearer which can extract coal from beds of 0.7–1.3 metres.

About 15 years ago the Donetsk Coal Institute of the Ukrainian Ministry of Coal Industry designed a high technology cutter for the extraction of coal from thin beds. But without a construction department and tool making unit the institute itself could not produce it. The task of constructing the cutter was assigned to the Donetsk Coal Machinery factory under the Ministry of Coal. Once again this factory had no facilities for manufacturing it. Therefore to produce even a few initial coal cutters it was necessary to place orders with several machine-building factories. And to do this is not easy since factories are overstretched and unwilling to take on single orders. Finally, however, the cutter was made; it did well in trials and the question was raised of its mass production. The existing machine-building factories have a full book of mass production orders and it was not easy for them to transfer to the manufacture of new products. Moreover this cutter contained less metal (bad in terms of plan fulfilment!), was complex to make and therefore it was hard to find a factory that could prepare a prototype. All the same, eventually the order was placed with a new machine-building factory which lacked previous experience in complex machine development. Once more the project had fallen into inappropriate hands. Nevertheless the production of new cutters is now well in hand and they are being introduced into the mines. But 15 years have passed and the real economic impact has only just begun to be felt.

If we try to estimate the cost of this delay in design and production, it exceeds the total value of all the capital expended on coal machine-building in the Soviet Union and the total expenditure over many years on geological reseach. This would not have occurred had the Donetsk Coal Institute, the Donetsk Coal Machinery factory and three or four coal machinery-building factories been united into one scientific-production association. The cutter could have been produced in a few years and billions of roubles of state resources would have been saved. It should be noted that from the very beginning everyone was interested in such a machine. There were no competing organisations or opponents and all this occurred within one ministry. But even so, because of the methods of coordination of the institutes and machine-building factories the introductory process proceeded extremely slowly. In circumstances where the way is blocked by inter-institutional barriers, and when new technology is challenged by a major institute offering a competing solution to the technological problems involved, the matter may drag on for years.

Of course such scientific production associations do not provide the only way of integrating science and production. In many cases design and research organisations can be included within large production concerns, thereby strengthening the factory-based science sector. A good example may be taken here from certain East German plants, incorporating about 90% of all scientific establishments in the country. This has enabled East Germany to accelerate its scientific and technological progress and to solve its many production problems relatively rapidly. A sufficient example of this is the Karl Zeiss plant which supplies its products to more than a hundred countries. We are also making use of this experience and many formerly independent institutes and construction departments are being turned into large productive concerns.

An enormous quantity of scientific technological work has been accumulated in the Soviet Union. There is no little scientific research whose application can create a scientific revolution in production in the several branches of industry. We have many highly efficient prototypes which are widely admired at technical exhibitions. What is at issue is how to advance all these scientific and technical ideas and models into production and into wide use in practice. Only in this way can science have any real and growing economic impact.

In the West one often hears the following question: How can the Soviet Union accelerate its development with declining amounts of hard currency as a result of the falling oil price which makes it impossible to buy new technology from the West? People asking this question start from the premise that progress in the Soviet Union can be realised only on the basis of technology bought from the West. Fortunately this is not the case. There is a fairly high level of scientific research in the Soviet Union and this is no secret to Western scientists and specialists. For a long time the Soviet Union has had outstanding scientific establishments in the sphere of mathematics, physics and some areas of chemistry. The situation was worst in biology where the fallacious views of Lysenko held back the development of modern genetics. But even in this area, the lag has been substantially made good. The achievements of Soviet geologists, climatologists etc. are also well known. There are currently more than 5,000 research institutes in the USSR, with more than one million research fellows. The total number of people working in the sphere of science and related areas is about 4.6 million. While there have been many shortcomings in the development of Soviet science due to the backwardness of the technical base, to the inefficiency of some organisations and the institutional isolation of many scientific establishments, nevertheless enormous amounts of scientific work in advanced technology are still going on.

Numerous examples can be given of this. Recently during a trip to Japan I visited a well known metallurgical factory, one of the most advanced in the world, situated on the artificial island Ogisimo. At this factory dry coke processing is being carried out under USSR licence. Continuous casting of steel is also being carried out there under licence purchased from the USSR. All these techniques were invented twenty to thirty years ago while Soviet metallurgical science has now advanced considerably further, especially in horizontal continuous processing and domed blast furnaces.

Or let us consider the substantial body of geological work such as the sinking of mine shafts. The USSR, which developed and introduced a fundamentally new technical system, has the world record for sinking mines. The average monthly speed for sinking a 60–70 metre shaft is the fastest in the world. Other Soviet technologies are also well known. Examples include the AN-124, the most economic plane with the greatest payload in the world, capable of carrying 180 tonnes, a helicopter with a payload capacity of 20 tonnes; the most powerful electronic hardware; modern hydroturbines, extrusion presses, Ivanosk processing centres which are widely demanded in the world market, shaped plastic components, rolling mills for making steel, roles and conveyor belts for mass production, etc. Thus there is a great deal that can be developed further within the USSR relying on Soviet scientific technological progress. In most branches of science and technology, progress in the USSR will be based on Soviet achievements.

Of course no country in the world, including the USSR, can be the most advanced in every field. There has always been mutually advantageous international scientific, technological and economic cooperation and we like any other country participate in it. However, the volume of new technology and licences purchased by the Soviet Union was in fact much less than that purchased by other industrialised countries of the West. So the Soviet Union needs advanced foreign technology no more or less than the USA, West Germany or any other Western country.

The main problem lies in the fact that the Soviet Union is seriously behind in the application of the most advanced applied science and technology. For example, the continuous process for the casting of steel, first developed in the Soviet Union and introduced by the Novolipetsk metallurgical factory, is actually less used in the Soviet Union than in other countries. The Japanese were the first to buy the licence for the process from the Soviet Union. And currently more than 90% of Japanese steel is cast by using this process, while in the USSR less than one quarter of rolled steel is produced in this way, the lowest for all developed countries. In Japan the Soviet method of dried processing of coke is being used on a massive scale, but in the USSR it is scarcely to be found. And unfortunately there are many other similar examples.

The poor take-up of Soviet technology not to mention Western advanced technology is connected with shortcomings in scientific technological investment policy, and with a flawed economic system. Because of erroneous investment policies, the rate of annual renewal of the existing stock of machinery, equipment and technology has remained at roughly three per cent. With such a rate of renewal, satisfactory scientific and technological change could not be effected.

The existing structure of production also creates many barriers to the more rapid application of the achievements of science and technology. Many branches hold reserves which could be rapidly put to work in making some of the latest products, and in new and experimental production, and because of this the time needed to develop a new product is protracted. The rewards and motivation are insufficient for developing new technology more rapidly and for product innovation. The organisational structure of the economy is such that in many cases science is divorced from design, while design departments are divorced from production, and it is difficult to bridge these gaps. Time is being lost, and the economy of time in conditions of rapid technological and scientific change is an important indicator of efficiency. Lenin said, "He who wins time, wins everything." This has still not been taken as a guideline by Soviet economic planners. Now with *perestroika* these shortcomings are beginning to disappear, and fundamental measures are being implemented to integrate science and production.

5 NEW INVESTMENT POLICY

For the application of science and technology to make a real economic impact on production, old technology and machinery must be changed for new and the whole economy must be technically re-equipped. Technological reconstruction and the acceleration of re-equipment in all branches of the economy are most important components of our economic strategy at this stage. A new policy for investment and structural change is needed, which will have three main features. Firstly, it must involve the transition from capital investment that takes place mainly in new construction to the extension of technological reconstruction and the re-equipping of existing enterprises. Secondly, it must involve a change in the relationship between categories of capital investment in resource-procurement, and processing and consumer branches, with guaranteed priority given to the development of resource conserving technologies. Thirdly, less capital must be invested in increasing the sheer volume of production, and more in improving the quality of products, the meeting of social needs with fewer goods but of better quality.

In a word, the whole structure of capital investment is to be fundamentally changed, reorienting it from extensive development, i.e. focusing extra resources on intensive methods of production and increased efficiency in resource use. This suggests a concentration of investment in those branches of the economy which give the highest return and which best guarantee the acceleration of scientific and technological progress. Consequently the structure of the economy must change substantially. This structure was formed in line with reliance on extensive methods of production and therefore excessive weight was placed on the branch producing raw material, the production of traditional materials and on ageing technology. The repair and maintenance sector has hypertrophied.

In the new conditions of structural reform the transition of the economy to an intensive path of development is envisaged, aiming at increasing efficiency in production. The degree of refining of primary materials must grow sharply and preference must be given to the development of branches requiring high technology input – machine building, information industry, chemistry, biotechnology. Development of new materials must have high priority. In all branches there must be a rational use of resources and infrastructure. The whole economic structure must become more flexible and capable of rapid application of scientific and technological achievements. It must undergo *perestroika* to ensure a consistent rate of acceleration of the socio-economic development of the country. Let us consider these questions in more detail. Above all it is essential to escape from the stereotypes of past economic management, in which new construction was considered as the main way to extend production, despite the fact that many existing enterprises had not been re-equipped for many years. New annual inputs into the existing capital stock were insignificant as the data on written off and replaced equipment for 1985 reveals:

Written off/replaced in 1985	Total value of replacements as % of capital stock	Of which machines and tools
For all industry	1.3	2.3
For machine building and metal processing	1.1	1.9

This kind of situation leads to many undesirable consequences:

1) Excessive growth in expenditure on repairs because of the ageing condition of the existing capital stock. In 1985, 35 billion roubles was spent on repairs. In many types of machine expenditure on repairs substantially exceeded expenditure on new equipment. In metallurgy the annual value of repair work was more than the total capital investment.

2) Since most capital investment was directed at new construction this attracted workers from existing production; and whole sections of production were left undermanned. The number of new jobs substantially outnumbered the potential increase in the number of workers. Therefore increasing numbers of jobs remained unfilled and personnel changes increased. The cost of unfilled jobs in the economy has topped an estimated 200 billion roubles (out of the total value of the capital stock in the economy of 1.6 trillion roubles).

3) Insofar as productivity has stagnated and no technological improvements have been made the number of manual jobs has not fallen. New jobs have not always been mechanised despite the considerable capital investment being made in production. Now there are about 50 million manual workers: i.e. roughly one third of all the workers in industry, more than a half of those in construction and three quarters of those in agriculture.

4) Because of the outdated nature of a large part of the existing capital equipment and because unfilled jobs lead to less than full capacity operation, a worsening of the capital-output ratio occurred in the economy. Thus the capital-output ratio in the national income worsened in the 1971–75 period by 16% and in the 1976–80 and 1981–85 periods by 15%.

Here are some examples:

In the last three five-year periods 50 billion roubles of capital were invested by the Ministry of Metallurgy. Most of this investment was made in new construction and none of the necessary attention was paid to reconstruction and technical re-equipment of enterprises. It can have been no coincidence that this Ministry tended not to fulfil its plan in this period.

The Kuzbass coal industry offers a further example of the misguided attitude to reconstruction. Up to the mid-1970s this coalfield was developing well. It has extremely favourable geological conditions – an unprecedented concentration of coal in a small area, with extensive fields lying close to the surface. Volumes of coal output were systematically increasing, productivity rose and production costs fell. Capital construction and continual reconstruction were undertaken by development teams in each mine. Kuzbass shaft construction was carried out by highly specialised organisations of the Ministry of Heavy Construction. There were 15 brigades working on the sinking of mine-shafts. Most coal was situated between shafts and close to the surface and it was extracted by using efficient technology. Thus costs of transporting the coal were minimal, guaranteeing good ventilation and facilitating the preparation of new districts of extraction.

Then the Ministry of Coal undertook an ill-considered reorganisation. It transferred the mine construction organisations from the Ministry of Heavy Construction and put them under the Ministry of Coal. Specialised development work was abolished. Development workers now within the Ministry of Coal immediately began to be used for ongoing duties of coal extraction and work on deepening and sinking further shafts was ended. Only two out of fifteen specialised brigades remained and the skills and traditions of rapid mine-shaft sinking were lost and tools were squandered. As a result when the higher levels in the mines became exhausted they were obliged to transfer to extraction of coal by drift mining, i.e. to find the necessary layers in lower shafts and to transport the coal to the surface across these slopes. The expenditure on transport thus sharply increased, ventilation of shafts deteriorated and new layers became more difficult to prepare. Now up to one half of all coal in the Kuzbass is extracted from drift mines, and 53% of mines require urgent reconstruction. To try to set right the system of coal working, and to overcome the state it has fallen into over the last 15 years, 100 new shafts need to be sunk in the Kuzbass alone. Shaft-sinking brigades are urgently being set up for this purpose. Where there were two before there are now five, and appropriate equipment, including foreign machinery is being acquired. but time was lost, reconstruction of mines was abandoned and as a result the Kuzbass did not fulfil either the 1976–80 or 1981–85 period plans for coal extraction. Moreover, despite increased open cast extraction output levels stood still. Productivity fell annually by an average 2% and production costs systematically rose. The situation has only begun to improve in the last two years.

The way out of the situation for coal, as for other branches of the economy, is by the acceleration of technical reconstruction and the re-equipment of enterprises with new technology. One third of current resources in the total volume of capital investment is spent on reconstruction. In the 1986–90 period this share is to be increased to at least a half. The volume of new construction should fall and it will be undertaken only when all the possibilities available for increasing production from existing investment are exhausted. After due consideration, certain projects will be rapidly developed whereas others will be stopped totally or temporarily halted. A general inventory of capital goods is to be undertaken and programmes are to be worked out for future technical reconstruction of every branch and every enterprise. The proportion of capital stock that will be rejected as obsolete, especially from the more active section of the economy, is to double in a short time. This will mean the renewal of more than one third of the productive plant with up to 50% new machinery by the end of 1990.

Emphasis must be placed on resource conservation in the new investment policy. In the Basic Projections of Economic and Social Development of the USSR, the target was set of meeting 75%–80% of fuel and raw material consumption through economies, thereby stabilising the share of capital investment in these sectors of the economy. This share of capital investment is still rising. Capital investment in fuel, metallurgy, timber and building materials industries, i.e. in the predominately raw material based branches was 33% of total industrial investment in 1975, 36% in 1980, and 40% in 1985. The required investment per tonne of fuel and raw materials extracted continues to grow also because of the worsening of geological and economic conditions. Of all capital investment in mining more than 90% goes towards maintaining previous levels of output and this percentage is still growing. At the same time the price fixed for a tonne of fuel or a tonne of basic raw material is two to three times less than the cost of its extraction. This makes it essential that economising is widespread and that there is a general introduction of resource-conserving technology.

Many branches have the capacity to increase their output without increasing inputs, by more rational use of fuel and raw materials. Thus enterprises and associations in the electronics industry have ensured growth in output for the 1981–85 period with an absolute reduction in their consumption of metals. Reductions of up to 20% have been realised through the transition to products that consume less material. One example is the transition from the electric generator series 4-A to mass production of the series AI with equivalent capacity, in which the energy output of the generator has been substantially improved without increases in the cost of material inputs. The annual economic saving from this is by now more than 200 million roubles. The introduction of a series of powerful turbo generators, with water cooling systems and using 15% to 20% less materials but with improved output and availability, is also having a big effect.

One more example, from 1975 to 1985 the output of the timber, cellulose and paper industries increased by 30%, although the area felled during this period dropped from 395 to 356 million cubic metres, as did wood pulp (from 313 to 275 million cubic metres). In other words the volume of production per unit of timber felled grew by more than 40% during this period. In spite of this we can properly criticise this sector for its mistakes in the overall use of timber resources. The output of final products per thousand cubic metres of input is two to two and a half times below that of the best world levels. So there is still plenty of scope for improvement.

It will take a great deal to change the currently very wasteful economy into a resource-conscious economy. Consumption of oil-based products must be radically reduced. The truck fleet must be given diesel engines; and oil refining and processing facilities for liquid coal-gas must be expanded. Great savings in fuel should be made by the technological reconstruction of thermal power stations and the introduction of centralised heat supply in place of the hundreds, and thousands, of primitive boilers. Expenditure on fuel oil must be reduced several times and lower quality and cheaper fuels must take its place. Throughout the metallurgy industry there must be up to 100% utilisation of all usable constituents. In the construction sector, by using better building methods the weight of buildings and equipment can be much reduced and many tonnes of materials saved. Metals will be increasingly replaced by plastics and by serviceable non-metallic materials.

As the new advanced technology is being developed with the help of whole systems of machines, equipment and instruments, so machine building is playing a key role in the re-equipping of the economy and in the implementation of the scientific and technological revolution. We have proposed a fundamental change in attitude to machine building plants. A shattering critique was made of the existing situation in which only about 5% of all capital investment made during the 1981–85 period went into machine building, i.e. 20 times less than into the branches of production for which the machines were built. 18 times less resources were directed to the production of machines for agriculture, 23 times less for machines in light industry and food production, 28 times less for heavy machinery and transport, 47 times less for chemical and oil machinery, than went into the corresponding branches which were requiring the machinery

In the 1981–85 period the emphasis placed on machine building actually declined in terms of overall capital investment. The volume of capital investment in machine construction in these years rose by a total of 24% only. This tendency must be reversed. A resolution on the reallocation of resources has already been passed. Specifically, an additional 6 billion roubles have been reallocated from agriculture to machine building. It has been resolved that in the 1986–90 period capital investment by machine building ministries shall be increased by 1.8 times compared with the previous period. In 1986 alone capital investment in machine building increased by 17% and in technical reconstruction and re-equipment by 30%, i.e. by more than in the preceding five years.

A large increase in capital investment in machine building, above all in the technical reconstruction of existing enterprises, will push up the rate of replacement of productive capacity in these enterprises from the past level of 2% a year to a rate of 8%–9%. It is proposed that in the 1986–90 period no less than 40% of all metal-working equipment in machine building factories will be replaced, and new computers, processing centres and modern automated production lines will be installed. This means extensive changes in the range of machinery produced. While in 1985 3.1% of machines were replaced by new models, in 1986 4% were changed, in 1987 7.6% and in 1990 this figure should be 13%. The new, modern machines will give one and a half times to double the productivity, more reliable performance and use 12%–18% less metal per unit of output. While in 1985 only 29% of production came up to the standard of contemporary world demand, in 1990 80% or more should do so.

Thus our strategy is to ensure in the first place an increase in machine building, and to proceed to the mass production of a generation of new technology for all branches and on this basis to carry out the fundamental technological reconstruction of the whole economy. Recently the Central Committee and the Government have passed a number of resolutions to strengthen the development of important branches of machine building, through flexible automation and robot-technology, rotor and conveyor belt production lines, computers and machinery for light industry and food processing, and many others. Particular attention will be paid to micro-electronics, computer technology and tool manufacturing, and to the whole information technology sector which has such a decisive influence on the efficient use of labour and on the technology systems in all their branches. Thus, it is machine building that lies at the heart of the technical reconstruction of the economy, and it in turn depends above all on the acceleration of scientific and technological progress.

The technological revolution is making new demands on engineers and technicians as well as on the general system of education and training. In the April 1985 Central Committee meeting the important matter of the occupational prestige of graduate engineers was discussed. In the light of the requirements of the new technology, the decline in occupational prestige of skilled engineers is unacceptable. The average wage of an engineer 20–25 years ago was one and a half times to twice that of the average worker. Now in the construction industry as a whole it is often lower than a worker's wage, while in industry as a whole it is practically the same. Workers' operations and workplaces during this period have become three to four times better equipped, whereas the work conditions for experts in construction and technologists, not to mention other categories of graduate engineers, have changed very little. Only in a few very advanced enterprises is there a computer assisted system of project design, and computerised construction and technological processes. Experimental production, where new engineering ideas can be tested, has been very poorly developed. At the same time, the flow of paper has grown immeasurably, resulting from the requirements of multiple agreements and the complexity of construction and project documentation. The very title "engineer" has come to be used for so many careers that it has lost a clearly defined meaning. It is hoped now to elevate the role and authority of graduate engineers, construction experts and technologists, to raise the material and moral motivation for their work. A first step in this direction has been taken with the acceptance of a resolution on improvements in the system for determining the salaries of scientific workers, construction experts and technologists. Scales of pay have been raised and additionally the right has been established that an incentive element can be introduced of up to 50% based on individual creative input . The titles "Engineer of Merit" and "Technologist of Merit" have also been introduced.

Many hopes for raising the efficiency of engineering work rest on the *perestroika* of higher education. In the recent period higher education has been alienated from the science of the academies as well as from the needs of the real world. These shortcomings are to be ended. The training of specialists, above all of graduate engineers, has been linked to requests from the organisations which will require these engineers in the future, and which will pay for the resources used in the provision of training. This approach will facilitate the immediate renewal and strengthening of the technological base of the higher schools which are seriously in need of improvement. The widest possible use is to be made of modern computers in education. At the same time staff of the Academy of Sciences will become more widely involved in university teaching. Research centres like the Physics and Technology Institute in Moscow and Novosibirsk University are establishing education departments to help with students' specialisation. The practical training of students must also be greatly improved, so that would-be specialists can become familiar with the work they are to undertake in the future.

To conclude this section we wish to underline the fact that we aim to achieve an advanced scientific and technological position together with the highest levels of productivity. It in the light of this aim, that every innovation, each reconstruction project, each new construction scheme and the plans for the development of whole branches of industry, will have to be examined.

6 THE RADICAL REFORM OF MANAGEMENT

The June 1987 meeting of the Central Committee decided the key question of the *perestroika* of the Soviet economic life: implementing a radical reform of management and reform of the whole economic system. Possibly no single Plenary meeting in the past was prepared for with such care. The Law on State Enterprises was drafted by a large group of specialists including directors of enterprises and academics. The project was based on nationwide discussion, which drew upon 180,000 suggestions, additions and proposed amendments. A special commission worked hard to consider these suggestions. The draft law was, as a result, substantially re-worked and then submitted for discussion to the Central Committee.

Simultaneously the Soviet government began working out proposals to execute its decisions and for the necessary regulations concerning fundamental *perestroika* of institutions, ministerial branches and local management. After difficult and lengthy work eleven resolutions were prepared. Based on the Law on State Enterprises, these proposals contained measures for *perestroika* of planning, price formation, finances and the banking system, systems of material and technological supply, authorities' duties on social and labour questions, the work of the State Committees for Science and Technology, the restructuring of the ministerial branches of the individual republics as well as of local authorities, and the reshaping of the management structure of the Council of Ministers of the USSR[10]. The proposed decisions of the government were distributed to the participants in the Plenary meeting of the Central Committee which approved them in their broad outline. It was recognised that a comprehensive document would have to be prepared for the Central Committee on radical *perestroika* of management of the economy and of the economic system. This document, entitled "Radical *perestroika* of Management of the Economy," was accepted by the Plenary meeting and put forward as the basis of long-term policy.

The preparatory materials for the Plenary meeting underwent quite detailed examination. More than thirty speakers discussed them. Many valuable suggestions were made and the experience, especially recent experience, of the first steps towards *perestroika* was examined. The Plenary meeting did not restrict itself to an examination of specific questions in the radical reform of management. Broader problems of management were scrutinised against the wider task of *perestroika* of the whole economy and social life. The general course of *perestroika*, and what could be learned from successes and failure, achievements and shortcomings were thoroughly analysed in Gorbachev's opening report. This report laid the foundation for discussion of key problems in the reform of management.

A new concept of management was first put forward at the April 1985 Central Committee meeting, for management to correspond to contemporary conditions and to the developing needs of Soviet society. This concept, of course, did not arise from nowhere, but developed and brought together the experiences of the Soviet Union and of other socialist countries in fashioning their management and economic systems with the ideas of academics and the suggestions of workers in the field. The important thing here is that questions of management were for the first time considered as a strategic matter, and put forward at a new historic stage of development of Soviet society, a stage of accelerated socio-economic development.

According to the resolutions of the April 1985 meeting leading on

[10] The Soviet Union consists of 15 Republics each with its own republic Government. There is a division of responsibility between these governments and the governments of the Union, i.e. the Council of Ministers of the USSR. (ed.)

to the XXVII Party Congress, various experiments with new economic methods were undertaken in some enterprises and even in whole branches or sectors of the economy . These first steps in the *perestroika* of management, above all at the enterprise level, clearly showed that a total reform was necessary and that no real impact would be gained from *perestroika* of some branches while leaving others as they were. Granting independence to enterprises was only achieved in many sectors with great difficulty, because of the retention of the old practice of assignment from the top down of even the smallest tasks, the inputs required, as well as the method of fixing prices. An enterprise was often crushed by the system of finance and the petty intervention of the banks. As before, predominantly administrative methods of management operated in the ministries and local authorities. The question of a general *perestroika* of management was put on the agenda because without this it is impossible to advance.

It also became clear that reconstruction of economic life is very closely linked to *perestroika* in other spheres of social life, particularly those of politics and ideology. It is not possible really to restructure the economy including management, if the work of party organisations, the local and national authorities, and information agencies is not substantially changed and if a corresponding socio-political, moral and psychological climate is not created in society to accompany *perestroika*.

The transformation of the economy by intensifying scientific and technological progress and by strengthening social justice has come up against the barrier of the existing system of management. It is this that has acted as a brake on Soviet society's advancement. Radical reform of management is in effect the key to the acceleration of the socio-economic development. The new economic system must be one that will accelerate and stimulate the transition towards intensive development and return all branches of economic management to meeting more fully the demands of the people. This is why the June 1987 Plenary was of such exceptional significance. It summed up the stage reached in the discussion and completed the outline for a wholly new system of management. Now a most exacting time is opening up, the period of actual transformation of the system of management. During the coming two to three years up to the end of the current five-year period, a completely new system of management has to be developed so that we begin the 1991–95 period with this new economic system in place.

What does the radical reform of management really involve? First, what it does *not* mean. It does not mean the renunciation of the various achievements of socialism. Our society is developing along socialist lines and there are objective laws governing its development on which the new economic system will still be based. We are talking of the supremacy of socialist (primarily public) ownership, of planned and proportional development, of the deployment of labour, of the principle of democratic centralism in management and of commercial production and market relations etc. Not only are these and other laws and categories of socialist economic management not being altered in the *perestroika* of management, but on the contrary, they are being developed and enriched. The principle of "more socialism" enunciated by Gorbachev infuses all aspects of the general transformation of the economic system.

Secondly, what does the radical reform of management positively imply? What radicalism and what revolutionary changes? Basically it means the transition from administrative to economic methods and the development of industrial democracy, i.e. through making a reality of socialist ownership, planning and democratic central- ism. An especially important turning point in this occurred at the June 1985 meeting of the Central Committee with Gorbachev's address on questions of the acceleration of scientific and technologi- cal progress. In accordance with the resolutions of the XXVII Party Congress, a major economic initiative to meet social needs implied the abolition of the residual principle in allocating resources to the social sector.

Administrative methods of management are based on a schedule of commands which make up the state plan being handed down each year from on top. This, which is the basis of the economy's command system, is now to be scrapped and the allocation of tasks and plans from the top down ended. From now on enterprises and associations will work out and approve their own plans. They will not be subject to the approval of any higher authority and there will be absolutely no allocation of planned work. Enterprises, propo- sing a plan for the following year will firstly build up an order book on the basis of consumer demand. Some consumers will be state organs, in which case their orders will be state orders. Such orders will take up a part of total production but in time this share will be reduced. It will mainly comprise arms production, state-directed construction and the most essential products needed by the government. State orders will be much less involved in the production of consumer goods and of items for the service sector. Here production plans will be formulated in the majority of cases only on the basis of trade orders, which means that they will be based on consumer demand. It should be stressed that even the system for state orders will not be the old command system. An order suggests the existence both of a seller and of a customer, between whom an agreement is concluded with *mutual* obligations. The state body which makes an order must not only guarantee payment for the order but also supply to the seller if necessary the appropriate technical documentation, the capital investment, and the permits for any scarce, centrally allocated inputs, and may have to assign foreign currency for the purchase of raw materials or other necessary goods from abroad etc. In foreign (including capitalist) countries, the system of state orders has a long history. As a rule state orders guarantee higher profit from production and a guaranteed sale of the product. When the economic system is well established, enterprises would compete for state orders and therefore provision will have to be made for competitive tendering.

Having built up a full order book, an enterprise will take account of its economic indicators, turnover of products, some at government prices and some at free prices, related to the norms fixed well before the beginning of the next five year period. Payment for resources is to be provided for and payments into the state budget, the ministerial funds and to local authorities. Where necessary, credit and bank assistance can be obtained – all this so that the working collective can determine its self-accountable income[11] and be individually responsible for its disposal. The wages fund is determined by coefficients which depend directly on the trading results of the end activity of the enterprise. If an enterprise undertakes a non-intensive workplan, does not make enough contracts and has less total orders, then both its wage fund and the profit left over at its disposal will be that much less. From this profit (with the addition of receipts from the depreciation fund), new

[11] This is the income that in capitalist economies would be called profit, that comes from the enterprise's own cost accounting after taking into account the payments here outlined. (ed).

investment will be made in science and technology as well as other extra payments determined according to set norms of economic proportions.[12] Then the distribution of the profit between housing, social and cultural construction and material incentives can be worked out.

Once every five years, an enterprise receives from a higher body overall estimates for the next five-year period and the fixed economic proportions in which its income is to be divided. These figures should not be seen simply as a new system of top-down allocation by central state planning. First of all they are not detailed like the current state plans, which include hundreds of indicators for each enterprise. The figures, starting from the estimated need for a given product, indicate the minimum level of efficiency expected and set tasks of a social character to guide the planning of the enterprise. But these figures should not be directive in nature, nor should they bind the working collective to any particular plan. They leave to the enterprise a wide choice of decision on particular products as well as partners with whom to make contracts. It is also important that these figures are given in advance of work being set up for the five-year period and that very detailed plans are made not only in the five years but for each individual year.

This fundamentally new system of planning starts from the premise that enterprises and associations are to become independent, self-accounting, self-financing and self-managing. These four characteristics all involve the responsibility of the enterprise, and imply a completely new economic situation for the basic production units in the Soviet economic system. Only in these conditions can the working collective of an enterprise really be master, owner and director of the resources of production available to it.

Enterprises are changing over to full self-accounting, in which all expenditure must be covered by income. What does full economic accounting mean? It may be contrasted with partial economic accounting. Currently enterprise income covers only running costs, while at the same time a significant part of capital investment of the enterprise comes from centralised resources. Full economic accounting, above all, implies that there are no subsidies so that the income of an enterprise from production covers both its running costs and its capital expenditure.

[12] These norms are defined in footnote 4, page 24.

Another aspect of full self-accounting is related to the levy each enterprise pays for all types of resources used in production: for land (including all natural resources), labour and capital goods. Currently, no direct payment is made for the use of land or labour resources. If payment for the use of land is related to the differential rent[13], then the payment for the use of labour resources should primarily compensate for the actual expenditure by society on the reproduction of the work force. This greatly exceeds the size of the average wage and also incorporates education, social expenditure, state subsidies in retail prices or rents etc.

A key issue in the transition to economic methods of management is the specification of the norms of economic proportions which are becoming important regulators of the activity of enterprises. It is clear that these proportions must be stable and long-term, lasting a minimum of five years. But this is not all. Proportions can relate both to individual enterprises or a whole universe. If individual coefficients are separately established for every enterprise given the level of its economic indicators, then effectively these proportional norms would barely differ from directive planning. The administrative nature of the indicator would remain as before. Set in January 1987 the economic proportions in the car industry, in tool making, in oil refining and processing began in this way, as a part of the transition to self-financing. The norms simply expressed in a different form the old schedule of commands under the five-year plan. The experience of self-financing in the enterprises of these branches of industry clearly showed that no notable improvement in the rate of growth of efficiency was achieved. These branches are not working any better than machine building enterprises similar to them which have not transferred to self-financing. In a word, the mountain has been in labour and has brought forth a ridiculous mouse!

---

[13] Differential rent is an income from land ownership based on the different quality and location of different lands since the value of the output will be higher on the better quality or better located land with the same capital and labour applied. In Soviet conditions, where land is a state monopoly, to ensure the most economical use of scarce resources like good land, the state should charge a differential rent. It could presumably, like landlords elsewhere, charge a rent even for the least good land and show that David Ricardo, the British economist who first argued the question in 1817, still lives. (ed.)

This could have been predicted, because the method set for adopting individual enterprise proportional norms meant the retention of administrative methods of management, albeit in a more modern form. It is clear that with individually assigned proportions the best enterprises find themselves in a worse situation, a higher percentage of their profit being deducted for the budget, while sloppy, backward enterprises gain all the advantage of staying on as they were, at the expense of the better enterprises. Projected expenditure from the past was based, or rather not based, on the fact that it would be automatically covered. For example there was a plan to reconstruct the ZIL car plant from the state budget. Money was not spared and expenditure on the reconstruction was enormous. The resulting new lorry with the same freight-carrying capacity as the old one was heavier and the cost of producing it rose. Furthermore, together with the investment of enormous resources and the reduction in the output of cars, a growth in the number of workers was even envisaged after the reconstruction. Gorbachev has criticised this type of reconstruction project. In this case the project was consequently reworked, cutting the projected number of workers but necessitating further additional capital investment. I think that had the ZIL reconstruction project been financed through credit, to be paid in the same way that foreign car companies work (paying 8%–12% annually for the debt incurred), this reconstruction project would have worked out very differently, since the viability of the expenditure would have had to be assured. As things stand, almost all the profit from the inflated prices for the uneconomic and obsolete lorries currently being produced was left to the ZIL car plant in its transition to self-financing. This profit goes towards financing the reconstruction. In other words, the state budget financing system has been preserved and the state receives a scanty profit. Whereas, to take another example, in the case of the enterprise KAMAZ, which does not for the time being require reconstruction, the state receives from it not only a large share of profits but also a large share of amortisation without so much as guaranteeing the conditions for simple reproduction of the capital stock, postponing this in effect to the indefinite future.

The whole situation will look completely different if general norms of economic proportions are introduced for each branch. For example, all enterprises, in any branch, regardless of profitability and wealth, are obliged to assign one half of all profit to the state budget and may then keep the remainder. It is clear that the more viable the enterprise, the better position it will be in. A single rate of tax on profit operates in many Western countries. It appears to be an effective method of stimulating increasing profitability. As a rule, bank credit should become the source of funds for undertaking major reconstruction or new construction. And it will be possible to obtain such credit after demonstrating the profitability of the intended measures, taking into consideration factors of time, efficiency etc.

In conditions of full self-accounting by enterprises the *perestroika* of prices, of the credit system and of the system of material and technological supply, all become fundamentally important. Enterprises can only be independent if proper mechanisms for wholesale trade are introduced, including direct commercial links between enterprises. An enterprise must be able to choose its own suppliers. Indeed the existing centralised supply system is the main repository of administrative methods of management, for this goes into even more detail than in the administrative directives issued to enterprises. It completely deprives enterprises of room for manoeuvre and freedom of action. Thus a change in the centralised supply system of resources for production is possibly the most essential measure for a transition from administrative to economic methods.

What is hindering this change? First of all it is the existing pricing system. As an example, in many areas the price of fuel oil is lower than the price of coal. And if the sale of fuel oil is changed to a wholesale system, it will turn out to be more convenient to use than coal in power stations etc. However, from an overall government viewpoint this is not at all desirable. On the contrary, we need radically to cut down the consumption of fuel oil. The USSR currently consumes annually around 200 million tonnes, four times as much as the USA. Thus the price of fuel oil and indeed of other types of fuel and raw materials, needs to be raised in line with world prices.

It is very important to differentiate clearly among prices for certain products according to their quality and usefulness. A radical reform of the pricing system is needed to cover wholesale prices, tariffs, purchase prices in agriculture, retail prices, etc.

Let us assume that prices are calculated correctly and correspond to the necessary costs, taking into account the costs of all inputs, differentiated according to quality and efficiency. Can the transition to the required wholesale trading system really be guaranteed in this way? The answer must be no, not really, because, in addition to prices, there is also the question of the money used to purchase the goods at these prices. A transition to wholesale trading is not possible while there is a surplus of money in the economy. This surplus is created by credit, which until recently has never been strictly repayable. Since collective and state farms alone owed the banks almost 100 billion roubles, it is obvious that such a sum could never be repaid. This unearned money has in effect to be given to the farms, and to be written off in their accounts.

A further source of unearned money is the state budget, into which turnover tax is paid before the goods are sold. But goods may lie on the shelf. Yet the money for them has already appeared in the budget and is being spent. A total financial and credit reform is needed to bring money and material turnover into relation with each other, to return credit to its true role by ensuring that it is reimbursable and economically beneficial to banks and enterprises which practise self-accounting.

The reform of prices and of the finance and credit system will create, in my opinion, the economic preconditions for a widespread change from the allocation system of supply to a wholesale trade supply system. The existing shortages which are the reason for the centralised allocation system are mainly due to the shortcomings of the economic system itself – incorrect prices and surplus money. Thus, as we put these things in order, many of the shortages will disappear. The shortages are also partially structural and are linked to the insufficient development of production in many branches, which has occurred because of a lack of connection between production and demand. Production has developed independently, guided by its own indicators. Therefore many more types of some goods are mass produced than consumer demand dictates, with less production of others. Time is needed to bring production into line with the structure of consumer demand. We will therefore be obliged temporarily to keep to a restricted allocation of certain resources in short supply. But wholesale trade will become the main way in the future for enterprises to obtain their means of production. Quotas for materials will gradually be phased out until they play only a subsidiary role.

The development of wholesale trading suggests a significant broadening of the socialist market and the stepping up of market relations. Socialist enterprises will enter the market as commodity producers. To make the socialist market into a mechanism that effectively evaluates the social usefulness and efficiency of an enterprise's products, competition between enterprises must be ensured, and the effective monopoly of certain enterprises in some sectors of production must be broken. Special efforts must be made to achieve this, so that there are parallel producers in the market of all the goods involved. Cooperative enterprises must also compete as, in some cases, must self-employed people. The socialist market is a regulated market in the sense that the prices for the most essential products will be set centrally, i.e. fuel, electricity, the most important raw materials, rolled steel machinery, and some consumer goods. This is done to give the government power over the rate of growth of prices and the means to stave off inflation, and to prevent enterprises from raising their prices in these cases. However, price formation will be considerably decentralised: a growing share of goods will be sold by contract and with freely set prices. Besides this, through the system of economic proportions state bodies can influence the market by economic methods, organising or encouraging additional production of certain goods, while restricting less efficient production.

In my opinion, the hardest problem to resolve in the *perestroika* of the economic system is to ensure the direct interest of working people in the final results of their labour. I cannot but share the distressing impression I had during a recent business trip to Austria. There as in other Western countries shops are literally groaning with goods, with new types of bread or milk products being invented all the time, and hundreds of types of cheese, sausage etc. on sale. Packaging is being constantly changed to make it more attractive. I stayed, however, at a hotel situated in the special area set apart for Soviet citizens. Here there was no restaurant or cafe and I headed towards a shop in the area to purchase some things for breakfast. The products were, naturally, on sale for Austrian shillings and the prices similar, as I later checked, to those in Vienna.

Imagine my surprise when I saw empty shelves in this shop: milk, as the sales assistant told me "was not available", bread had sold out, the choice was meagre, and I felt quite at home. Moreover at the checkout there was a twenty minute queue. Yet fifteen minutes walk away was an enormous shop with shelves stocked with goods, where sales assistants looked avidly after all the needs of every shopper, recommending this or that purchase. By this example I want to point out that the presence of well-founded prices, the elimination of surplus money, the establishment of wholesale trade and finally the presence of all the necessary goods does not lead automatically to ensuring the availability of goods for enterprises or for the population at large. One further condition is required. It needs to be profitable to meet social needs. In the case I have given the income of employees in our shop did not depend at all on the volume of sales or the degree to which consumer demand was met. The key point is the direct dependence of wages on results. In principle, as will be shown below, the system of full self-accounting and self-financing for enterprises enables this to be done.

The starting premise, the foundation of *perestroika* is the transition of basic production units to full self-accounting, when the government ceases to take responsibility for the accounts of an enterprise and it in turn ceases to be bound to the government. The wage fund, and from that the average working person's pay and the resources for the social development of the working collective, will now directly depend on an enterprise's results. In such conditions the enterprise and its working collective must take economic decisions on their own and be materially responsible for them. This means that administrative interference in the enterprise's affairs, such as occurs now, becomes inadmissible. It also means that the work of planning has to be fundamentally restructured.

Planning must concentrate above all on the substantiation of economic proportions, prices, finance and credit facilities and incentives, plus restricted and shrinking state orders. Of course planning will also involve the allocation of the use of centralised state resources, the creation of new branches of production, major projects, transport infrastructure, reconstruction of towns etc. All this demands the concentration of the activities of the State Planning Office and of other planning authorities on long-term, strategic issues and the renunciation of the current manner of regulating activities. Day-to-day economic activity is to be the job of associations and enterprises. In the light of this change the branch ministries also need to be fundamentally restructured. They must become scientific and technological bodies, planning and economic headquarters of their branches, refraining from trivial intervention in the work of the enterprises. Similarly local authorities must refrain from high-handed methods of sending working collectives out on field work and involving them in supplying their offices with services and utilities or getting assistance from their builders without compensation for expenses. As we say "everyone must carry his own suitcase".

All the same, opportunities for regional authorities in the new economic system are greatly increased. It is possible to manage efficiently when you have the resources you need. Local authorities can be relied on as sourcing agencies in the new system. Local budgets will be drawn up according to economic proportions by the assignment to them of payments from enterprises' profits for the use of resources in the region, both land and labour. So the size of the local budget is linked to the efficiency of local enterprises. There will also be included in the local budget part of the turnover tax levied on the sale of local goods, excluding wine, spirits and tobacco. Local councils currently control agro-industrial complexes[14] and regional construction organisations and are thus invested with a major role in the field of production of widely needed goods and in general social development. I believe that in the future a significant proportion of minor and medium enterprises across all branches of industry will also be transferred to local control.

As a consequence, local authorities have many opportunities, including the creation of cooperatives and the encouragement of self-employment, to ensure the broad economic and social development of their region. But for this they must end their dependence on hand-outs and look more keenly about them for local possibilities and local reserves. Local authorities have been granted extensive legal powers. But many authorities have not as yet exercised their rights, complaining that everything remains as it was with the real power still preserved in the ministries etc. They have forgotten that powers are not simply given but must be taken. There are others which have taken them up, like the enterprise urban executive committees, which are using the housing and social funds of

[14] Agro-industrial complexes in the Soviet Union are structural units of the national economy that incorporate branches engaged in agricultural production and the processing, transportation, storage and sale of agricultural products. (ed.)

institutions; like certain regions and provinces, which are undertaking campaigns to protect the environment; like individual republics and local authorities, which are showing great enterprise in developing agricultural and housing construction, or substantially improving the nutrition of the population, or the supply of goods in the shops and the reduction of queues for housing. But, regrettably all this is still an isolated and not a widespread phenomenon.

The inertia of many local authorities is associated with the lack of developed democracy. Authorities are not yet experiencing any pressure from working people who should be replacing sluggish leaders by those who are more active and daring, learning from neighbouring regions where there are better supplies, where more housing is being built, and attempts made to improve the environment. It is therefore the development of democracy, as was justifiably pointed out at the June 1987 Plenary meeting of the Central Committee, which is the main condition for *perestroika* of management, including both branch management and regional management. It is just through the development of democracy that working people are taking part in *perestroika*. The increased role of working collectives in enterprises, especially in the transition to the appointment of their leaders by election, is the main form of development of industrial democracy.

At the current stage in the conflicting combination of democracy and centralism, expressed in the single principle of democratic centralism, preferential consideration must be given to the development and deepening of democracy, just as in preceding stages a deformation occurred and centralism suppressed the democratic principles of management.

With the transition to economic methods, the central leadership of the Soviet economy will take on a new look. It would be wrong to associate centralism only with the directives and command methods of management, where the form substitutes for content. In the new conditions centralised tasks for the whole economy can and must be decided by economic methods, and by more democratic means. Consideration of people's economic interests is essential, with the recognition of workers' ownership rights to the means of production. Economic methods are effective when they are based on people's interests. We must learn to manage via people's interests.

I am far from implying that the management system described is fully adequate for the acceleration of the socio-economic development of the Soviet Union. We shall, in time, probably move to a more efficient management system. I understand and in many ways share the radicalism of many comrades, who consider that the proposed economic and management systems have been formed as a result of a struggle of opinions, of contradictory assessments and are a form of compromise between those who want to change the system of management through revolution and those who remain in favour of its evolution. This view is probably not without justification. But something else needs to be taken into consideration. Stability is needed for a transition to a new economic system and the enormous responsibility for correct planning rests on us. We all recognise that one wrong step in *perestroika* of the economic system will result in losses of many billions of roubles, and that no one will assist the Soviet Union. With the existing level of knowledge and research we must move to an economic system which can guarantee the acceleration of development, the transition to intensive methods and increased quality of production. Perhaps we are not altering management as profoundly as we would have liked, but we will be able to make the improvements, and deepen and develop them in the future. One thing is clear, that life and economic activity require deep revolutionary changes. We have a fairly clear-cut programme for the *perestroika* of management. A new stage is beginning and our whole future life depends on its outcome.

7 PLAN AND MARKET

In the journal *Novyi Mir* a piece appeared recently from the Soviet economist Popkova entitled "Whose pies are lighter?" Although confused and seeming like a stream of consciousness the piece defined the nature of socialism as being a centralised society in which the market must not be developed and used to meet people's needs more fully and so end shortages. The market, the author asserted, is a characteristic of capitalism and only under capitalism can shortages be avoided and the market come to be full of goods. The author concludes that there is no third alternative. This primitive view of a socialist economy is fairly widespread in the Soviet Union and more so in the West. In our opinion, this point of view is wrong and contradicts not only theory but practice.

Commodity production and market relations have been characteristic also of socialism. These relations are by no means inherent only in a capitalist economy. Commodity production and market relations have come about over centuries, commencing long before the rise of capitalism in the period of the break-down of early communal systems. In ancient Greece and Rome there were fairly well developed markets, and a money system operated. Market relations were also characteristic of the later feudal societies of the Middle Ages.

Without doubt the full development of market relations occurred under capitalism, when these became universal. In a capitalist society everything is bought and sold, not merely everyday goods, but land, natural resources, whole enterprises and organisations. And in addition to the market for goods there is a stockmarket for capital. Labour also becomes a commodity insofar as there is a fairly free labour market where there is unemployment. Internationalisation has strengthened market relations and made them worldwide. In the post-war period the integration of international capital has intensified with the rise of transnational monopolies.

The rule of commodities under capitalism, however, cannot negate the indisputable fact that commodity production and money existed before capitalism and exist under socialism as well. Commodity production and market relations arise when producers are individualised and there is a division of labour. In such conditions goods are exchanged to meet social needs. Under socialism the division of labour is well developed and deepens and widens further according to the degree of development of the productive forces. Within the framework of public ownership, which predominates in the Soviet economy, the individualising of enterprises and economic organisations is relative. This is linked to the fact that common public ownership gives the rights of possession, use and distribution of resources to individual enterprises and organisations in managing their businesses. In the recent Law on State Enterprises it is laid down that the state is not responsible for the debts of enterprises, but neither are enterprises under obligation to answer for the debts of the state. By law enterprises are accordingly being transferred to full self-accounting, self-financing and self-management.

Under socialism there exist also cooperative enterprises and organisations, including collective farms, based on another cooperative form of socialist ownership. Once, quite unjustified efforts were made in the Soviet Union to abolish cooperatives. Now cooperatives are reviving in industry, trade and other sectors and continue to develop in agriculture. Cooperatives, as a flexible form of organisation of collective labour, have some definite advantages and a promising future. Alexander Chayanov, the theorist of world renown on cooperative forms of economy, wrote about this as long ago as the 1920s. Although innocent, he suffered during the period of repression under Stalin's cult of personality. Recently after a petition by the scientific community, he was fully cleared of all accusations and his famous works are now being prepared for publication.

Self-employment, which is to be developed in socialist conditions is individualised by its very nature and assumes separation of producers, the division of labour and the exchange of commodities. Any interrelation between producers and consumers who buy goods they need with their wages or other income, is also by its nature individual. Finally, the Soviet Union and other socialist countries are participating increasingly actively in international trade, and this leaves its impression on market relations in the country. The conditions for the existence of commodity production and market relations in the USSR are not of transient importance but part of the long-term development of a socialist economy. Therefore the Party programme, passed at the XXVII Party Congress and designed for the next 20–30 years, refers specifically to socialist enterprises as commodity producers and to market relations as being inherent in our social system.

Quite a different issue is the new content of these market relations under socialism. The point is that in the exchange of commodities relations are established between people. These can be between private capitalist owners or monopolies and the population, as is characteristic of capitalism, or between socialist enterprises or cooperatives and the population as under socialism. Commodity production, the market and market relations in the socialist conditions of the Soviet Union, vary greatly. But in contrast to capitalism commodities and money relations are not universal categories. Land and natural resources cannot be bought and sold. Since there is no unemployment and the economic base of society accords with socialist ownership, there is no labour market. A market for capital is not envisaged as part of *perestroika*. There are no plans for a Soviet stock exchange, shares, bills of exchange or profit from commercial credit.

A socialist market is a government-regulated market. Through the prescription of set economic proportions, fixed wages and a system of state finance and credit, the monetary income of the population is regulated. On the other hand, prices for most essential products are also to be set by state bodies. Major capital investment and other economic levers and stimuli are in the hands of the state and can be directed at greater or lesser production of certain goods and thus have a major influence on the market.

Up to now the market in the Soviet Union has been both restricted and deformed. Most means of production have been centrally allocated by the state through a material and technical supply system. They are not freely bought and sold. The market is still one in which there are persistent shortages and consumer demand, especially for high quality goods, is not being met. The system of pricing is excessively rigid and centralised, so that prices may not reflect reality because they do not correspond to the the costs incurred and efficiency in the production of the goods. Since in the past, many types of cooperatives were not permitted to develop and self-employment was not encouraged, representation of commodity producers in the market was incomplete. In such a distorted marketplace the grey economy became widespread with its uncontrolled mechanism for distributing goods and incomes. The so-called black market also grew and speculation became increasingly rife.

During *perestroika* market relations in the USSR will be deepened and broadened. Above all the market is set to more than double in size thanks to the transition from centralised material and technical supply to wholesale trade in means of production, including direct commercial links between enterprises. In this way a well-developed market in the means of production will be created, and the proportion of centrally set prices will be substantially reduced. Centralised pricing will be retained only for the most essential products, to control their rate of growth and to stave off inflation. At the same time the scope of contracted and free prices will grow significantly.

Let us look in greater detail at measures for the development of cooperatives and self-employment. Cooperative ownership in the Soviet Union is a type of socialist ownership based on collective labour. All members of a cooperative are economically equal, with no employers and employees and no exploitation of labour. Lenin attached great importance to the development of cooperatives and one set of his last writings, considered as his will, is particularly devoted to cooperatives. Lenin considered cooperatives broadly in many forms, adapted to various sectors of the economy. Formerly cooperatives were widespread not only in agriculture in the form of collective farms but also in trade and marketing, and many other branches of industry. In the 1950s for no reason manufacturing cooperatives were abolished by decree. Cooperatives were largely removed from trade, food provision and the service sectors. In the 1950s and early 1960s a massive process began of transforming collective farms, normally the less-developed ones, into state farms. All this resulted in a significant reduction of cooperative ownership. While in 1939 collective farm members and cooperative craftsmen made up 47.2% of the population, in 1959 the figure was 31.4%, while 1986 data show 12.1%.

Simultaneously administrative influence by the state on cooperatives was intensified, particularly affecting the collective farms. The system of planning and material supply, and even the financing and credit system, barely differed from those applied to state enterprises. It is true that the choice of the collective farm chairperson rested with the workers, but this was usually a mere formality. Many collective farms were unprofitable and the state covered their debts. Thus members of the cooperative were not liable for the results of their work and wages were generally similar to those paid in state enterprises and were not really related to the economic achievements of the cooperative.

Yet, there are many opportunities for raising the efficiency of production on the basis of cooperative ownership and their potential is far from exhausted under the administrative methods of management. Moreover the advantages of cooperatives could never have been apparent under these administrative methods. For, in this sector more than any other, the efficiency of a cooperative's work depends on its independence, its responsibility for its own budget, self-financing and self-management. As the ongoing *perestroika* of management and the transfer to economic methods are implemented, the role of cooperatives will substantially increase.

The cooperative sector is in fact expanding beyond all others. This was limited to agriculture and fisheries in the recent past, but in the manufacturing industry, trade, food provision and services, cooperatives can now operate successfully. In this new environment for cooperatives a revival is taking place in several sectors of the economy. For example several hundred manufacturing cooperatives have started, while cooperative cafes, snack bars, car repairs, flat repairs, house builders have all begun to be established.

However, the development of cooperatives is still limited even though the cooperative movement is gradually gathering force in the few months since the new law came into operation. It is the poor system of supply that is hindering this growth. With an almost total absence of wholesale trade there are insoluble problems in obtaining necessary resources and materials. The credit system for cooperatives is still not developed and they have no united organisation yet to defend their interests. But these are temporary difficulties which will be overcome.

How large a role can cooperatives play in the economy? There are currently 26,700 thousand collective farms in the USSR, incorporating 12.6 million peasant homesteads. Collective farms produce about 40% of all goods in the countryside including half of the grain, two thirds of the cotton, almost nine tenths of the sugarbeet, more than half of all the milk, around one third of the meat, wool, potatoes and vegetables. Roughly this share of agricultural production will be maintained in the future. Manufacturing cooperatives have considerable potential. Judging by other socialist countries where cooperatives are developed, their share could reach about one quarter of all consumer goods, one third of foodstuffs and up to a half of all services. But we are still a long way from such figures. Cooperatives occupy a significant place only in Soviet retail trade, with about 27% of all turnover in current prices. Cooperative restaurants and the like enterprises hold roughly a one fifth share of this market. Recently the network of cooperative food shops has substantially grown. These cooperatives have begun increasingly to purchase the produce of collective farms and their members at agreed prices and to sell them through their shops.

With the transition from administrative to economic methods of management the attitude to cooperatives is changing. Instead of the command system of management, the economic interests of cooperatives are being taken into account and economic norms are being established for them. This gives wide freedom in the choice of work, and the principle of self-management is being strictly observed. All this is resulting in increased productivity of cooperative labour and in the successful development of cooperative ownership.

A Law on Self-Employment was passed on 1 May 1987. The law permits self-employment without hiring other workers and leaves a wide sphere for cooperative activity. The law does not define these spheres but permits individual activity wherever it is not explicitly prohibited. Self-employment in the production of fire-arms, medicines, drugs and weed-killer is not permitted. Extensive rights to regulate self-employment have been given to local authorities. There has been a major breakthrough toward rapid expansion in places where local authorities have actively pursued policies of extending self-employment. Individually run taxis have appeared on the streets of many towns, self-employed doctors and nurses have increased in number, production of handicrafts and the whole gamut of services developed. Self-employed workers now number tens of thousands and I believe their numbers will grow very considerably.

A definite restriction on the growth in numbers of the self-employed lies in the fact that in many cases self-employment is possible only as a second occupation or in free time. Pensioners, students, women with children and housewives can all become self-employed. Local authorities can now grant permission for full-time self-employment especially when it relates to the production of needed consumer goods. I assume self-employment will expand primarily in the service sector. It will of course play an auxiliary role to state and cooperative enterprises in this sector. I do not think, however, that major changes will occur in the social structure of Soviet society as a result of the appearance of numerous as it were private producers.

Certain misgivings are being expressed about the possibility of excessively high incomes arising from self-employment. To counter this there is a progressive income tax levied on the self-employed. This tax is constructed in such a way as to provide for earnings through self-employment which are close to those of workers in state and cooperative enterprises. It is however understood that through more intensive and higher quality work these earnings can be higher.

The development of cooperatives and of self-employment will supply the socialist market with many goods, and bring the higher flexibility and competitive potency needed to satisfy social needs. The essential attribute of a market is consumer choice. The advantage of a market is lost when monopoly occurs. To give the market its economic effectiveness, competition between producers making similar or the same goods is crucial. Under *perestroika* this question is being given special attention. Monopoly of particular lines of production has to be ended and parallel enterprises or economic organisations created. When designating enterprises as

economically effective we now apply the term "economic emula-
tion", to express the distinctive form of competition between
enterprises in Soviet conditions. The growing socialist economy can
never become capitalist. Since there is no hired labour, business-
owners, exploitation and commodities are not a universal category.
There will not be an uncontrolled market. In the light of this the
relationship between the plan and market must be examined.

A socialist economy is by its nature planned. Indeed it is based on
socialist ownership with state ownership as its main form. The
means of production of society, particularly the land, material
wealth and enterprises belong to the whole people, through which
their administrative bodies systematically manage them and seek to
make good use of them.

Thus the social formation of a planned economy from top to
bottom as in Soviet society is overriding and universal. This
formation will be conserved even with *perestroika*, but it will take
on some new features and, most importantly, new forms to
implement the realisation of a planned economy. Planning for the
development of the economy will in part be realised through the
market. In the market place commodities obtain the social recognition of the consumer – they are bought or rejected. Social valuation
is given to the production costs of the goods. Thus the market place
acts as a key additional regulator of production within socialist
society.

People ask the following question: is the development of a
socialist market a step on the road to capitalism? From the above it
will be quite evident that the answer to this question is categorically
"no!" We are not developing capitalist production, but a socialist
market with a new content and system of operation in a socialist
economy. Similarly we are asked: what about "market socialism",
does the ongoing radical reform of management in the USSR equal
a step on the road to a "market economy"? Here the answer
depends on what is understood by the terms market economy or
market socialism. If by this is understood the universalisation and
general spread of the market place, an economic system in which
everything is bought and sold, then naturally we are not moving
towards such a system and never will since this would not be
socialist. In China during their economic reforms the term "planned
commodity economy" is being promoted. My attitude to this term is
two-fold, again depending on the meaning ascribed to it. I have

tried to describe the place of the market in a socialist economy, its important though limited character. But is this how the market is understood when the whole economy is called a commodity economy? Let us recall what was said earlier, that in the Soviet case a significant number of prices of goods are not determined in the market.

In our radical reform of management the relationship of plan and market is being fundamentally changed. It is changing because the whole centralised system of planning is being looked at differently. It is changing because the market sector is being developed and extended and a new unity and interaction of plan and market is beginning. Plans are being implemented by proportional norms and contracts and not by commands.

In the new system of economic management prices become a basic point of reference. Enterprises and associations will evaluate the results of their work through the pricing of their products. The existing system of prices does not give a true valuation because prices do not reflect social costs and the economic efficiency of production. Up to now this common denominator has been lacking in the Soviet Union.

For historical reasons the prices for natural resources and agricultural products have been depressed, since these did not include rents and a realistic valuation of the labour used. Low prices for fuel and raw materials in the past stimulated their wider use in production and assisted their growth. The depressed prices for agricultural products re-allocated resources from agriculture to industry, although subsidised prices guaranteed foodstuffs to the less well-off families. Currently these depressed prices are acting as a brake on development. Low prices for fuel and raw materials led to waste and impeded resource conservation and economies in their use. With prices at these levels, many geological enterprises and even whole extraction branches (like coal mining) are unprofitable and their losses are simply covered by grants from the state. Depressed prices for agricultural products, where their production is relatively costly because of low productivity, have also been covered by state grants. This impairs the stimulating effect of prices on the development of agriculture.

During the *perestroika* this situation must be fundamentally changed. A radical and total reform of price formation is envisaged as well as a revision of all types of prices; wholesale, purchase, retail and supply tariffs, into a unified coordinated system of prices. A substantial increase is intended in the prices of fuel and raw materials, relating them to world levels. At the same time subsidies on the price of goods will be substantially cut. In agriculture prices will be constructed so as to take into account the real cost of fertiliser inputs, of machinery and other equipment, formerly sold to agriculture at depressed prices through state compensation for the actual cost of production of these products.

Prices must be constructed in such a way that improved quality and more efficient production becomes highly profitable. Obsolete products which do not meet contemporary demands of efficiency should become unremunerative and unprofitable for enterprises to produce. In many countries prices are set so that they drop by 30% for products of 10% lower quality.

Although under the last revision of wholesale prices on 1 January 1982 and in the ongoing improvement of price formation certain advances have been made, it is nonetheless still remunerative to produce obsolete machinery. It is possible to name hundreds of examples where enterprises produce such machinery and make large profits. In particular, light industry deserves severe censure from the point of view of product quality, yet the level of profitability of this branch is the highest – more than 25% (the relation of profit to cost of the capital stock and material resources). The oil refining industry has the worst indicators for processing, using the most costly hydrocarbon as an input and yet it is showing profitability at about 15%.

The state of affairs in ferrous metallurgy is often criticised, as is the unsatisfactory quality of the rolled iron. Yet the profitability of ferrous metallurgy has grown from 7% to 11% in five years. Similar examples, relating to different branches of production and specific enterprises could be multiplied. In a word, what is needed is for prices to facilitate more rapid introduction to industry of all that is new and advanced, forcing economic planners to improve their technology and to economise.

During the reform the procedure for establishing prices is being changed. Under the former administrative system of management, prices for many products were set centrally by state bodies. Out of 24 million types of goods and services offered in the USSR, about 500,000 prices were set centrally by the Committee for Prices. For the remainder, as a rule one-off or short-run products or goods sold locally only, prices were set by other state or local bodies. Less widespread was the practice of prices based on agreement between producer and consumer and rarer still were free prices, set according to demand and supply. These free prices operated only in the collective farm private markets. In the consumer cooperative chain of Cooptorg shops prices for meat and some other food products also reflected supply and demand.

The way prices were set under the administrative system of management was designed to cover producers' costs and give them a normal profit. But these prices were rarely reviewed, perhaps once in 7–10 years. During such a period major changes occurred in expenditure patterns and sometimes once profitable branches became loss-making, as recently occurred in the coal industry. State prices for coal do not compensate any longer even for the production costs of extracting the coal, which makes coal mining generally unprofitable. With the implementation of the reforms intended for the 1989–90 period the whole method of price formation is to be radically changed. The number of prices set centrally is to be reduced, that is, to comprehend only the more essential staple products. And, moreover, they will not be set in a voluntaristic fashion. Rather they will be based on social costs and will take into consideration the cost effectiveness of production and the level of world prices shaped by the relations between supply and demand. The prices will be reviewed at least once every five years and will be closely tied to the indicators of five-year plans. Should the conditions change sharply prices will be reviewed before the end of a five-year period.

At the same time the sphere of contractually set and free prices will rapidly expand, since now enterprises themselves will decide on their own development plans based in turn on agreements with consumers. Thus to a large extent prices will be a matter of agreement. It is possible then that the state will set up a certain method for calculating prices, and the Prices Committee is being invested with the task of assessing the rationale for contractual and free prices. In particular, speculative price increases aimed at excessive profit will not be permitted. Special measures will be taken to combat monopolies. It can be seen that a process of democratising the whole of price formation is underway.

To ensure that production really leads to the satisfaction of consumer needs a number of measures are proposed to strengthen the influence of the consumer on the technical level and quality of production. One of the main impediments to scientific technological progress lies in the existence of shortages. And these shortages are not primarily caused by too little being produced. Their main underlying cause rests in the lack of any real feedback between consumer and producer. In other words shortages are generated by the working of the economic system.

The existing system itself gives rise to shortages where the consumer is simply an adjunct of the producer, where the consumer has no freedom of choice, but confronts a centralised distribution of products quite heedless of their quality. To support this statement I will present a hypothetical example. Let us suppose that the entire population's need for sugar is wholly and fully met. Nobody hoards bags of sugar at home. Now imagine a situation in which from 1st January of the following year the open sale of sugar is abolished and sugar is to be given out according to applications which must be made well in advance. It is difficult to estimate how much sugar a family requires to meet its various needs, which can include jam-making, providing for guests, as well as for unforeseen demands. Therefore every family will try to obtain the maximum quantity of sugar so as to meet in full whatever needs may arise. And if these applications are likely to be pruned then every claimant will consciously increase the quantity of sugar demanded to guarantee a supply for all eventualities. All these applications will be collected and totalled and in all probability the volume of sugar production will turn out to be quite insufficient. The applications will have to be reduced. A shortage of sugar will arise in the country, while in every home bags are being stored up and gradually everybody will accumulate enough sugar to last for many months to come.

I have introduced an intentionally simple example. But imagine a present-day enterprise: it must make applications for rolled steel and other materials long before the plan of production for the following year has been determined. Not yet knowing the details of its final plans, these applications are naturally exaggerated. Much is acquired that is not needed. So difficult is the existing bureaucratic method of passing on unneeded resources to another enterprise, that it is easier to leave the unneeded materials in the storehouse. Thus shortages gradually accumulated and stocks grew in enterprises and organisations of materials that were withdrawn from circulation. This is why the transition to wholesale trading, associated with an increase in available resources and an increased role for direct links between enterprises to make economic contracts, has such major significance. Expanding the range of consumer choice is also envisaged by the organisation of competition between manufacturing enterprises.

The transition to wholesale trading is a crucial part of a radical reform of management. The centralised material and technical supply system is the very opposite of trading, and is the basis of the administrative method of management. It deprives enterprises of any choice in the products they acquire and manufacture. Formerly the view prevailed that a transition to wholesale trading would only be possible when persistent shortages had been overcome. Time passed, production grew but shortages were not eliminated. And if one is to wait for the elimination of shortages and only advance the transition to wholesale trade in line with the development of production, it will be necessary to wait a long time. It has now been understood that it is the whole system of material and technical allocations which itself generates shortages. This means that the total satisfaction of demand is not a precondition for the transition to wholesale trading but this transition should be implemented as part of the reform of management.

It is intended to make wholesale trading into the main channel for the actual supply of the means of production for enterprises and organisations. By the year 1990 no less than 60% of all production in the country is to be allocated through wholesale trading and by 1992 this share will rise to 80%–90%. In this context wholesale trading is understood to comprise multi-channelled trade including direct commercial links between enterprises as well as links through freely selected intermediaries, operating themselves as self-accounting wholesalers. Vertical links predominated in the system of top-down material and technical allocations. It was necessary in order to get delivery to resort to a higher organisation which gave the instructions for the delivery of any product you wanted. But now instead of these vertical links mutually beneficial horizontal trade links are being forged.

If we accept that the most fundamental part of radical reform is the transition from administrative to economic methods of management then the basic measures needed still lie ahead of us, namely: the reform of price formation, changes in the finance and credit mechanism, the transition to wholesale trading and to direct links instead of the centralised material and technical supply. One measure without the other will not give the anticipated result and will simply not work. We are not yet able to transfer to wholesale trading because there is still a great deal of excess money actually unused in the accounts of the enterprises. Enterprises therefore will be tempted to throw all their money into buying up to increase their stocks. This occurred during previous experiments with the idea of preferential supply, when enterprises immediately rushed to store metal for "emergencies". The present total value of stocks in the economy exceeds 460 billion roubles. We also cannot transfer to wholesale trading with the existing prices. You cannot try to cancel reservations for fuel oil which is priced so low that in many regions it is more convenient to burn it than coal. Even now the USSR burns around 200 million tonnes of fuel oil a year whereas in the USA consumption has fallen to 50 million tonnes because of its high price.

Here I have touched on a very important question concerning the reforms of the finance and credit system. Practical aspects of it have been looked at ahead. Here we will look at one of the most important tasks of this reform: bringing the circulation of money into line with the actual turnover of goods in the economy; and filling in all the cracks and holes through which surplus money seeps. One channel is the counting of the tax income the state gets from enterprises before goods have been sold to consumers. In particular, this occurs when financial bodies receive tax for turnover before the commodities are actually sold. Another channel is the budget deficit. To balance the budget credit is created. The most important source of surplus money, however is credit itself. For many years credit has grown much faster than the volume of production. In some years the volume of credit increased by 15–17% when output grew by 3%–5%. Often credit was granted to low profit, non-cost effective enterprises which wasted the credit and could not repay. This was true of a large proportion of collective and state farms. As a result the line between credit and financing has faded. Credit has lost its basic distinguishing characteristic – that it should be recoverable.

Surpluses of money have exerted a strong influence on the market and this has been one of the major causes of the persistent shortages of supply in relation to demand. It should be noted that the socio-

economic dimension of the problem of shortages is quite insufficiently researched in the literature. The sole exception to this is the
book by Ya. Kornai, a distinguished Hungarian economist whose
work is well known to Western specialists.

Thus it is intended that an extensive wholesale market for the
means of production will gradually be created during the price
reform and the reform of the finance, credit and material supply
systems along with the transition to wholesale trading. Associations
and enterprises will obtain economic freedom in the production and
sale of their products and new relations will be established thereby
between the plan and the market. It will take two to three years to
prepare and introduce these reforms, which are intended to take
hold during the years 1989–90.

8 AN OPEN ECONOMY

External trade occupies a smaller place in the economy of the USSR than in that of most industrialised capitalist countries. In 1986, for example, the proportion of exports in the national income stood at 12%, while this indicator for many capitalist countries and socialist countries of eastern Europe was 40%, and even 50%. The low proportion of external trade in the USSR primarily follows from the fact that the country is large and rich in a wide range of natural resources, so that many needs are satisfied through its own production. It has been mentioned earlier that the USSR is perhaps the only country in the world which can meet in full its needs for all types of fuel and the vast majority of raw materials for industry.

Nevertheless, it should be recognised at once that the contribution of external trade in the development of the Soviet economy is set too low and the volume of exports and imports does not correspond to the level of development of production. This situation is linked to the one-sided and not very effective structure of exports and imports. Fuel and electricity predominate (about 53%) among Soviet exports, other raw materials (ores, timber) account for about 9%, while machines, equipment and vehicles make up only about 14% of the total value. With regard to imports, foodstuffs and raw materials to produce them make up a considerable share (more than 20%), metals and manufactures for them account for more than 8%, industrial goods for mass consumption about 12%, while machines, equipment and vehicles make up a litle over one third of all imports.

Because of the predominance of fuel, chiefly oil and gas, in the export structure, Soviet exports to other countries fell during 1986 by 8% and again in 1987 owing to of the drop in the world prices of oil and gas. Although these prices have somewhat stabilised the Soviet Union will experience difficulties for a number of years to come even with stable international fuel prices. This is because in its trade with socialist countries the price for oil is set at an average of the world prices for the preceding five years and this will be falling for a further three to four years.

Any consideration of the cost-effectiveness of exports immediately reveals the poor share of exports supplied by machinery and equipment. The share of these exports has been falling sharply from 22% in 1970, 19% in 1975, and 16% in 1980 to less than 14% in 1985. Not only does the Soviet Union export less machinery than major western countries but less than many relatively small countries. It even exports less than some underdeveloped countries. Of course this does not correspond to the actual volume of machine construction, in which the USSR is second only to the USA. And it is the export of machinery and equipment, in particular sophisticated machinery, which is the most cost-effective. The recent relatively low prices for raw materials and the barter of growing quantities of exported fuel and raw materials for imported machinery and equipment have meant that our exports are not as effective as they should be. Therefore the proportion of machinery and equipment exported to the socialist countries and the west must be increased significantly. The basis for this is now being created by the radical technical reconstruction of machine building, the improvement of its quality and competitive capacity, and the systematic renewal of production prototypes.

The proportion of goods for export which involve intensive processing must also be increased, as against the current predominance of the export of unprocessed raw materials. The export of processed chemical products in particular could be substantially raised, linked with the development of the chemical industry based on oil, gas and chlorine, and sulphur compounds. It is more profitable to export cellulose and other products of timber chemistry than export unprocessed timber or wood chips.

The conclusion from all this is not that exports of oil, gas and raw materials should be reduced. All countries in the world which have large natural deposits and good technical and economic conditions use their exclusive rights to these deposits and by exporting raw materials derive a differential rent. The Soviet Union also derives such an income insofar as the yields of oil deposits, situated mainly on dry land, are fairly high compared with the oil yields in the USA and some other deposits. Of course, the yields and economic outlay in the Soviet Union are less favourable than those of the Near East. But in general the conditions for extracting our oil deposits are much better than in the North Sea or Alaska. The Soviet Union also has the richest deposits of natural gas in the world.

Thus there is nothing intrinsically wrong in exporting raw materials if there are sufficient resources in the country for the present and subsequent generations. Sweden, one of the most developed countries in Europe, exports iron ore mined from its unique Kiruno deposit. Canada exports a great deal of timber, and so on. It should be noted that many Soviet people are anxious about the large export of fuel and natural resources, particularly oil, gas and timber. They fear that we are robbing future generations. I do not share this view. Mining technology will without doubt be perfected. Our children and grandchildren are hardly likely to want us to leave them more than half of the oil reserves, and in many deposits two thirds. irrevocably in the ground. I believe that they will in fact return to many deposits which we consider exhausted.

Moreover, Western Siberia is not the only source of oil in the USSR. Recently a large-scale Caspian province of hydrocarbon raw materials was opened up for production. It has outstanding gas deposits like the Astrakhan and Karachaganaksk fields, and the vast Tengiz oil deposits which make possible great increases in oil yields. The Caspian deposits contain much hydrogen sulphide and other valuable compounds and these can be used not only as a source of hydrocarbon but as a chemical raw material base. The development of these new deposits begins in the 1986–90 five-year period. Up to the year 2000 this region will provide tens of millions of tonnes of oil and tens of billions of cubic metres of gas annually. A powerful gas and oil chemical industry is being created, new towns are growing up as production and the social infrastructure are created in this region.

For more than three decades deposits of oil and gas have been discovered also in Eastern Siberia, in the northern Irkutsk Region, Krasnoyarsk Province and south-west Yakutia. Exploitation of these deposits will begin in 1991. Thus with such reserves the annual amount of oil and gas going for export is only one hundredth of one per cent, which is no problem. Earnings in hard currency from the sale of fuel and raw materials go towards strengthening the economic development of the country and the growth in the well-being of the people. They are, consequently, not being wasted as far as subsequent generations are concerned. On the contrary, favourable conditions are thereby prepared for their entry into life.

Turning now to imports, their structure also must be fundamentally changed. The weakest link is the import of large quantities of grain, meat and dairy products. With the accelerated development of agriculture we will most probably be able gradually to discontinue such imports. There is great potential in the Soviet Union not only to extend the production of grain, but to secure its more effective use as fodder for livestock, as seed and material for flour-based goods. There is still serious waste in this sector. Because of extremely low prices for bread, (1 kg of black bread in the USSR costs 0.16 roubles) it is convenient to feed bread to livestock which is then being sold as meat in the collective farm markets at prices two to three times the state retail prices for meat, i.e. six to eight roubles per kg. The low price of bread also leads to the wasteful use of bread by households.

But much more important is the uneconomic use of grain in the unbalanced fodder for livestock. Fodder is often deficient in protein while the grain is used in an insufficiently processed form. As a result the cost-effectiveness of fodder is reduced and to increase the yield in animal weight requires one and a half to two times more fodder than rational feeding methods. The transition to new more effective strains of livestock can also result in major economies in the use of fodder, particularly of grain.

Another unfavourable aspect of the Soviet import structure is the large-scale import of metal manufactures, particularly semi-finished and finished pipes. Meanwhile the Soviet Union produces 112 million tonnes of rolled steel, more than in the whole of Europe, and much more than in either the USA or Japan. The question once again is one of wastefulness, irrational use of metal, the inefficient structure of production and the lag in the technical development of metallurgy. All this is a temporary phenomenon and it is being rectified. Imports of metal manufactures can, in our view, be reduced substantially. At the same time, we need to import more modern machinery and a variety of consumer goods for the population. It should be noted though that we buy some machines and equipment from abroad at triple the price at which they could profitably be produced at home. The USSR has the most developed mining industry with the greatest amount of construction in the world including excavation work. Nevertheless for many years we have been purchasing bulldozers, excavators and other mining and digging equipment in massive quantities, even though, by using a small share of the resources we waste on purchases, it would have been possible to secure their local production. At last we are doing this, but why has it been necessary to throw away so much money on this when it could have been done much earlier?

Here is a fairly typical example. When the South Yakutia coal deposits were developed and the Neryungri open cast pit was dug there, a plan was drawn up to carry out the rock with 180-tonne dump-trucks. The plan itself could be questioned on economic grounds, since there are other more effective means of shifting rock; and nobody in the world was producing 180-tonne trucks in anything like the numbers suggested. They therefore had to be specially constructed for Neryungri conditions, taking into consideration the 50-degree frosts, and the more powerful engine needed for the steepness of the roads. As a result the cost of one truck ran to up to two million dollars. Many tens of them were needed. Then, despite the USSR being the leading advanced excavator producer, no excavator to load 180-tonne capacity trucks was to be found within the Soviet Union. 20 cubic tonne excavators were eventually purchased abroad at a cost of five million dollars but have performed poorly in the harsh conditions of Yakutia. Furthermore, this excavator made a large terrace in the rock so that our normal drilling machines became inadequate. New units were purchased with the result that many additional hundreds of millions of dollars were spent on the purchase of machinery which for much less cost could have been fairly rapidly developed in the Soviet Union.

When the foreign currency situation became worse and it became clear that the foreign machinery had not proved appropriate to Soviet conditions, although costing three to four times more than the same Soviet machinery, an order was eventually placed with the

Belorussian Vehicle Factory and it began to produce 180-tonne dump-trucks. As President of the Scientific Council of the Academy of Sciences concerned with the problems of the Baikal–Amur railway, I have visited Neryungri almost every year and I once assembled the drivers and asked which vehicle was better – the American or Soviet, which cost four times less for the same load-bearing capacity. Opinions were divided but it seems that the Soviet vehicle has proved to be of roughly similar quality. An order was also placed with the Ural Machine Factory, a factory with a great tradition of producing large excavators, and it built 20 cubic metre excavators fairly quickly. After some refinements they were no worse than the imported excavators at a third of the price and worked the pit successfully.

In the period I have described, all the newly acquired machinery was paid for by the state and supplied to the ministry and to the enterprise rather as a gift would be. Dependence on hand-outs and attempts to "live off the state" prevailed. Many ill-considered purchases of foreign equipment have been made in this way, some of which turned out simply to be unneeded or incomplete. Therefore the value of uninstalled and idle equipment has grown, especially in the oil and chemical industry where whole factories have been purchased. Meanwhile indigenous chemical machine building has been ill-treated, starved of resources and not directed towards producing the equipment needed. To quote a recent example, much foreign equipment was brought in by agreement with firms from Finland and other countries for the construction of the Astrakhan gas refining complex. These firms in fact ordered part of the equipment from Soviet factories, e.g. the Volgograd Oil Machine Building Factory, which reproduced the equipment supplied to us from the West, but much more cheaply and to the same quality. Yet this factory has been expanding very slowly while at the same time hundreds of millions of roubles are being spent on the purchase of almost similar equipment.

Today the attitude to machine building has fundamentally changed. As stated earlier, the rate of growth of capital investment has quadrupled, full technical reconstruction is being implemented and machine building enterprises are being treated as a high priority. Yet it does not follow from all this that the volume of imports of machinery and equipment should be reduced. On the contrary, the volume of purchased machinery and equipment must increase, but only of those types of machinery and equipment which it is more effective to buy than to produce ourselves.

The question is mainly one of the international exchange of machine building production. We not only need to purchase machinery and equipment but also to sell it in increasingly large quantities. Many Soviet factories have good experience and long traditions in this business. It is sufficient to refer to the large export sales of the Belarus tractor from the Minsk Tractor Factory, the once considerable interest of foreign consumers in the Neva motor vehicle factory, foreign purchases of ships and tankers from the Kherson shipbuilding association which sail the seas under Greek, English and other flags, etc. But the volume of these sales is small against the enormous size of Soviet machine building.

When considering the problems of developing and increasing the cost-effectiveness of exports and imports we assume it is advantageous for the USSR to develop its external trade. This view is an integral part of our new strategy. As Gorbachev has declared, we are against autarky and for the development of international economic and scientific technological relations. The USSR is to develop these relations for two main reasons. On the one hand, it improves the cost-effectiveness of the economy, making use of the advantages of the international division of labour; on the other, for broader foreign policy reasons it helps strengthen trust between states and advance the cause of peace. Characteristically, rapid growth of Soviet external trade has occurred during years when international relations improved. During the 1960s the volume of the USSR's external trade with the West grew two and a half times in comparative prices and in the following 5-year period to 1975 it doubled again, a total increase of five times over a 15-year period. But as the cold war wind blew and the world situation became more complex, growth in the volume of external trade slowed down sharply. In the following decade 1975–85 external trade with the West increased by only one third and in the last 5-year period it has simply stopped growing. The cold war has resulted in a situation in which the total volume of trade between the USSR and the USA is currently less than half that of USSR trade with Finland, and the volume of the USSR's external trade with Japan is substantially lower than with Italy. We buy and sell more goods from and to the Federal Republic of Germany than to the USA and Japan combined, although it is not long since the volume of Soviet trade with the USA and Japan was higher than with any other western partners.

We wish to develop external trade with all countries, including the West, and, as it was in the recent past, to have trade outstrip the growth of the Soviet economy. The economy should become increasingly open and the proportion of external economic exchanges grow so that the Soviet share in world trade corresponds to its role in world production. Today, while the USSR's share in world industrial production is roughly one fifth, its share of world trade is only one twentieth. This gap is a product of history; 30 years ago the USSR's share in the world market was even less. Then, however, as part of a general improvement in international relations, there was a period of rapid expansion of Soviet external economic and scientific relations. These developed rapidly, particularly with the socialist countries, but also with western and developing countries. Long-term trading and economic agreements were concluded with many states, envisaging the doubling or even trebling of external trade every ten years. Satisfactory procedures were created to facilitate these economic relations, and appropriate forms were found for large long-term deals through compensation agreements, whereby foreign firms together with Soviet organisations concluded large joint enterprise ventures using foreign credit. Payment against these credits was made subsequently by the supply of products after the enterprises started operating.

There is quite a list of large-scale deals with a noticeable positive influence on the development of the Soviet economy. A classic example is the building of the Volga Car Factory in cooperation with the Italian firm Fiat, designed for an annual production of 660,000 light vehicles. The factory's first conveyor belt was set in motion three years after construction started. The factory very soon reached planned levels of output, and the Lada cars have proved successful in Soviet conditions. They have changed the look of Soviet towns, substantially affected the life styles of many Soviet families and sales of them account for a considerable share of internal trade turnover. Almost one quarter of the output of these cars is sold to other countries, above all to members of CMEA[15]

[15] Council for Mutual Economic Aid (CMEA), which used to be known as COMECON, is responsible for coordinating the external trade of the Soviet Union, the Eastern European socialist countries and Cuba and Vietnam, but not China. It also discusses joint ventures and some division of labour in manufacturing among the several partners. (ed.)

(The Council for Mutual Economic Aid) – the integrating economic organisation of socialist countries.

A new stage in the development of the USSR's external trade relations has now opened up. After years of stagnation and standstill in this sphere, a much greater acceleration and dynamism are being shown. A whole new approach has been worked out to develop the USSR's external economic relations. To begin with, a fundamental *perestroika* of the management of external trade was introduced. In the past the monopoly of foreign trade lay in the hands of the Ministry of Foreign Trade. Producers of exports or consumers of imports – enterprises, associations and even management bodies in the branch ministries – had no direct outlets into the international market. There was no effective economic mechanism to encourage external economic activity. A small share of the hard currency from the sale of their goods abroad was assigned to enterprises and associations to be kept in special accounts. This could be used by them for the purchase of necessary equipment or materials, once again through the Ministry of Foreign Trade. But, as a rule, there were considerable restrictions on using these accounts and therefore producers were not really interested in receiving hard currency.

Payment for exports was based on internal prices and not tied in any way to the price on the international market in which the goods were sold. These prices were normally higher than analogous prices for Soviet goods. Since higher quality was demanded of export goods there were higher costs for the inputs involved. Internal prices for export production did not usually compensate for these increased outlays and in self-accounting terms production for export was unprofitable for enterprises. Worse still, however, the export production plan was under special supervision and managers were severely punished when the plan was not fulfilled. There was therefore no desire among managers to supply goods for export. Schedules of tasks were handed down from above for production for export. Being divorced from the market, producers but poorly understood the need for quality goods, and did not take the demands of the world market into consideration during the production process. Thus it was that exports came to centre on fuel and raw materials where the problems of quality and adaptation to market demands were less acute. The export of complex products was held back, particularly of various kinds of machinery, and so their share declined.

The situation was even worse in relation to imports. Imports were made at the expense not of the enterprise but of state resources. The tendency was to live at somebody else's expense. Decisions to import were not taken on an economic basis but in an arbitrary manner. In these conditions imports were frequently ineffective. The whole economic mechanism for international economic turn-over was extremely inflexible. An enterprise could not get hard currency credit for needed equipment even to produce goods for export. To obtain such credit a separate request was needed for funds, the enterprise being left unsure over many months that its application would be granted. No tie existed between hard currency received for exports and internal money. Transfer prices for exported goods in the accounts of the enterprises were lacking and therefore it was difficult to determine the cost-effectiveness of international economic relations.

Besides the Ministry of Foreign Trade, the State Committee for Economic Relations also engaged in international economic activity, concentrating primarily on the construction of enterprises, installations and joint ventures abroad. Also, the International Division for Scientific and Technological Relations was active in foreign trade. The bodies connected with economic and scientific and technological relations with other countries were not combined organisationally in any way and they functioned in an uncoordinated manner.

The new economic policy pronounced at the April 1985 Plenary meeting of the Central Committee contained a new international economic policy as its main component. A new system was founded for managing all the international economic activity of the country. A permanent division of the Council of Ministers of the USSR was created, the State External Economic Commission (GVK), to head up all international economic activity in the country. This is chaired by a special deputy chairman of the Council of Ministers of the USSR. The Ministry of Foreign Trade's monopoly has been abolished and twenty-one ministries and institutions have been given the right to operate directly in the world market. Foreign trade agencies from the Ministry of Foreign Trade have been handed over to these relevant ministries and institutions. Thus for example, the export agency for selling cars and accessories has been transferred to the Ministry for the Car Industry.

Besides this, seventy associations and large enterprises in the USSR have received the right of independent entry into the world market. Foreign trade divisions are being created within these associations and enterprises. Moreover, all enterprises and economic organisations have been granted the right directly to enter the socialist countries' markets and organise direct contacts with corresponding enterprises in other socialist countries. The work of the External Trade Bank has also been reorganised and it is obliged under the new regime to grant credit in foreign currency to producers of goods for export. All procedures have been eased for trade specialists to travel abroad.

The whole economic mechanism for international economic relations has been changed. Among the economic norms established for enterprises, one is concerned with regulating the share of hard currency earnings that the enterprise may retain. For the Volga Car Factory and other enterprises this proportion is set at 70 per cent, which has sharply increased the working collectives' motivation to expand exports and raise efficiency. The number of associations and enterprises with the right to enter the world market at this stage is limited. Experience must first be gained and only then will this right be more widely granted.

We attach special significance to the possibilities within the USSR for joint venture enterprises with foreign companies. The necessary laws have been passed regulating the procedure for organising such enterprises. The share of foreign capital in these enterprises must not exceed 49 per cent. It is a prerequisite that the manager of the joint enterprise should be a Soviet citizen. Soviet labour laws are to extend to workers in such enterprises. A joint enterprise is liable to a moderate tax of 30% on profits and the remaining part belongs to the partners. It is divided between the partners in proportion to the capital invested. Foreign firms participating in joint enterprises can export their share of the profit in foreign currency, but on transferring money abroad they are liable to an additional 20% tax. In most cases these joint enterprises are being organised for export production, so that the enterprises' hard currency viability is achieved. Alternatively, joint enterprises can be aimed at the production of goods which replace imports previously purchased for hard currency. In this case the source of the currency repayment of profits to the foreign partners comes from the resources saved on imports. Around three hundred proposals were received from foreign firms in the first six months after the opportunity to create joint enterprises was announced. Understanding has been reached on some of these proposals and concrete work is underway to put them into effect. The fact is that this is a new departure for the Soviet Union and we are inexperienced. The organisations and people involved are perhaps being excessively cautious and feeling their way, which is perfectly natural at this stage. As experience is gained and the cost-effectiveness of joint enterprises is confirmed, it will, of course, proceed more rapidly.

The absence of a convertible Soviet rouble complicates the organisation of joint enterprises. For various countries and goods different exchange rates have been set. But the great number of these rates and the intricacy of the calculations makes matters difficult and complicated. I believe all the same that effective forms of joint enterprise will gradually be found. They are particularly important for branches of machine building and instrument making, in the chemical industry and in the production of consumer goods. The high level of basic research in the USSR is well known, as are the considerable achievements in several areas of technology. Sensible development of this potential, in arranging for new production using foreign capital and technology, should produce a considerable impact. In the joint venture organised for the production of new medical technology by "Mikromed", a joint Hungarian-Soviet enterprise, production can be aimed both at foreign and home markets. The Soviet market is huge, enabling joint enterprises of optimum size to be set up with relatively low production costs. In order to receive the necessary foreign currency for the functioning of a joint enterprise, part of the output could be sold abroad. The proposal of the Italian firm Fata for organising a joint enterprise in the USSR to produce fridges had precisely this aim.

The Soviet Union is open to a variety of proposals. For example, an enterprise can produce goods for the internal market and with the earnings from its sales the foreign partner could purchase Soviet goods for export, all without direct use of foreign currency. The possibilities are manifold. In the system of international economic and scientific relations, the contact with socialist countries, above all CMEA members, should be clearly singled out, but there will also be new openings with western and developing countries.

The socialist countries occupy a leading position in Soviet international trade turnover (67% in 1986) and the CMEA members' share was around 60%. The value of foreign trade with these countries in 1986 was 80 billion roubles and with western and developing countries 43 billion roubles (29 billion roubles with the west and more than 14 billion with developing countries). The Soviet Union's most important international economic relations (each representing 9%–10% of the USSR's international trade turnover) are with the GDR, Czechoslovakia, Poland and Bulgaria. Hungary and Cuba each constitute 6%–7%, Romania and Yugoslavia 3%–4% and VietNam, China and North Korea roughly 1% each in the total value of Soviet foreign trade.

Economic and scientific technological relations with socialist countries are wide ranging. A broad programme of economic integration of these countries is under way and a common socialist market is being established. A complex programme of scientific technological progress jointly adopted by the CMEA countries is playing a key role in the development of these relations. The programme envisages a whole range of joint measures to conduct research and technological development and to organise production in five main areas – nuclear energy, new materials, new technologies, electronics and biotechnology.

Soviet trade turnover with the CMEA fell from 37.9 billion roubles in 1985 to 29.0 billion roubles in 1986 because of the sharp fall in prices in the western markets for fuel, raw materials and several other goods. In this one year exports fell by 5.5 billion roubles and imports by 3.4 billion roubles. So imports exceeded exports by 2.8 billion roubles (in the preceding years a balance between imports and exports had been maintained). Changes in the situation of the world capitalist market have negatively affected Soviet external trade with developing countries, the overall value falling from 17.2 billion roubles in 1985 to 14.4 billion in 1986. Exports exceeded imports. Besides strictly trade relations the Soviet Union has been giving economic and technical assistance. Help has been given in the construction of industrial enterprises and other projects, and in the supply of equipment and materials for them in fifty countries, made up of thirteen socialist countries and thirty-seven developing countries.

The Soviet Union trades with 145 countries in total and gives economic and technical assistance to 74. It is therefore understandable that it should wish to take an active part in the international bodies which regulate economic relations. The USSR has submitted a proposal to join the General Agreement on Tariffs and Trade (GATT). This possibility has not been ruled out given time, nor in fact has cooperation with the International Monetary Fund and the International Bank for Reconstruction and Development. The Soviet Union was also one of the initiators of the Helsinki Agreements, in which measures for economic security and cooperation were provided for in the so-called "second basket". The Helsinki Agreements support mutually beneficial economic relations and are directed against discriminatory measures in foreign trade. It is unfortunate that this "second basket" of agreements is being systematically broken by the USA. A special body (COCOM)[16] was created to impose various restrictions on listed goods being traded by western countries with the USSR.

A memorable example is the ban by the US Government on the supply to the USSR of equipment for the construction of the gas pipeline from the gas field in North Western Siberia, Urengoi, to the western borders of the USSR. In order to complete the contract on time the Soviet Union had to develop urgently the production of gas pumping stations and organise production within the Soviet Union of a particular type of pipe laying equipment and other machinery. Nevertheless the 4,500 km pipeline from Urengoi to Western Europe was built in one and a half years and brought on stream ahead of schedule. I do not know if this case taught the USA and other counties anything. For, the fact is that, although similar discriminatory measures against the Soviet Union do cause temporary difficulties, ultimately they lead to the organisation of new types of production in the USSR and reduce the country's dependence.

An important long-term question, the resolution of which could greatly intensify external economic relations, is the question of the convertibility of the rouble. Currently this is not possible as the existing structure of internal prices differs sharply from both the socialist and non-socialist international market levels. But in 1989–90 we are undertaking a total reform of prices. Wholesale, purchase

---

[16] COCOM is defined in footnote 21, page 208.

and retail prices will be changed and world prices taken into consideration. The structure of prices in the Soviet Union will then more closely correspond to world prices. In particular, the reform will banish the enormous difference now existing between the prices for fuel and food stuffs which are set too low in the USSR. A much greater differential will be allowed on prices for goods of higher quality, which also corresponds to the world tendency.

During the review of measures taken for the major *perestroika* of management at the June 1987 Meeting of the Central Committee, the question of convertibility of the rouble was presented as a long-term objective. When the new pricing system has been established in the Soviet Union it is my opinion that this question will be addressed more closely. Firstly it will be possible to establish a convertible rouble in relation to the currencies of the socialist countries, made easier by their similar types of economies and the existing processes of economic integration. As to a convertible rouble in relation to the capitalist countries, this can hardly be resolved in the near future, since such a resolution is linked to structural changes in the development of the Soviet economy. But I believe that eventually this question also will have to be answered.

A first measure could be the introduction, along Hungarian lines, of an internally convertible rouble, that is the establishment of a rate for the rouble and other currencies according to which enterprises and other organisations could exchange the rouble for foreign currency, and some currency earned from the export of goods and services could be exchanged into roubles. With a balanced economy and mutually beneficial relations with other countries it is always possible to select rates for the rouble and other currencies so that the overall currency balance will be guaranteed. The cost-effectiveness of all international relations will grow in this way since this balance will not be two-sided but multilateral. A transition to internal convertibility would greatly increase the flexibility of international economic relations and introduce large numbers of new enterprises and organisations to international trade. It will associate the cost-effectiveness of external economic relations with the full self-acccounting and self-financing of enterprises. On the other hand, a transition to internal convertibility will raise the status of the rouble and its purchasing power, and so strengthen the country's currency.

The Soviet Union is searching for new forms and methods of economic management. This search extends not only to the resolution of internal economic problems but to the whole system of external economic and scientific and technological relations. In all these, new approaches, unorthodox solutions and an emphasis on economic cost-effectiveness are essential.

9 THE ENTERPRISE: INCENTIVES FOR SELF-DEVELOPMENT

The administrative system of management of enterprises took the form of planned instructions set by command from above. Every enterprise was obliged to fulfil these commands. The whole incentive system was also based on the fulfilment or over-fulfilment of plans. On the other hand, the failure to fulfil a planned instruction led to withholding of bonuses, reduction of wages, and in the case of systematic failure to fulfil the plan the enterprise director and other managers were dismissed from their posts and deprived not only of higher pay but also of those special privileges accorded to managers. In these circumstances the enterprise resisted as far as possible being set a very demanding plan, concealing its reserves and potential capacity. It tried to get a reduction of plan targets to make them easier to fulfil and over-fulfil. In this way the interests of the higher authorities were in constant conflict with the interests of the enterprises and their workers. The more so because the main form of economic planning was the annual plan, set by the level achieved in the past. If this level was high and the enterprise had achieved considerable success in the preceding year, then the new plan set was more demanding. By contrast, if growth was small, and there were difficulties in fulfilling the plan, then the plan was based on such past annual results.

This approach did not motivate collectives to reveal their reserves, or to exceed the targets of the plan if they could help it, because this brought on them larger demands that were harder to fulfil in the following year. Evidently the administrative system of management was not directed to meeting the economic interests of working collectives; rather the opposite, it thrust on them a method of operation which was in opposition to the interests of both society and of the collective itself. But the administrative system did function with all its shortcomings and defects and did produce some definite results. It forced an enterprise to increase productivity and to improve the several indicators of achievement. As all these contradictions accumulated, however, this system came increasingly to act as a brake, caused a reduction in the rate of economic growth and encouraged the tendency towards extensive development – the attempt to get hold of more resources while producing less products.

In the new system of management, the economic system will fundamentally change. Management will be based on economic methods taking the economic interests of working collectives into consideration. In this matter key significance is attached to the question of incentives for self-development. We are bringing to an end the system of compulsory direction of tasks and of allocations made in the plan from the top down. Now the working collectives themselves are working out their own plans and setting them on the basis of an order book, with norms of economic proportions to act as levers and incentives. In these conditions what is it that will make them work well, accept and fulfil a demanding plan, improve efficiency and quality, accelerate scientific–technological progress and address social needs? The broad answer could be this. In the new economic system an enterprise must be placed in an economic context that makes it profitable for the working collective and every single worker in it to work well and effectively. With the most powerful incentive, economic interest, in operation, it is simply disadvantageous to work badly.

What does the new economic context consist of? Self-account-ability for the income of enterprises is playing a determining role in the new conditions in the stimulation of the collectives' activity. For it is from the share of the enterprise's income which will remain at the disposal of the collective that are to be drawn the wages, incentives and resources for social improvement and for the development of the enterprise itself. The enterprise must above all find a customer for its products to obtain the income for which it is accountable. So that not only this one enterprise but others shall also produce the appropriate output, the following must be guaranteed: the output must be of the proper quality, the costs of production must be borne by the consumer, and a corresponding service be supplied if it is concerned with technology etc. Consumer demand is one of the most efficacious stimuli for self-development. Everything starts from this.

In the former conditions of administrative planning and management, consumer demand was secondary. Orders and directives were handed down from above to produce a certain quantity of output. The sale was assured, the prices fixed from above, so that the sovereignty of the producers was maintained. The administrative system, as mentioned above, perpetuated an economy of shortages. In these conditions the means of production of the enterprise received the most attention. Would output be achieved were the resources sufficient and productive capacity adequate? These were the main questions. As long as output was achieved it would all be sold to the consumers. There was no problem of demand. This was as it were an economy of productive potential. To the question posed to an enterprise, a branch or the economy as a whole, why did your volume of production increase by only 3% last year? the answer, under the old system of management, would go like this: we were given insufficient raw materials, not enough capital investment, and we were unable to attract additional workers; therefore we could not increase production by more than 3%. Here the issue of meeting needs and demand did not even arise. It was taken as read that if additional output were achieved consumers would take it all. The nature of the economy of shortages has been clearly manifest in all this.

Now the case is quite different with production subordinated to the tasks of satisfying social needs and working according to consumer demand. Instead of an economy of productive potential and shortages, the economy is directed to satisfying demand and to working for the consumer. And to the same question: why did you only produce 3% more? a different answer will be given – there was no further demand for our output. But the answer will continue that currently we are reorganising our methods of work, changing the range of goods, improving the quality, and we hope that demand for this new output will grow and we will be able to develop more rapidly. As to resources, the enterprise purchases them by whole-sale trading according to its means. But means depend on the volume of sales, i.e. on consumer demand. Orders emanating from state authorities will play a definite role among consumer orders in the order book. These orders should be especially profitable insofar as demand is guaranteed, and allocations of any relatively scarce resources needed for these orders will be made, e.g. of foreign currency, centralised capital investment, certain types of raw materials, particularly those that have to be imported.

By producing to meet demand and selling at prices which are highly differentiated according to quality, and therefore stimulate the production of higher quality goods, enterprises will receive their earnings from the sale of their output. The gross revenue of enterprises will be formed by these earnings after material input expenses have been met (on raw materials, finishing, and even amortisation). From this gross revenue an enterprise makes pay-ments for resources used (natural resources and labour, and the use of capital stock), makes contributions to the budget, local authority rates and to ministry funds, pays off bank credit and any fines to contractors and makes any other payments due. The remainder is self-managed income at the full disposal of the enterprise's working collective, determining its well-being and further development. To receive a large self-accountable net income more goods must be sold, through increasing both the quantity and quality of produc-tion, and by trying to get higher prices. For this a competitive edge will need to be maintained against other similar enterprises and higher quality and a better technological level of output will need to be attained. All this is the precondition for a larger self-accountable income. The self-accountable income also depends on production costs. The lower the fuel, energy and raw material consumption, the larger the enterprise's income. Therefore the system of economic planning adopted will encourage economies in the use of raw materials and a reduction in their inputs.

It is also very important to accelerate the turnover of stocks by each enterprise. If surplus stocks have accumulated, whether of resources or of manufactured output, then part of the enterprise's means are amortised and a share of its income is lost. Therefore the principle of self-accountable income encourages acceleration in the turnover of working capital. Furthermore, the amount of self-accountable income depends on the amount the enterprise spends on resources. The more resources used for a given volume of output the higher will be the payment for them. If an enterprise, while disposing of considerable resources, undertakes a reduced plan and produces less, then it will make a larger payment per unit of output into the state budget and this will be unprofitable for the working collective. The fullest possible use of natural and labour resources and of capital stock and the highest cost-effectiveness is the most profitable way of working. A reduction in cost-effectiveness in the use of certain resources, a worsening let us say in the capital-output ratio will decrease the incomes of the working collective rouble for rouble. And on the other hand, an improvement in the capital-output ratio will provide additional payments into the self-accountable income.

The rate of payment into the state budget required for use of resources is set centrally. Throughout the economy or industry the rates do not on the whole vary from enterprise to enterprise. But in its work the enterprise, in accounting for unit costs, can in fact reduce these payments with increased output or on the contrary suffer an increase in payments if the enterprise fails to realise fully its potential. The net deductions from gross revenue for the budget and ministerial funds come from the enterprise's income that is self-accountable. The greater an enterprise's profit, the greater the income at the disposal of the working collective. The rates fixed for these deductions must not then be set on the basis of an individual enterprise, but for whole branches and sectors of the economy. Thus whoever works better and with more profitability will augment the size of their self-accountable income.

Close relations with the banks are becoming very important for the effective functioning of an enterprise in the new system of management. It will be advantageous for an enterprise to draw on credit and this will increase its self-accountable income if the credit is well used so that profit is increased at a greater rate than the interest paid on the credit. If credit is obtained without good reason so that it does not enhance the profit of the enterprise, then it will simply be deducted from the enterprise's self-accountable income. Thus in the new system of economic management an enterprise becomes interested only in the effective use of credit. For its part the bank, having itself gone over to full self-accounting, will be interested in granting credit only to those who can use it effectively. It will be important for the bank not only to have the credit paid back in due time but with interest that will add to its own self-accountable income.

Lastly, in the formation of self-accountable income there is a balance of payments and fines between enterprises and organisations. When the enterprise fails to fulfil the conditions of a contract it pays a fine to compensate for the damages which the other party to the contract has borne. In turn the enterprise may receive a certain sum back through fines owed to it. Where there are many such connections between self-accounting enterprises, fines may in certain situations add up to fairly impressive sums, which seriously affect the amount of self-accountable income. In this way an enterprise is encouraged to fulfil contracts on time and to meet agreed standards of quality in order to avoid fines. As is evident the orientation toward self-accountable income is a fairly strong incentive for working collectives to work effectively. Thereafter when the size of the self-accountable income is determined, the motivation of the working collective as a whole and of individual workers is linked directly to the way their wages are worked out. The key point is to set a direct relationship between results and the wages and other financial remuneration of the working collective.

There are two basic systems for the economic regulation of this relationship. One way to do it is through a system of profit incentives. This is currently the main one in use. The essence of this is that wages are determined according to some kind of economic proportion, which can be fixed in various ways, where production costs and profit are clearly separated. A part of the profit is channelled to the state and a part is assigned to the incentive funds of the enterprise. Great significance is attached to the financial incentive fund, but everyone knows that the incentive fund of the enterprise cannot be very large. If one assumes an average 10%–15% profitability and takes into account the part of this profit which is deducted for the state then the incentive funds are formed from the remaining share of the profit. On average in industry the incentive fund makes up one twelfth of the wage fund. In the best enterprises, for example in Sumy, this fund reached 15%. But on average no such figure is attained. Yet as a stimulation the 8%, 10% or even 15% added to the wage seems to be insufficient. The incentive fund offers a purely subsidiary incentive; it is the basic wage that must play the main motivating role. To make the basic wage dependent on results is the key problem. It is easy to see that now under the method of centrally administered proportions this link is very tenuous and the actual impact of good or bad management is shared between state and enterprise. I propose to appraise the situation through some actual examples.

A lorry filled with concrete arrives at the factory gates; nobody unloads the concrete and it sets. Three hundred roubles are lost. Who pays this three hundred roubles? Will this affect any actual worker? If we go through this case following our existing system, we shall see that ultimately most of this loss will fall on the state, some on the enterprise development fund and a very small share, imperceptible to the workers, will come from the wages and incentive funds. Or, again, let us say that a director has extended the management staff without improving the enterprise's results. The state bears the whole loss. The collective does not sense this. Neither wages nor the workers' incentive fund are in any way reduced. To take a further example, imported equipment was purchased. It was not unpacked and was left out in the yard. Its cost was, say, 0.5 million roubles. Who pays? Under the existing system it is the state which actually pays. This, like the previous example, contradicts the fundamental principle that the state should not be responsible for enterprises' bills.

There is another system, a fairly rigid one, which ensures that the state does not pay these expenses. This is a system of collective contracting, to be operated in all enterprises and working collectives. The system is very simple: income is received, expenses are reimbursed, payment for resources is deposited regardless of whether they are being used or not, other deductions for the budget are implemented, credits and fines are paid and development funds are set up. What is left is for workers' incomes. So if concrete is unloaded and sets in the yard of a cooperative this means that every member of this cooperative must relinquish a part of their pay. If an additional person is taken on this means that the wages of the remainder must be cut to make up this person's wage. If a new machine is received and is not used, this means that people pay for it out of their income, including its amortisation. This system is ruthless and rigorous but it will immediately show that in many spheres one third of all machines and half of all tractors are actually not needed for production, and many surpluses in the use of metal, fuel, etc. will surface at once. Overmanning will also appear in enterprise management and in auxiliary and service departments.

Thus there are two competing systems. I am not calling for the system of collective contracting to be immediately made the main one, but this should be the main direction for development and experimentation. In this context there is the interesting experience of No. 18 Moscow Region Construction group of enterprises, headed by an enthusiast for collective contracting, N.I. Travkin. In October 1986 the Central Committee approved this experiment and recommended the widest possible use of this form of economic management. The system of collective contracting is complex and fairly difficult to run. A well-founded level of remuneration depends on setting the correct price, which we still do not know how to determine, and on correct financial and other arrangements. The other system based on profit is more easily regulated but it is less effective.

The best example of the first system based on incentives from profit is the self-financing experience of the Sumy "Frunze" Factory, which was particularly effective. A much larger proportion (52%) of the growth of net output does not go into the wage fund. The incentive fund, however, is one third of total labour remuneration, double the average. The association's development fund is also high and stands at 5% of the value of the capital stock (7% is projected for 1990), i.e. they can actually undertake the renewal of their capital stock in line with the highest world standards. The enterprise is profitable and motivation to work well is strong. But I fear that the majority of enterprises transferring to self-financing will not attain such standards, and the incentives will be accordingly weaker than in Sumy.

The transition of an enterprise to collective contracting eliminates the contradiction inherent in the current system. Various forms of organisations and collective labour incentives are developing on the initiative of workers and the ITP. These include collective contracting. But the whole system of fixing the wage fund from above contradicts the basic principles of the contract. If all the subdivisions of an enterprise make a contract, this contradiction would show up immediately. A very important moment in the system of profit incentive is the choice of the economic proportions to be used in determining the wage fund. The attempt to establish a proportional norm for wages related to the gross indicators of output is a survival of the past administrative system of management. The volume of gross output can then be increased simply by greater consumption of materials in production and this will therefore not motivate the collective to economise on material costs. During the experiments made in preparation for the transition to new systems of economic management, a system was tried out for establishing proportional norms for determining the wages fund which were linked to the value of the net output over and above what had been laid down. This revealed the complexity of calculation in the system, the possibility of variations in value, depending on what was added by cooperatively organised supplies, and the difficulty in checking the trustworthiness of the accounts. All this revealed the inadequate cost-effectiveness of this basis of calculating proportional norms although the norm for the proportion of wages did help to reduce the materials consumed in production and did not have the shortcomings of the norm based on gross output.

Related to this, in many branches of production a system began to be developed for calculating proportional norms dependent on the actual value added. This is a better basis although it has shortcomings which include the fact that the value of net output is not wholly representative of the results of economic management by the working collective, while the objective is to link wages directly to results. In particular, the value of net output does not take into consideration the extent of the enterprise's use of resources, shown in the payments for resources. The value added does not fully reflect the interaction of enterprises with the bank and between each other (through the payment of fines etc.). In our view the best indicator for determining the wages fund by proportional norms is to relate it to the self-accountable income, insofar as this better than any other indicator reflects the end results of the activities of the enterprise. With this approach, a rapprochement occurs of the two forms of incentives for the enterprise – from income or from profit – since both these systems have their basis in the self-accountable income.

Another question concerns the nature of the proportional norm for generating the wages fund. It may be expressed as a proportion of the self-accountable income (or another indicator related to income generation) or calculated incrementally from the growth of income achieved. Incremental norms by their very nature are geared to an attainable level. An enterprise has a certain basic wage fund and the question, when there is an incremental norm, is merely how much to increase it by. For example, taking a norm of 0.5 of growth for the wages fund in relation to growth of the self-accountable income means that if this income grew by one million roubles then the wages fund would gain 500,000 roubles. This growth in the wages fund is added to the basic wages over a planned period. Incremental norms are easily regulated. They guarantee more rapid growth of productivity in relation to wages, but do not effect substantial changes in the existing relationship of work and pay. Under such norms, if they were established individually for each enterprise, the best enterprises would find themselves in the worst position, since any advance they made would call for much greater effort than the same step made by a less effective enterprise. And even if this advance is made with greater effort the enterprise nevertheless would only receive the same rise in the wages fund as enterprises working less effectively.

The wages fund norm expressed as a proportion of the self-accountable income is more revolutionary in nature. It places all enterprises, good and bad, in an equal position. Whoever works better and earns more self-accountable income receives more from the wages fund for all enterprises. The whole question lies in how to link the size of the wages fund with the basic capital stock whose size is determined in ways quite unrelated to the enterprise's current performance. It may transpire that substantial differences in the level of wages among different enterprises will occur if this principle of calculation is maintained. This can be permitted only within certain very narrow limits. At present we will give preference to growth indicators in the setting up of wages funds, although we understand that proportional indicators based on income are a stronger incentive. But if growth indicators are applied sensibly they can prepare the ground for the transition to the more effective proportional indicators in the future.

In the new system of economic management the rights of the working collective and of the managers of enterprises in dealing with labour and wages are significantly broadened. The size of the wages fund is no longer set from above, but determined according to an economic norm established through the wages fund. But this wages fund is divided between the total number of individual workers . If the same results are achieved by fewer workers then each will receive higher average wages.

The state will implement an overall wages policy, mainly through a centrally established system of pay scales for workers (rates and scales, with differentials set according to qualifications through a reference book in which categories are ascribed to workers). The principles of norm-setting are also being established centrally. So is the system of salary scales for engineering and technical managers and for white-collar workers. The state is also defining the principles of workers' bonuses and incentives. Different types of additional payments for working conditions, regional coefficients for wages in regions with harsher working and living conditions, privileges for working in the far north, additional payments for night shifts, the length and nature of holidays etc. are all being established centrally. They are being determined by the state together with the All-Union Council of Trade Unions, which represents the interests of working people. This is the backbone, as it were, of the wages system. To flesh that out, the enterprise working collective has the right to introduce increases in the pay scales and rates for extra professional skills and for more productive labour and to introduce an effective system of bonuses etc. Therefore higher average wages for enterprises that work well will be created on the foundation of standard scales and rates by extra rises, higher earnings for agreed tasks and other bonuses.

In the current 1986–90 five-year period an increase in the scales of pay is already under way. Scales for manual workers are being raised by 20%–25%, and for engineers, technical and white-collar workers by 30%–35%. The higher growth in the scales for these last is linked to the significant lag that has occurred in their wage levels and the need to avoid the excessive levelling tendencies of the past. We do not consider it satisfactory that graduate engineers and technicians in construction on average actually currently receive slightly lower wages than manual workers and that in industry the wages of engineers and technicians are but 10%–15% higher than labourers' wages. With the transition to new pay scales and rates the correlation between work and earnings will improve here too. In contrast to the preceding measures, it is planned in the period 1991–96 to introduce pay rises in a new way, according to the means of the enterprises themselves, by tightening up the labour norms, additions for increases in productivity, economies in use of inputs, and the discovery of new resources and possibilities. This will give an additional incentive to raise both cost-effectiveness and quality.

Up to now we have considered how to create incentives for the self-development of whole enterprises, associations and their working collectives. Most people in the USSR work in relatively large collectives, since the degree of concentraion of production is fairly high. It is sufficient to say that the average number of workers per productive association or enterprise is more than 800, much higher than in other countries. Agricultural collectives are by now also very large. On average on a collective farm there are around 500 collective farm worker-members, and slightly more on state farms.

Naturally such large working collectives are divided up into smaller work units. A major problem is to generate not only the overall interest of a large working collective of a whole association or enterprise, but to interest the primary work units so as to reach down to each individual worker. In the past the interest of the individual worker was guaranteed by the widespread practice of piece-work payment. More than three quarters of workers in industry were piece-workers. Each worker was set a norm and a rate per unit and overall earnings were based on the fulfilment of the norm. The rate often increased for over-fulfilment and payment was on a sliding scale, giving strong motivation thereby to the over-fulfilment of norms. Otherwise, a bonus was paid on the fulfilment of norms and the additional achievement of agreed qualitative indicators. But with the mechanisation and automation of production and closer attention being given to the quality of output, the proportion of piece-workers declined and the number of hourly paid workers rose. To motivate workers paid by the hour in the results of their labour they were transferred to various bonus schemes. Further technical progress and the organisation of complex technical systems increasingly reinforced the collective nature of labour. A group of workers could only ensure technological progress and good results on the basis of concerted action and not on the uncoordinated productivity of single workers. At this stage, as distinct from individual forms of wage payments, new collective forms of organisation and labour motivation began to emerge – in work teams, brigades, etc. Forms of collective labour arose from below on the initiative of workers themselves and on democratic principles. In this way contract-based brigades and, later on, contract groups, even whole enterprises, came to be organised.

Contract forms of work have a long history in our country. They trace their origins to the cooperative organisations characteristic of pre-revolutionary Russia. In peasant Russia, rural inhabitants did not live on homesteads but in villages, and many types of work, particularly construction were not done by families but with the involvement of the other villagers. Gradually seasonal work away from the village developed and *artels*[17] were formed which undertook certain jobs for remuneration. An artel worked under a collective contract. The client negotiated with the whole artel and paid for the work when it was completed. The earnings were then distributed among the members of the artel. The artel worked cooperatively, its members usually moving from task to task, combining several skills, i.e. what today would be called a combination of trades. The artel form of labour organisation and the motivation of payment by final results, was for that reason effectively abolished and authorised only in the case of individual piece-work. Hourly work, as mentioned above, came to predominate.

However, people remained attracted to the artel form of work. This collective form of work has now been reviving on a new technological basis. The first worker brigades receiving payment for work done appeared in the construction industry and quickly spread to other branches. They displayed their cost-effectiveness, guaranteeing higher productivity and better final results. Several state resolutions were passed to increase the number of such brigades, but usually this important matter was approached in an administrative spirit. The ministries began to set plans for work brigades. Reporting to higher authorities was introduced and the important task was turned into just the next official "campaign". Brigades were created officially but as a formality, without their purpose being thought through. Conditions were not created to ensure their high productivity. The expected effect of the transition to brigades as a form of labour organisation was not therefore obtained. Of course among the large number of officially organised brigades, there were brigades in name only, where in fact many workers continued to work individually and were paid individually.

What are the characteristics of an authentic collective contract?

---

[17] The *artel'* is a traditional form of Russian peasants' cooperative for carrying out a specific craft or trade, often while away from their villages. Led by an elected elder, it worked as a team, sharing its income and where necessary collectively providing food and lodging to its members while they were away from their villages, and for their general welfare needs and support. (ed.)

A working collective is created to fulfil a complete job of some kind to obtain a final tangible result. The first condition of effective organisation of collective labour is that its objective should be clear-cut. Another indication is its independence and self-management. The collective chooses its own methods of working and the division of labour among its members. It must function on a democratic basis. The head of the collective must be freely elected. In relatively large collectives a chairman and a council are elected and a large collective may be subdivided into sections. Payment for contract labour is mainly made on the basis of the results of the work done, for example among builders for every house completed. Among brigades of dockers the final results are the loaded or unloaded ships.

A collective's work is formalised in a contract. The contract is, as a rule, concluded with the administration of an association or enterprise. The contract defines both parties' obligations. A crucial part of the contract is the setting of the price for the brigade's work, which the administration is obliged to pay on receiving work of appropriate quality and on time etc. A collective contract is extremely appropriate for self-accounting and self-managing organisations. Revenues from the collective's work must cover expenses. The cost of materials used is subtracted from the earnings and therefore the collective has an interest in economising in their use. Machinery and other basic capital equipment are leased to the collective and it pays according to fixed rates. This will give the collective an interest in using machines, equipment and other stocks efficiently. What remains of the income makes up the collective's wage fund. Within the collective wages are distributed on a democratic basis, setting a coefficient for the labour input of each worker, with proportional wages. The whole wage fund can then be divided up in line with these coefficients. Or it can be done differently: with each worker paid according to his appropriate pay scale and additional payments distributed according to the coefficient of labour participation.

The transition to collective forms of organisation and labour incentives make new demands on all producing enterprises, both as to their planning and management. It is only necessary that each collective be given a clearly outlined field of work, and an uninterrupted supply of raw materials to fulfil this work. Essential machinery must be transfered to the disposal of the collective and the contract collective's arrangements will have to be worked out with the factories producing the equipment they need. The system of inter-factory planning has to be changed. Planning must now be oriented towards the achievement by every contract collective of the results that they have decided on. The structure of the enterprise's plans comes from the decisions of the contract collectives themselves.

Some contract collectives in the 1960s showed exceptional results. For example, in agricultural production in Kazakhstan, a contract collective was created under I. Khudenko, previously a Ministry official. He gathered highly qualified specialists in plant growing into a collective, which achieved seven to nine times higher productivity than regional averages, with home-produced machinery, exceeding even American levels. The work of this collective shows what increases in productivity in agriculture can be made in Kazakhstan and thus how poorly resources were in fact being used there. The leaders, who were responsible for the misuse of resources began then to persecute Khudenko, the farm he organised was broken up and finally, through forgery and deception, a trumped up charge was made against him and he died in jail. Public opinion stood by him, letters were circulated in support of Khudenko. T.I. Zaslavskaya and I also wrote a letter to the First Secretary of the Central Committee of Kazakhstan, D. Kunaev, but to no purpose. Only now has the Khudenko case been reviewed and the new leadership of Kazakhstan is organising contract collectives on his principles with the participation of the people who worked with Khudenko.

Clearly the fate of Khudenko did not befall all the highly productive collectives. But many advanced experiments had their wings clipped. The existing administrative system of management tore down any economic formations that were alien to it, especially in the form of self-managing contract collectives. Now, with the implementation of a radical reform of management, on the other hand, favourable economic and organisational conditions are being created for the revival of several different forms of collective contract. These are being organically inserted into the new system of economic management, and are you might say propping it up from below.

We have already accumulated a rich experience of economic experiments including those concerned with work organisation and motivation. What then have they shown? Analysing the various experiments one comes to the conclusion that if an experiment does not touch the broad mass of the working people, specifically the workers and the skilled engineers, it will have little significant impact. A large proportion of the experiments and systems which we introduced were, if one can speak one's mind plainly, organised from the top down. When conditions of economic management of an enterprise changed, it affected the director and the works management significantly, but the main mass of the workers was not affected at all or at least barely affected by the changes.

I visited more than thirty enterprises which were undergoing major experiments during 1984–85, and asked workers on the shop floor the question: "How's your experiment going?" The usual reply was "What experiment?" The Director or his Deputy accompanying me would say "How is it you don't remember? Haven't we discussed this at meetings? The notices about this experiment are all over the shop floor." Then the worker began to remember something. To all intents, though, for the worker at his bench, almost nothing had changed. It is true that for a small number of workers a slight rise was introduced in the pay scale. The vast majority of workers continued to work with no changes whatsoever.

By contrast, if the innovation to the economic mechanism affects the workers' wages, the impact is enormous. Here is a typical example. On the railway system the 1986 planned increase in productivity of 2% actually reached 7.5% (in the previous five-year period average growth in productivity was 1.6%). How did this happen? The answer lies in the extension of an experiment carried out on the Belorussian railway system to ten main routes in the USSR at large. The Belorussian experiment permitted a drop of 12,000 workers over one year, giving an 11% increase in labour productivity. Why? Because the essence of the new system lies in encouraging flexibility between trades with the resulting growth of productivity and the improvement of other labour indicators. It directly affected the interests and earnings of all workers. Some people studying the evidence pointed to several negative aspects – in some places the surplus was reduced, elsewhere other things went wrong. But any complex issue has pros and cons. The final result is what matters.

In the Novosibirsk region forty-six factories and the sections of fifteen enterprises were transferred into contract collectives, including the managers and graduate engineers. Many introduced the new relations as a formality and were unsuccessful. Nevertheless, average productivity rose 15% or 2.5 times faster than previously in all the units involved. And where there was a business-like approach to this transition growth of productivity rose by as much as 20%–30%. This included conveyor belt production and light industry, where apparently there were no new resources available.

Under the Shchekinskii method of work[18] operated by about one hundred enterprises the rate of growth of productivity was on average doubled. This, better than what we said earlier, was the target we were setting ourselves for the 1986–90 period of accelerating the rate of growth of productivity by one and a half times. A very interesting experiment was tried in ten transport organisations where the new methods introduced affected the wages of delivery drivers making it unremunerative for them to sell petrol on the black market or make long-distance trips with empty trucks. The main goal of the incentives was the strict meeting of orders. The percentage of orders strictly met according to the contracts agreed with clients rose from 86% to 99.8%. About 3% of motor vehicles were decommissioned and the number of drivers decreased by 2%. Fuel savings of 18% were made over the year.

To sum up, where economic reforms directly touch people's economic interests there is an explosive effect. This testifies to the enormous potential in unused resources which can be mobilised by increased cost-effectiveness by the correct use of material incentives.

[18] This method was worked out at the chemical plant in Shchekino Tula region.Its essence is that the wages fund was assigned to the enterprise and if the planned results were achieved with fewer employees they were given a rise in salary. This gave workers an incentive to be flexible between several trades and to maintain equipment with fewer workers, and this led to a high rate of growth in productivity.

10 *PERESTROIKA* FOR PEOPLE

In the final analysis *perestroika* is being implemented for people. And the main criterion of its success must be the fuller satisfaction of the material and spiritual needs of the Soviet people. This is the primary aim of the planned acceleration of socio-economic development in the country. The sole source of increase in the material well-being of the people lies the growth of the country's national income. In 1985 national income reached roughly 570 billion roubles.* Approximately 80% of the national income, i.e. more than 450 billion roubles annually, is being directed at increasing personal and social consumption, i.e. for current necessities, housing and welfare. The resources for meeting these are the sum total of the wealth created, i.e. the quantity of material goods consumed by the population.

The potential scale of the social programme to be implemented depends on the rate of growth of the national income. If annual growth of the national income continues at 3%, then this will be in round figures 17 billion roubles, and of this 12 billion roubles will be for consumption. From this total figure the needs of the year's newly born members of society have first to be met. In recent years the Soviet population has been increasing by approximately 2.5 million annually. After these extra numbers are taken into account 8–9 billion roubles are left to improve the living standards of the whole

* One rouble equalled approximately $1.5 in January 1988. (ed.)

population, equalling on average a little over two roubles a month per person. With such limited means our social programmes to increase the well-being of the people are quite unrealisable. It would be different if the rate of economic development grows to 4%–5% as planned, then the total annual increase in the national income will be 23–29 billion roubles and what is available for consumption will be 17–21 billion roubles. Taking the extra population into consideration there may be twice as much to assign to the implementation of social programmes. This is very important because a number of pressing problems of social development face Soviet society.

Firstly, *the supply of foodstuffs in the country must be improved.* Up to the 1970–75 period the consumption of food products in the Soviet Union rose systematically, particularly for high quality products – meat, milk and dairy products, eggs, vegetables and fruit – against a reduction in consumption of potatoes and flour-based products, as can be seen in Table 8.

Table 8: *Food consumption in the USSR, 1950–75* (per head per year)

Item	1950	1960	1970	1975
Meat (kg)	26	40	48	54
Dairy products (as kg of milk)	172			316
Eggs (no.)	60			216
Fish products (kg)	7			17
Vegetable oil (kg)	3			8
Sugar (kg)	12			41
Vegetables (kg)	51			89
Potatoes (kg)	241			120
Flour-based products (as kg of flour)	172			141

However, in the past ten years, because of the slowing down of socio-economic development, the composition of the diet has changed little in terms of quality. The important task facing us is a substantial improvement in the diet of the population in accordance with the Food Provision Programme of the USSR, passed in 1982. Generally speaking, the nutritional value of the Soviet diet needs to be improved roughly one and a half times.

In order to resolve the problem of food provision, the lag in the development of agriculture needs above all else to be overcome and its development greatly accelerated. During the 1981–85 period the volume of agricultural production rose by only 6% and therefore to improve the Soviet diet it was necessary to resort to large scale food imports. Each year more than 40 million tonnes of grain were bought abroad, mostly for fodder, and more than one million tonnes of meat. These negative tendencies are to be overcome. In the current five-year period the volume of agricultural production is to increase by 14.4% which will enable the purchases of foodstuffs from abroad to be significantly reduced.

The tasks for 1986–90 envisage the increase of gross yields and production in agriculture as shown in Table 9 (in millions of tonnes).

Table 9: *Agricultural output of the USSR, 1985–90 (in millions of tonnes)*

	1985 (actual)	1986 (actual)	1990 (planned)
Gross yields			
Grain	191.7	210.1	250–255
Sugar-beet	82.4	79.3	92–95
Potatoes	73.0	87.2	90–92
Vegetables, melons, gourds	28.1	29.7	40–42
Production			
Meat (by slaughtered weight)	17.1	17.7	21
Milk	98.6	101.1	106–110
Eggs (in billions)	77.3	80.3	80–82

A first major step towards this end was made in 1986 as can be seen from the figures. The volume of agricultural production increased 5.1% partly through increases in the grain yield but especially through the rise in livestock productivity. This made it possible to cut food purchases on the world market, including grain, by half, and simultaneously to make an appreciable improvement in the people's diet. But this is only a beginning. Efforts to accelerate all food production need to be stepped up significantly, including those in farming itself, in the food industry and in the trade in foodstuffs.

To balance effective demand and supply for meat and dairy products a substantial increase is envisaged in the prices charged to consumers through the implementation of the retail price reform. The prices for these products in state shops are set centrally. The last time they were revised was in 1962. Since then collective and state farm workers' earnings have grown more than three and a half times but the growth in productivity rose by less than two and a half times because of unsatisfactory farming practices. The use of capital in agriculture production rose sharply. This led to a rise in the cost of production of agricultural products, especially of meat and milk. Their production resulted in losses and moreover the size of these losses increased every year. As a result, retail prices are below the purchase prices paid by the state.

The losses involved are covered by state subsidies which have been growing steadily. Currently the subsidies on meat and milk products alone have reached almost 50 billion roubles a year (against the total state budget for 1986 of 433 billion roubles). For each kilo of meat sold in a state retail shop, the state pays around three roubles to bring the average consumer price down to one rouble 80 kopeks per kilo. Similarly the subsidy for one litre of milk sold at 30 kopeks amounts to around 25 kopeks. With such subsidised retail prices the demand for meat and some types of dairy products could not be met. Therefore in some regions of the country the distribution of meat and of butter is rationed. In the face of the increased demand for meat the price in cooperative shops is, as a rule, two or more times higher than the state prices, while the price in the collective farm private market is two and a half to three times the state price. This of course is far from satisfactory. The subsidised price of meat and dairy products distorts the range of products available and has negative social consequences. The fact is that well paid families consume more meat and dairy products than do the more poorly paid. They therefore receive a greater subsidy from the state. As a result the inequalities are actually increasing. A reasonable and well thought-out increase in prices for meat and dairy products will end this social injustice.

The June 1987 Plenary meeting of the Central Committee emphasised that the reform of retail prices must be undertaken democratically. This means that its provisions, including the proposed new prices for meat and dairy products, are to be widely discussed with the population before being implemented. It goes without saying that in a socialist country the population must be fully compensated for such large increases in retail prices. We have experience of such compensation. In the post-war years, when ration cards were abolished and retail prices rose, the so-called "bread bonus" was introduced, which was paid on top of wages. A similar bonus will probably be introduced along with the increase in prices of meat and dairy products. At the same time, the retail price may be reduced for many other consumer goods.

Table 10: *Future goals for improving the diet of the Soviet people/ population* (average annual figures of food intake in kg per head)*

	1986	1990 programme	Needs established by dieticians
Meat and meat products	62.5	70.0	78
Milk and Dairy products	332	330–340	405
Fish and fish products	18.4	19.0	18.2
Eggs (units)	285	260–266	292
Sugar	44	45.5	40
Vegetables, melons, etc.	103	126–135	130
Fruit and berries	52	67–70	91
Potatoes	108	n.a.	110
Bread and flour-based products	133	n.a.	115

* From *SSSR v tsifrakh v 1986*, Finance and Statistics edition, 1985, p.21; *Prodovol 'stvennaya programma SSSR*, Politizdat, 1982, p.11; *Problemy povysheniya urovnya narodnogo blagosostoyaniya*, Scientific Research Institute of Labour, 1982, p.24.

Another important aim is to *increase the production of goods and services for the population so that market demands can be met.* Effective demand is still not being fully met, especially for high quality items in a whole range of different goods. The improvements in quality that are being made in textiles, ready-made clothes and shoes are absolutely inadequate. The population refuses to buy many of the items produced and therefore stocks in the retail and wholesale trade and industry have risen, while in the 1970s the volume of stocks declined. Measured in days of average disposals, these stood at 96 days in 1980, but this figure had increased by 1985 to 118 days.

In 1987 serious efforts were made to improve the development of light industry and consumer goods. Much larger resources were allocated to enterprises producing machinery and equipment for light industry so that they could rapidly renovate outdated technology. Simultaneously light industry and retailing were transferred to new economic management. From now on centralised plans in the form of directives to produce certain goods are not being given to enterprises in light industry. They are working out their plans on their own on the basis of orders. Linked to this, an increased role has fallen to trade fairs at which deals between shops and industrial enterprises are made. Shop workers have also been transferred to the new conditions of economic management and their material interest in meeting the population's demands more fully aroused.

These measures have above all had an effect in reducing the previous increase of stocks in the shops. Long unsold goods have been sold off to the public at reduced prices. At the same time the range of products is changing for the better. The important point here is not so much the quantity as the quality of consumer goods. This still leaves much to be desired and to raise standards of quality both administrative and economic measures are being undertaken. A discount is being given on prices for substandard goods and in contrast an extra charge made for high quality, competitive goods. Freedom to set their own or contract prices for new goods has been granted to collectives so that they are encouraged to produce higher quality goods and novelties and to renew their range of goods. Public demand is also being taken into consideration more thoroughly in the setting of prices for imported goods. At the same time, stricter administrative measures are being applied in the formal acceptance by the state of the produce of some enterprises. State inspectors at such enterprises are exercising a special control of products, checking the quality and technological progress against specifications and testing batches of goods. State inspectors have wide-ranging powers and the right to reject products if their quality does not correspond to required standards. So the first steps are being taken towards improving the quality of products but there is clearly a long haul ahead.

Another major task ahead is the creation of a *modern service sector*. This sector is still extremely poorly developed. The total value of sales totals 10 billion roubles, which is only 3% of the value of retail commodity circulation. Also, in the past this sector was increasing slowly – in the period 1981–85 the service sector volume grew by a total of 25%. In the 1986–90 period it is to increase by 50%. During 1986 alone the volume of paid services offered to the population grew by more than 10%. In the future the aim is to exceed significantly the plans in this area for the current five-year period so as to achieve increases of 15% or more each year.

The provision of basic consumer durables to the urban and rural population of the USSR has been growing fairly rapidly. Currently 95% of families have a television, 90% fridges, 70% washing machines, 65% sewing machines and one in seven motorcycles and motorscooters. Every year roughly 1.5 million light vehicles for personal use are sold for a sum of 12 billion roubles. The situation is not so good in the provision of tape-recorders, cameras, vacuum cleaners, air conditioners and electronics generally. But the important point is that the quality of many items does not meet modern requirements. This is particularly true of colour television sets, some makes of fridges and washing machines, bicycles and other items. The fact is that public demand has obviously to be met not only in quantity but in quality, and public demand is not being met fully because of the poor quality and range of goods which leave a large gap between demand and supply.

To some extent this is associated with the fact that the balance of the population's unspent money is growing rapidly, a part of which is being deposited into savings banks. In the 1971–75 period total deposits into savings banks increased 2.6 times faster than the growth in sales of consumer goods, in the 1976–80 period 3 times faster, and in the 1981–5 period 2.6 times faster. In the last two years total deposits have been growing by 20 billion roubles annually, exceeding the growth of the whole resources fund available for consumption in the national income. Overall deposits in 1986 were in excess of 240 billion, i.e. more than two thirds of the total volume of retail commodity circulation. The swift growth of savings bank deposits can be partially explained by the natural shift of the population towards the acquisition of expensive durable goods, cooperative flats and the accumulation of money for leisure purposes, etc. A significant part of this accelerated growth, however, is due to the accumulation of postponed demand because of the existing imbalance between monetary income and the opportunity to use it to acquire goods and services. The correction of this situation is one of the central tasks of the future, which requires the accelerated growth in production of goods and services that are widely used, with emphasis on their improved quality and range.

There is an acute social problem of *housing* in the Soviet Union. The aim by the year 2000 is to guarantee a separate flat or house with all modern conveniences to every family. Up to now this has been advancing with considerable difficulty. Much housing is being built in the Soviet Union. This is the fourth five-year period in which more than 100 million cubic metres of actual living space have been constructed each year.[19] In the last twenty years, that is, a total of more than 10 million flats were built in each five-year period, two million a year. But given the enormous size of the population, 283 million in mid-1987, the volume of housing being built per capita is not enough. We now build on average 110 million cubic metres each year. From this total the housing needed to meet the growth in population must be deducted, i.e. at least 35–40 million cubic metres. A certain proportion of the remaining 70–75 million cubic metres must be assigned to replace poorly equipped housing due to be demolished. The total Soviet housing stock now exceeds 4 billion cubic metres, so that an annual withdrawal of 5% is already equal to 20 million cubic metres. The remainder must be distributed among the existing population. This means that average housing provision is now only a little more than 15 cubic metres and the aim of providing every family with a separate flat or house can scarcely be achieved. This is especially true since public needs and expectations are growing, with many families and others looking for larger and more comfortable flats.

About 80% of the urban population lives in separate flats, but there are still many regions of the country in which provision of housing is much lower (one and a half or more times below the average levels). Moreover 40% of housing is currently privately owned and a large proportion of this does not have modern conveniences and is in need of renovation or even demolition. The improvement of the urban housing stock is proceeding faster. But here too about 10% of the flats are not equipped with running water, plumbing and central heating, not to mention hot water, which is lacking in one third of all flats. The situation in villages and rural areas is worse.

[19] Housing is measured in cubic metres in the Soviet Union. This means that the flats built in the last twenty years have averaged a little over 50 cubic metres per flat, that is having a floor space of roughly 20 feet by 10 feet. The average space per person of 15 cubic metres means that a family of four has 60 cubic metres, i.e. a floor space of roughly 24 feet by 12 feet. (ed.)

It should be noted that the proportion of total capital investment going into housing construction, including private investment has been falling for a long time. This proportion was 23.5% of the total volume of capital investment in the economy in the 1956–60 period. In the 1961–65 period it was 18.6%, in 1966–70 17.2%, in 1971–75 15.3%, in 1976–80 13.6% and only in 1981–85 did the proportion begin to rise again and to exceed 14%. Given the relatively low rate of growth of the national income, there will naturally not be the means to increase the volume of housing construction significantly, however greatly it is needed. The same is true for the construction of enterprises and institutions serving the population. Even less resources have been directed to this end than to housing construction, and the proportion of capital investment in this area has also been falling.

It is evident from all that has been said above that only through the acceleration of socio-economic development will we be able to resolve the problem of housing and related social, cultural and welfare provision in a relatively short time. Only 2.7% of a manual or white-collar worker's family aggregate income currently goes towards rent, the maintenance of houses and communal services, so that without giving up the advantage of low rent, it might be possible to attract more public resources into the improvement of housing conditions. In particular, a significant expansion of cooperative and private house building is envisaged. Until recently there was a tendency to cut down on individuals building their own houses whether wholly at their own expense or with the aid of state credit. While in the 1956–60 period more than six million flats were built by individuals, in the 1961–65 period the figure was only a little over 4 million, in the 1966–70 period around three million, in the 1971–75 two million, in 1976–80 less than one and a half and in 1981–85 even less. The proportion of cooperative construction is also still small, although in many towns the public demand for cooperative flats and privately built housing was not being met. In the country as a whole more than one million people are on waiting lists for cooperative housing.

Even during the short period of *perestroika* it has been possible to make serious changes in the attitude to housing construction at all levels . While the annual rate of completion of houses in the period 1983–85 remained stable at 2.0 million units, in 1986 2.22 million units were built. And 2.4 million are expected to have been built in

1987. There has not been such a growth of housing in one year in the Soviet Union for 20 years. This has provided the basis for an upward revision of our housing construction plans. The "Basic Directions of Economic and Social Development in the USSR" document at the XXVII Congress called for housing construction of 565–570 million cubic metres in the period 1986–1990. Later this was increased to 595 million cubic metres and again revised upward to no less than 630 million cubic metres or 126 million cubic metres a year. I believe that this figure will also be surpassed.

The complexity of the problem lies in the fact that while in the 1986–90 period the construction of schools and public health care centres is being increased one and a half times, at the same time greater resources are being allocated to the construction of cultural and social institutions and such projects. Yet the organisations available for construction outside the state enterprises are very limited. Therefore serious measures are being taken to develop and extend these so that at the beginning of the 1991–95 period an annual 140 to 150 million cubic metres of housing or even more can be completed. While we have been building two million flats a year, by the 1990s we need to build three million good quality flats and houses. We need to complete more than two billion cubic metres of housing or more than 40 million flats in the 15 years up to the year 2000. This would make it possible to resolve the housing problem as planned, that is to grant every family their own well-built flat or house.

As the population begins to live and eat better and is able to acquire more general consumer goods, *health* moves to the forefront of social values. In the light of modern requirements, the material and technical base of public health care, the quality of medical help and the provision of medicines to the population are all in need of major improvement. Thoroughgoing measures are needed and these are already stipulated for the 1986–90 period. There have been many achievements in the development of Soviet public health care, where free access is provided for all citizens to this vitally important service. But demand is growing and we cannot be at all satisfied with the fact that since 1960 the number of deaths per thousand of the population has grown by almost one and a half times. Of course, this is associated with the increase in the number of old people as a proportion of the population. However, there is also the opposing tendency for life expectancy to be prolonged as a result of progress in public health care, better nutrition, living conditions and leisure facilities. No significant rise in the death rate has been observed in many other countries with an ageing population. The indicator for average life expectancy is also comparatively low. In 1986 it rose to 69 years. There are clearly many problems in the sphere of improving the health of the population. Of course this can in no way be restricted to public health care, for we must change the whole quality and way of life, improving industrial safety and reducing the number of deaths on the roads.

Closely related to this, all the measures in the struggle against alcoholism and to eradicate drunkenness take on exceptional importance. In the two years since the Decree on the campaign against drunkeness came into effect (it was passed on 17 May 1985) the sale of alchohol in the USSR halved. There is no doubt that alongside other positive results these measures will directly show up in the improvement of the health of the population. Next, the problem of *improvement in the economic conditions of retired workers and all pensioners* is closely connected. In the 1981–85 period, for the first time, the number of individuals receiving pensions rose above 50 million and now stands at over 55 million. The USSR has one of the lowest retirement ages. For example, in the USA and the Federal Republic of Germany the pensionable age is 63 to 65 years and in the USSR it is 55 years for women and 60 years for men. Besides this many groups of the Soviet population, especially those working in heavy conditions or in the north, have the privilege of receiving a pension 5 to 10 years earlier. Pensions are fully covered by the state or by collective farms.

Since many pensioners retired in years gone by when earnings were lower, their pensions no longer correspond to contemporary conditions. People's needs, including those of pensioners, are growing all the time and it is therefore imperative to increase the pension in line with the accumulation of state resources at least for those with relatively small pensions. It is easy to see that this requires enormous means. If pensions are to be increased by a total of ten roubles a month, this will require almost 7 billion roubles a year; i.e. practically all the growth in the resources for consumption would go into pensions (minus the needs of the extra population), assuming the national income increases by 3% a year. It is clear that to solve the pension problem we must greatly increase the rate of growth of socio-economic development. A new pension law is currently in preparation, which while retaining the existing retirement age (55–60) will substantially raise the size of the pension.

The most important, indeed vital, benefit in our socialist society is the equal access of all citizens to *education*. Around 35 billion roubles annually are provided for education, more than 6% of the national income. In order to profit from the scientific and technological revolution and to train a new type of worker, expenditure on education must grow significantly. A broad reform of schools is being undertaken aimed at improving the quality of education, while simultaneously increasing its relevance to life, raising a new generation for useful work. The first stage of this school reform alone will require an extra eleven billion roubles. Means over and above this amount will have to be found to computerise education, including school education. The improvement of secondary specialist and higher education lies ahead as well as retraining and increasing the number of skilled workers. All this requires more and more resources and there is but one source for this – the national income.

Schooling, fully paid for by the state, is only one of the aspects of society's concern for children. There is a realistic possibility that in the very near future the population will be fully provided with a comprehensive system of creches, but again this will require additional funds. The strengthening of measures for maternity and child care is also planned. Child benefits for less well-off families already exist and around two million mothers of large families receive monthly benefit. As the standard of living rises it will be necessary to take measures to reduce the number of poorly provided-for families – many of which have several children so that even where the parents' earnings are reasonably high, there is nevertheless relatively less income per head. The *improvement of the living conditions for young families* is a serious matter in cases where they have not yet managed to acquire sufficient qualifications or work experience, are earning below average wages and at the same time have to get a flat, set up a home and raise a family. Here too, regular state help is needed on the basis that this help will be more than paid back to the state subsequently.

The plan to accelerate the growth in productivity will bring out the *problem of redeploying* workers who have lost their jobs. Already in the 1986–90 period the growth of productivity in many parts of industry, agriculture and the railways will outstrip the growth in production and the numbers of workers employed in these branches will fall. Towards 1990 more rapid rates of growth in productivity are planned well ahead of the volume of production in the economy as a whole; and the numbers discharged will be on a massive scale with losses of employment taking place. Besides this, the Law on State Enterprises envisages the closing down of some enterprises operating inefficiently and the redeployment of their workers with three months' wages while they find new jobs.

Naturally the question arises whether this will lead to the advent of unemployment in the USSR. The question is topical. So far during *perestroika* we have only just come up against the reality of this question. The problem of work placement has arisen most tangibly during the reduction of the number of jobs on the railways in the transition to new methods of economic management. Two years ago these new methods were approved for the Belorussian railways. In 1985 over one year the productivity on the Belorussian Republic railways grew by 11% and 12,000 employees were discharged. With the existing conditions of shortages of labour in the Belorussian Republic all of them were placed in jobs and there were almost no complaints. In 1986 ten more railways were transferred to the same methods of economic management and 125,000 people were discharged. In the placement of these people in jobs, especially in towns with no other well developed branches of production, certain difficulties were encountered; the more so since the labour agencies were not prepared for such a massive task of redeployment and retraining. In many places complaints arose and special measures had to be taken. The process of discharging workers can only increase. It should be noted that some Soviet economists in their articles and pronouncements allow for this possibility and some even talk of the desirability of "moderate" unemployment. These suggestions are explained as a way to strengthen people's incentive to work. People, they say, must work conscientiously to avoid dismissal with all its consequences. N. Shmelëv, a Doctor of Economics, expresses a similar position in his article "Advances and Duties" in *Novyi Mir* (No. 6, 1987).

I am opposed to a return even to moderate unemployment in the Soviet Union. In general it seems to me that with economic *perestroika* we should not need to give up any of the advantages won during the years of Soviet power, and the absence of unemployment is a major advantage of our system. Rather, on the contrary, in order to assure *perestroika* we must try to multiply the advantages of socialism. It may be that the presence of unemployment puts pressure on those who are working, makes them fear unemployment and so strive to work harder. But this is a capitalist method of influencing employees. What we need is to use a socialist approach and to develop our own incentives to work. The most important of these incentives is the socialist principle of distribution "from each according to his ability to each according to his labour". This envisages that society grants all citizens a job according to their ability and thereby meets the people's need for work and uses their capacities in the best possible way. On the other hand payment for work done depends on the quality as well as the quantity of the work. This means that whoever works badly should receive less than the worker who works well. If this differentiation is sufficient and is observed strictly then, without unemployment, the incentive to work well will be strong enough. It is in this way that we want to start now to end the general levelling process which developed in the past and to introduce well-founded differentials in wages dependent on results.

But can we give all workers who have lost their place a new job? Will unemployment not arise spontaneously despite our best intentions? I believe that there is a danger that it will, if we do not take special steps to deal with the problem. The opinion of those few economists that support "moderate" unemployment may in fact disarm us because it distracts attention from effective action in making new placements. From their point of view, it would be possible to avoid having to strengthen the work placement organisations and also avoid having to set up a system for retraining workers so that they can work more effectively in other jobs. There would also be no need to introduce an investment policy for job creation in some sectors of the economy and in some regions. Of course. there is much ahead of us to be done. Whereas previously, because of the slow growth of productivity the discharge of workers was a relatively rare affair, and in many regions a labour shortage persisted, the functions of the labour departments which exist in every town, region, province and republic were limited. The system for retraining workers and helping them to gain new qualifications was also insufficiently developed. But now it is different. Definite rights in finding new jobs must be given to these labour agencies, and where necessary retraining colleges need to be set up.

The transition to two-shift work, which has been started in many branches of industry, is an important method of increasing job vacancies for redundant workers. This move to two shifts is aimed of course not only at the placement of such workers but to ensure the fuller use of basic resources for production, especially of the new modern equipment.

It should be borne in mind in the coming 15 years that the problems of job placement will be resolved under specifically Soviet conditions, in particular the post-war demographic decline in the size of the population of working age. It is estimated that the growth in the working population up to the year 2000 will be roughly 20 million, i.e. less than in the past 15 years. A further special phenomenon stems from the extensive tendencies of capital investment in Soviet industry and other branches of the economy in the past. This has been the creation of surplus jobs. These can now be replaced from the labour force that is being freed.

Where necessary new vacancies will also be created entirely from centralised ministerial and state resources. This relates above all to the regions with labour surpluses, where the growth in the working population is rising at a faster rate, namely in Central Asia, Azerbaidzhan, parts of Georgia, Armenia, the Autonomous Republic of Dagestan and several other regions of the Soviet Union. In these regions new industrial enterprises are being established and the construction of manufacturing branches, especially in light industry, are receiving preferential treatment.

I believe that it is possible to assert confidently that *perestroika* of the economy, and acceleration of productivity will not lead to unemployment. Of course, this does not cover all the social problems. But it is sufficient to draw the conclusion that a major acceleration of socio-economic development must have the aim of fulfilling social programmes and increasing the Soviet people's standard of living. Indeed, it is the well-being of the Soviet citizen, the creation of conditions for his or her all-round development that must be central to the country's social and economic policy.

People usually judge the successes of *perestroika* according to the changes in their standard of living. Over the initial two years of *perestroika* fundamental changes have not occurred. Many foreigners visiting Moscow, its service sector and the shops and restaurants, quite reasonably ask the question – what has changed? They themselves reply that no real changes are visible in the supply of goods and in the development of the service sector.

There is in fact some foundation to this conclusion. We are as yet only at the beginning of *perestroika*. Very little time has passed and it is difficult to achieve radical changes for the better in such a short time, the more so since the backwardness in the social sector was formed over many years and it is impossible to end this lag in two to three years. Moreover, a population has a threshold of perception. If the sale of goods in demand increases by only 3%–5%, this will not really be perceived. Again it should be remembered that Moscow is not the whole of the Soviet Union. Its inhabitants previously had a preferential supply of foodstuffs and consumer goods. Therefore the changes in Moscow are less noticeable compared with those in other regions.

Let us look at the figures. The volume of consumption of goods and services has increased over the last two years by more than 10%. This is roughly one and a half times more than the changes observed in the preceding years. The sale of goods in one year, 1986, grew by 6%, including: meat products by 4%, dairy products by 6%, fish by 5%, vegetables by 8% and fruit by 20%. The sale of consumer goods rose even more, by 7%. These figures are corroborated by the natural indicators of sales through the network of shops, and also by per capita consumption figures. The consumption of meat products, for example, rose in one year from 61.7kg to 62.5kg, dairy products from 325kg to 332kg (in terms of milk), of eggs from 260 to 265, fish from 18kg to 18.4kg, fruit and berries from 48kg to 52kg, etc.

There are two further circumstances that must be taken into consideration in judging these figures. We could have increased the sale of food products further through growth of internal production but in fact over one year we almost halved the volume of imported foodstuffs instead, particularly of grain for fodder. Imports of industrial goods from abroad were also reduced because of the decline in hard currency earnings following the fall in the oil price. This held back a more rapid rise in commodity circulation.

The turnover of services that are paid for rose unprecedentedly by 10%, and excluding transport services by 15%. But since this sector is extremely undeveloped even this increase has remained barely perceptible. The unprecedented rise in housing construction for 1986 has already been mentioned. In one year 5.2 million cubic metres more living space (about 100,000 flats) was completed than in the preceding year. For 10.4 million people living conditions improved in that year. At the same time more houses were equipped with services and utilities, and the construction of social and cultural projects, schools, pre-school creches, clubs and cultural centres all increased. The construction of hospitals and poly-clinics increased by almost 20%.

Medical care improved somewhat, which was partly the cause of the fall in one year in the number of working days lost through illness and of an increase in life-expectancy (for the first time in 20 years). Deaths in the population of working age fell sharply from 738,000 in 1985 to 680,000 in 1986, inclusive of the drop from 228,000 to 180,000 in accidents, poisonings and injuries. This is mainly a consequence of the successful campaign against drunkenness. Infant mortality per 1,000 children born also fell from 26 to 25.1. This indicator is still very high, but the downward tendency is significant.

A definite change for the better in working conditions has occurred. This is primarily reflected in the decline in the number of manual workers, mainly of those doing heavy work. The intellectual needs of the people have been noticeably better met, since *perestroika* in the media is proceeding vigorously. It has truly become more interesting to be alive. Although, then, there are some positive changes for the better, we are far from satisfied with them. It is possible and necessary to do more and at the June 1987 Meeting of the Central Committee the aim was clearly spelled out of tackling more seriously the problem of satisfying the everyday needs of the people, so as to make every Soviet family feel within two to three years that there have been favourable changes in the provision of foodstuffs and consumer goods, in better housing, in higher incomes and in better health care and education.

11. *GLASNOST, DEMOCRACY, SELF-MANAGEMENT AS THE DYNAMO OF PERESTROIKA*

The development of democracy and the involvement of workers themselves in management is of decisive importance for the radical reform of management. We have seen that the failure of past economic reforms mainly resulted from the fact that these reforms were conducted from the top down, by order as it were, without sufficient development of initiative from below and without the broad participation of working people. We are not permitting such mistakes during the conduct of the current *perestroika*. The policy is to combine measures for reform of management from above with the involvement of the mass of the people in *perestroika*. The development of democracy, i.e. of people's self-management, is inherent within the the socialist system of economic management. V.I. Lenin put forward the principle of democratic centralism as the foundation of the economic system of socialism. He showed this principle to be a combination of centralised direction of the economy by the state towards the solution of the key tasks of development, so as to guarantee the public interest, together with the initiative of the people, allowing for local conditions and the development of democratic principles in management.

The peculiar and extreme conditions in which socialism was built in the Soviet Union (industrialisation, war, restoration of a ruined economy), have led to a deformation in the application of the principle of democratic centralism. In the first instance, what should have been its secondary aspect, that of centralism, was over-emphasised to the extent that it suppressed democratic principles of management. This was indivisibly associated with the prevailing administrative system of predominantly command management. As the Soviet socio-economic system became more complicated, the administrative system of management became broader and deeper. The number of management bodies proliferated. The number of links in the chain of management ramified and the administrative network itself increasingly deteriorated into a self-aggrandising system. Each management body, each department, followed its own self-interest, reflected in the effort to increase the role it could play. In this way departmentalisation arose and developed. Correspondingly, local bodies strengthened and accentuated their narrow local interests. A complex, cumbersome, interreacting administrative system arose. Suffice it to say that the highest executive body in the Soviet Union, the Council of Ministers of the USSR, directed more than one hundred ministries and departments, working separately from each other. Besides this the fifteen Republic Councils of Ministers would turn out for the meeting of the Council of Ministers of the USSR. Yet the Council of Ministers for the RSFSR (The Russian Soviet Federal Socialist Republic) held no responsibility for the problem of developing heavy industry, nor for most of construction, nor for the railways and air and sea transport. Therefore all local bodies (and in the RSFSR there are 71 autonomous republics, separate provinces, administrative regions and two cities, Moscow and Leningrad, subordinate to the Union) bypass the Council of Ministers of the RSFSR and report directly to the Government of the USSR with all their many problems.

An inevitable corollary of this system of management was bureaucracy – at the opposite pole to democracy. As part of the current radical reform we have to break this administrative system and offset the tendency to bureaucracy by changing over to a fundamentally different system of management based on the use of economic levers and incentives and on the development of democracy. It is well-known that the masses are the main force in history. It is their agitation which most powerfully influences transitional moments of social and economic development. The people, the working masses, were the main actors in the October socialist revolution. It was because it was a people's revolution that it was not put down by bayonets during the years of foreign intervention when the people successfully defended their Soviet power.

In the wide scope of its tasks, and in its novelty, the contemporary *perestroika* is truly revolutionary and it is this revolutionary nature which ensures the active participation of the broad masses of workers in *perestroika*. It must be noted that in contemporary society the role of the individual has greatly increased, as the basic force of production and the conduit through which these productive forces are developing. With the scientific and technological revolution the creative potential of individuals has begun to play a key role. Now every working person has not only his or her own strength but also that of elaborate machines and equipment. For example, in the USSR every worker has on average 90 h.p. at his or her elbow. In these conditions a great deal more depends on a worker's qualifications and attitude to work than before when technical levels were much lower. Also, contemporary production is collective in character. People are not isolated in their work, separate from one another, but work in a single technological production system. Therefore failure in one place, inadequate organisation and bad coordination of work, lead immediately to loss in pace and efficiency.

The events of recent years have demonstrated very graphically how much depends on the individual. The series of scandalous and tragic mistakes by the management and personnel at the Chernobyl Nuclear Power Station led to improbable, one could almost say impossible, results: the reactor was destroyed, there was radioactive fall-out and people perished. The direct damage caused alone amounted to two billion roubles. In accordance with the law managers were sentenced to a long term – up to 10 years – prison sentence for criminal negligence. The chemical plant explosion of harmful substances on the bank of the River Ruhr in West Germany and the poisoning of this river, the tragic events following the release of harmful chemical substances at Bhopal in India, the catastrophies that have struck large airliners and ships, are a far from complete list of the disastrous "accomplishments" of the hand of man, when modern technology is used unskilfully.

But people are not only the producers. They are at the same time the final consumers of their products. Social development has led to the appearance of many new needs. Human needs have become more elastic, more changeable and more diverse. The adaptation of production to the satisfaction of people's growing and changing needs is a sign of our times and in this too the growing role for the individual is reflected. It is not only that modern production and technology make demands on the individual, on his and her level of education, qualifications, discipline, ability to work in a collective, intelligence and creative attitude, but it is a fact also that the individual in return makes no less demands on modern production and technology. This technology must be safe, and must not not inflict damage on the environment. Working with this technology must be attractive to people and help to increase their qualifications. Production itself must increasingly be aimed at the direct satisfaction of human needs. It is this contemporary increase in the role of the individual that poses anew the question of people's participation in management.

There is also the question of self-management in the socialist conditions of the Soviet Union. Public ownership is the basic form of socialist ownership – of the land and its minerals, and of the state factories. These are the collective possessions of the whole society. The potential danger in this is that the property belongs to everyone but to no one in particular. The individual or group feeling of ownership is deadened. The attitudes to public property that may arise is that it is nobody's business, with many difficulties arising as a consequence. Workers may use public resources uneconomically, they may work less well in the social economy than for themselves. The attitude to machinery in state factories is quite different from that, say, to personally owned cars.

One of the most important problems of an effective system of economic management under socialism is the problem of inculcating in every worker the feeling of being a co-owner. No single measure can succeed in doing this. A whole integrated system of measures is needed. There is the relative separation of some parts of public property, which are then assigned to particular enterprises and workers collectives and given to them to keep, use and dispose of. There is also a correctly organised system of wages, closely tied to the final results of economic management. But these results are indivisibly bound up with the efficient use of socialist property. There is also the creation of a social infrastructure in enterprises and working collectives, so that people take care of themselves and link their lives with the work of their enterprise. The transition to self-management is the most important means of strengthening the feeling of ownership, so that the workers themselves feel that they are in charge of the socialist property allotted to the collective, something that is theirs and not someone else's.

In the new system of economic management the rights of working collectives have been greatly expanded by the Law on Socialist Enterprises passed in June 1987. The working collective now determines the development policy of the enterprise. It also establishes the plan of development for its enterprise, including the plan for the five-year period. Plans set by the collective are final and are not subject to the approval of any higher authorities. The collective determines the way the enterprise uses the self-account-able income which it has earned. It scrutinises particularly the way the enterprise's funds are used in the technological research and development fund, the social development fund and the financial incentives fund.

The working collective carries out its functions both directly at meetings of the whole working collective and through democrat-ically elected Councils to represent its interests. The decision to broaden the rights of the working collective was not taken dogmatically, but on the basis of generalisation of the experience accumulated at individual enterprises in the Soviet Union. At the Kaluga Turbine Factory, for example, a council of brigade leaders, representing the working collective's interests, has been operating effectively for many years. The fact is that here collective labour brigades were genuinely organised. Each brigade elects its brigade leader, so that the brigade leaders' council is a democratically elected body. The factory has major productive and social results to its credit and, moreover, the long-term development policy of the enterprise is in the main the responsibility of the brigade leaders' council.

For the first time working collectives are being given extensive rights such as the right to elect the manager. This affects the election of managers of all ranks: the brigade elects the brigadier, the workers and section foremen the section head, the working collective of the factory elects the director of the factory, and the whole working collective of the association elects the General Director. These elections are planned as a creative process. They must be preceded by public competition for managerial posts, with a preliminary selection made by, say, the working collective council. Each candidate then meets with the workers in the sections, departments and enterprises, attends meetings and meets with representatives of public organisations. Each candidate for the post of manager draws up a programme of action and presents it to the working collective. Secret elections then take place with votes cast for a specific person, whose particulars and potential are known, and for a definite development programme for the enterprise.

The idea of appointing managers by election has already been taken up by many working collectives. Even before the official acceptance of the Law on Enterprises these elections were being organised independently in many places. Interesting events occurred for example at the Riga Car Factory. This factory produces the RAF microbuses which gained popularity in their day, but had eventually ceased to meet the increasingly sophisticated demands as needs changed and technology developed. The factory was in a deep crisis and stopped fulfilling the plan. A new leader was needed. Under the aegis of the newspaper *Komsomolskaya Pravda* a nationwide competition was held for the post of director of the factory. A total of four thousand applications was received from all corners of the country and a commission was specially created composed of car construction specialists (from the Ministry of Car Industry), from the factory and from local bodies. About thirty candidates were shortlisted. They studied the factory and made their proposals for it. On the basis of a detailed examination of these more concrete data the list of candidates was further reduced to eight. They came to the factory, familiarized themselves with the work, stated their views on how to improve the situation and finally the working collective in a secret ballot selected its factory director. This turned out to be V.L. Bossert, an energetic young manager, 35 years of age, who up to then was working as the manager of the Omsk Factory, a major producer of gear-boxes for the Moskvich car. The collective supported the candidacy of this new director and gave its views on his programme for the full reconstruction of the factory and the design of a new model of microbus which would be on a par with world standards. Having elected the director, the collective began to work intensively and soon fulfilled the plan. The number of claims for replacement of defective goods was reduced. The financial situation of the enterprise improved, people started to receive prizes and work motivation grew. Parallel to this, work continues on designing a new car and reconstructing the factory.

This experience has proved to be successful and it has caught on. Based on the RAF factory's example, tens and even hundreds of other enterprises have organised elections for directors. Success is assured wherever this is carried out not as a mere formality, but where competition is guaranteed, where time is given and conditions are created for the preparation of imaginative programmes of development for the working collective, and where people really feel they are participating in the advancement of their enterprise at management level. In discussing the question of appointment of leaders by election, we have studied attentively the experience of other socialist countries, Bulgaria and Hungary. In Hungary in particular, this democratic mechanism has been very effective. In re-election for the post of director 8% of former directors were voted out, but 92% had their competence at management confirmed by the collective. In this way the quality of managers has been improved.

The transition to self-management is organically linked to the democratisation of the whole of social life in the Soviet Union and the development of *glasnost*. Great changes are taking place in Soviet society. The work of the mass media, newspapers, journals, radio and television has radically changed. *Glasnost*, openness and truthfulness have advanced. Criticism and self-criticism are developing. Shortcomings and those who have caused them are being exposed and at the same time the best experiences and achievements of *perestroika* are being advertised. Freedom of the press has been expanded and unions of creative workers have been transformed. In the Writers' and Film-makers' Unions there has been a change of leadership. All these unions have begun to live an active creative life.

Political democracy is also developing. The voters are being given the opportunity to express their opinions about a large number of candidates for election to Soviet authorities. The work of officials is now conducted in an environment of *glasnost*, with responsibility and control exercised from below. Leaders are informing the population of issues of interest to them. All this raises the consciousness of the working people and makes them participants in the changes that are occurring in Soviet society.

Of course, the process of democratisation flows in an intricate and contradictory way. Froth forms from time to time on the surface of the stream of new initiatives. There are cases when people want to use *glasnost* and democracy for personal ends, gaining popularity or settling accounts with opponents. The election still occurs of leaders who make no demands on the rank and file. In some cases, using *glasnost* and democracy, a minority may try to thrust their will on the majority. Different opinions and approaches in society are inevitable, and must be treated with patience. As they say, total unanimity only occurs in the graveyard, and in no way in a living society, especially not one in a transitional and exacting period of its development.

For example, some working people consider that the measures taken in the struggle against drunkenness are insufficient. Yet these have been major and radical measures. Over two years they have led to a halving of the sales of alcohol. But some citizens are in favour of total "prohibition" in the USSR. They are in a minority. But among them there is a small number of noisy demagogues, who have taken on themselves the role of expressing "public opinion". Although they are nothing of the sort they make speeches of condemnation, organise public meetings etc. This, of course does not further the business of *perestroika*. It is only important that under the pretext of combating such extremist outbursts, which take advantage of democracy, no moves have been permitted towards the curtailing of *glasnost*, nor towards the creation of excessive control or administrative interference. There is still none of this. On the contrary, democracy is developing and expanding. Comrade Gorbachev has put forward the requirement that democracy should be studied. Methods of work must be changed so that workers are again able to work in conditions of *glasnost*, criticism and self-criticism.

In the life of the Soviet Union public opinion is playing an ever increasing role. Writers, academics, experts, workers are actively voicing their protest at certain decisions and actions of ministries, departments and state authorities. This was how it was in the public campaign against the project to reverse the flow of some northern rivers southwards and to create large irrigated areas as a result. In accordance with government decisions the project was not only prepared, but practical work on the digging of channels was begun and the construction of reservoirs to direct a proportion of the flow of northern rivers of the European part of the country to the south, into the Volga. In the draft Basic Directions of Economic and Social Development in the USSR for the 1986–90 period, which was published for discussion before the XXVII Party Congress, there is a requirement that work continue on the reversal of a proportion of the flow of northern rivers to the south. In newspapers, journals and at meetings many writers and academics took part in the discussion of this point. In particular, the President of the Academy of Sciences of the USSR, Academician A.L. Yanshin, and other academics submitted an article to the newspaper *Pravda* on the untenability of this project for economic and ecological reasons. Our letter was published together with a letter from the Director of the Institute for Water Problems of the Academy of Sciences of the USSR, and corresponding member of the Academy of Sciences, G.V. Voropaev, who in reply stood up for the cost-effectiveness of this river reversal scheme.

Public efforts were not in vain. For, when it was discussed at the commission on the draft of the Basic Directions, a decision was taken to exclude the proposal as not yet fully substantiated. But digging continued. Further efforts were needed for the issue to be examined at the Presidium of the Council of Ministers of the USSR. I attended this discussion and spoke up but opinion was divided. Nevertheless the majority of the leadership, including the President of the Council of Ministers, N.M. Ryzhkov, sided decisively against the continuation of work. As a result a resolution was passed to discontinue all work and planning on the scheme. Almost one hundred million roubles already spent were written off. The departmental self-interest of the Ministry of Water Management and Land Improvement had cost the state dear. But many billion roubles of further expenditure were averted, and most importantly the natural environment was protected and no irrevocable harm was done to it.

In the USSR now new laws have been passed concerning public discussion of major projects and this practice has been widely developed. A recent typical example is the five-month long discussion of the draft of the Law on State Enterprises and Associations. We have already seen how numerous amendments were introduced into this law. These concerned mainly the expansion of the rights of working collectives, the redistribution of means from the fund for development of the enterprise into the social development fund for additional housing and cultural construction, the cancellation of the proposed proportional norm for the formation of an engineers' and white collar workers' wage fund on top of the general wage fund norm. There has been endless discussion on the categorical insistence of the Ministry of Finance and many planning authority representatives on the need for separate regulations for the wages of engineers and white collar workers. This is a long story drawn out over many decades. Restrictions were imposed from above on enterprises on the initiative of the Ministry of Finance, limiting their expenditure on the salaries of administrative workers. The economic planners fought against this. Finally a compromise was accepted. This was to set a proportional norm not for administrative workers but for all engineers and white collar workers. But this norm was in conflict with scientific and technological progress, which often involved an increase in the share of engineers and white collar workers in the overall staff composition. Once again a desperate struggle was crowned with success for the majority opinion. Now there are no such norms in the economic system and the working collective itself and its managers freely determine the share of the wage fund that goes to different categories of workers. Control from above has been removed and additional rights given to the working collective itself.

One issue of major importance is how to combine democracy and discipline. Democracy is not anarchy and is unthinkable without discipline. It was Lenin who proposed the need for "Learning to unite the stormy, spring flood-waters of bursting democratism of meetings of the working masses with the *iron* discipline and *unquestioning obedience* to the will of one person, the Soviet leadership at work." The issue is how to combine collective decision-making and unified management, how to combine discussion with organisation so that accepted decisions are carried out.

Democratisation in the Soviet Union is considered as a decisive condition of *perestroika*. Through democracy the working masses are being involved in self-management and in becoming real participants in *perestroika* and its shield bearer. In this we see the guarantee of our success. Democracy in the Soviet Union is gathering pace. It will undisputably expand and deepen. Democratic forms of management will be perfected as we gain experience. It is entirely fitting that the All-Union Party Conference in 1988 has on its agenda the further development of democracy.

12 CAN THE SOVIET ECONOMY SUSTAIN A NEW ROUND OF THE ARMS RACE?[20]

An account of *perestroika* of the Soviet economy would not be complete without a response to the crucial question which is being demanded by the American administration – can the Soviet economy stand a new round of the arms race, or will a new "cold war" halt *perestroika*.

At certain times it has become evident that despite the enormous efforts made by the Reagan administration to achieve military superiority over the USSR this goal has not been achieved and the overall strategic military balance has been maintained due to the Soviet response. Then, the aim of economically exhausting the Soviet Union has moved to centre stage in the military and political strategy of the American administration. What this means is that right-wing adventurist forces in the USA are continuing to hope for some type of military superiority over the USSR, which could be utilised both politically and diplomatically in different crisis situations right up to inflicting a disarming and fatal nuclear strike.

Among right-wing circles in the West the opinion is widespread that the rivalry in military matters of the USSR with the USA and

[20] This chapter was prepared by the author together with Andrei Kokoshin, Doctor of Historical Science (Institute of the Study of the USA and Canada of the Academy of Science of the USSR) and Boris Komzin, Doctor of Technical Science (Institute of International Economics and International Relations of the Academy of Sciences of the USSR).

other NATO members and Japan will require greater relative expenditure of the Soviet Union and its allies and will inflict severer losses on the Soviet economy than on the American economy. The aim of economically exhausting the USSR by an arms race is being proposed with increasing frankness of late at the highest official levels. Casper Weinberger, as US Defence Secretary, stated in his January 1987 Annual Report, that the conduct of concurrent strategies favourable to the USA in rivalry with the USSR was the main task of his department until the end of the Reagan administration's term of office. A year and a half earlier the President himself, Ronald Reagan, in the same spirit had said, "... we want to develop as complex a weapon as necessary to force the Soviet Union into bankruptcy if it should want to find a defence mechanism against it." This opinion stems from fallacious premises concerning Soviet military doctrine and strategy, and is based on an inaccurate and tendentious interpretation of our military, scientific, technological and resource potential. It also does not take into account the socio-political and economic changes which have occurred in the Soviet Union.

First and foremost, the West reckons that the development of weapons systems and military technological potential will follow the same course, that the Soviet Union will respond to new American military programmes with similar programmes. This is particularly the case concerning the Strategic Defence Initiative (SDI) programme – the development of a vast anti-missile system, at the centre of which are a host of space stations. The supporters of SDI in the USA are doing everything possible to nudge the USSR towards the development of the same system, since the economic burden on the Soviet Union and its allies would, thus, be in relative terms considerably larger than for the United States, their Western European allies and Japan.

The Stealth aircraft programme has a similar function as do a whole range of other American and NATO initiatives. "To fight the Stealth bombers," Weinberger wrote in his report, "the USSR will have to make enormous investments over many years into new anti-aircraft defences, while the investment already made will very rapidly depreciate in value." The right-wingers in the USA and in several other industrial capitalist countries estimate that if the USSR is not bankrupted in this way, then at the very least this policy of the West will prevent the Soviet Union from implementing *perestroika*, from the democratisation of Soviet society and from realising its latest social policy.

At the bottom of the new spiral of the arms race lies an attempt of right-wing forces in the West to use the very latest scientific and technological achievements to develop and to mass produce qualitatively new sophisticated and technically complex types of weapons and weapons systems. Within the framework of this spiralling arms race almost total reliance is placed on equipping both the existing and the future systems and types of weapons with the new generation of computers, the "artificial intelligence" systems. It should be emphasised that these new weapons systems are aimed at surpassing current models many times over. Worse still, this new major spiral is on the point of extending the arms race into space, and this will lead to a new galloping pace of expenditure for both the opposing groups of states.

The realisation of these American plans and the steps which are called for in response is capable of leading to dramatic changes. The possibility of strategic stability will decline, even while the overall military balance is maintained. Uncontrolled and almost infinite rivalry in the use of scientific and technological achievements for military purposes will create a completely different situation of the closest inter-dependence between the security of all countries. Progress in the sphere of electronics and computers, in their mathematical range, in sensory devices and new materials, when used in the military sector without calculating the possible political consequences of their impact on the stability of the strategic military balance, will only serve to aggravate the destabilising effects of these weapons systems.

In the area of strategic arms, this results above all in the increased accuracy of rocket systems and their increased ability to hit small hard targets through the perfection of navigational and other satellite systems. The development of aircraft and missiles which cannot be detected by radar or by other means, makes them a first-strike weapon in their accuracy and suddenness of attack. The changes planned in strategic nuclear forces will sharply increase uncertainty and the risk of the outbreak of a nuclear war by accident.

No less dangerous is the proposed use of the new science and technology in conventional weapons. The development of reconnaissance strike complexes, highly accurate artificially intelligent strike forces intended for attacks on targets hundreds of kilometres away, which are almost as militarily effective as tactical nuclear arms, will also reduce the stability of the military strategic balance. For the successful use of the new non-nuclear strike forces will rely to an even greater degree than current weapons on the factor of surprise.

This means that any confrontation, for example in Europe, implies a confrontation of military strike forces in a state of readiness for combat. This sort of situation can be characterised as the most unstable possible. Even the slightest external disturbance can upset the balance and lead to an escalation of the conflict. In this way the exchange of conventional weapons would differ little in its consequences from the use of nuclear strike weapons, especially in Europe, where more than 150 nuclear reactors are situated, the destruction of even a few of which would be a catastrophe for the whole continent. But the important point is that the development of large space-based anti-missile systems in the SDI programme and of anti-satellite systems means a further significant reduction in the stability of the military strategic balance.

The question of whether the USSR can stand another round of the arms race, when applied to the new spiral urged on by right-wing circles in the USA and other capitalist countries, should be considered in a broad socio-political and socio-economic context. Earlier, the debate was essentially about whether the USSR could raise the level of its military potential to enable it to confront effectively the military might of the USA. Now that the USSR has over a long period of time proved its capacity to sustain a military strategic balance with the USA, increasingly by perfecting the quality and by introducing new weapons, the economic and social aspect of the question is coming down to this: at what price can a sufficient level of defence and national security be achieved? The answer is that objective historical, economic and technological analysis shows that the Soviet Union has the necessary potential to ensure a sufficient level of self-defence.

This conclusion is borne out firstly by the fact that fundamental differences of political aims permit the maintenance of the military defence system for the Soviet Union and the security of its allies and friends at a lower cost than is required by the USA and its allies. Secondly the Soviet Union has large reserves of strategic resources and scientific and technological potential in research and development. Thirdly, through the new sources of economic growth that are arising from the ongoing *perestroika*, long-term positive influences on the socio-economic and political development of the country can be assured.

The Soviet Union's capacity to stand its ground in a new spiral of the arms race, to develop and to perfect its potential in science and technology, and to discover and use these resources efficiently so as to meet rising demand, depends on the overall state of the country's productive capacity and on the balance and dynamic of its social and political development.

The Soviet Union has a large productive potential. The volume of industrial production in the USSR is more than 70% of the United States. The consumption of electricity by Soviet industry has now reached more than 80% of that used by American industry. The USSR produces almost one and a half times more oil (inclusive of gas) and almost twice as much steel and cement. A purposeful concentration of resources is now characteristic of the Soviet economy. As the latest financial data reveal, average rates of growth of the Soviet economy are being maintained at a level of 4% a year and the aim is to raise this to 5%–5.5% in the future.

The development and production of modern weapons and military equipment are based on the intensive use of the results of research and development of prototypes, as well as on the adaptation of advanced technology, requiring high quality materials and skilled labour. A new round of the arms race will inevitably require from the competing countries the re-channelling of such resources to ensure the cutting edge of scientific and technological potential for the military branches.

In addition to references to the burden involved for the USSR in military confrontation, much is being made in the United States of the "lag" in research and development, in terms of projects which reflect the overall technological advance of the Soviet Union relative to the United States and other developed capitalist countries. In order to maintain and increase this lag, the USA is attempting to impede the development of Soviet cooperation with developed western countries in the sphere of science and technology by the introduction of restrictions on the transfer of technology within the framework of the activities of COCOM[21].

It should be recognised that the USSR possesses what is by all accounts a highly developed scientific sector. About 5% of the national income, i.e. roughly as much as the USA and substantially more than other developed capitalist countries, is spent on the development of science in the USSR. The Soviet Union occupies a leading position in the world in many branches of science and technology, e.g. in a number of areas of mathematics, theoretical physics, radio-physics, astronomy, and in aspects of space technology, lasers, electro- and diffusion welding techniques, and many others. The achievements in these areas reveal the potential capacity of the USSR to accelerate scientific and technological development, but also determine the real possibilities for the Soviet Union's equal participation in international scientific and technological cooperation.

The USSR is among the world leaders in electricity generating and electro-machine building and produces the most powerful turbines and generators for hydro-electric power stations in the world. In their technical specifications many Soviet electro-technology products for thermal power stations are as good as any foreign equivalents. In the Soviet Union the most powerful serial electro-furnaces are being built and used. It is generally accepted that the USSR is the world leader in the development of new methods of production of electricity generating with magnetic hydro-generators. The "Tokomak" principle for using thermo-nuclear fusion for the needs of electro-energy was developed in the USSR and received international acclaim and global distribution. Using these reactors thermo-nuclear fusion is being studied in the USA, Japan, Great Britain, West Germany, France and other countries.

The USSR has recorded major successes in the production of non-ferrous metals and in the equipment to refine them. The Soviet

---

[21] COCOM (Coordinating Committee on Multilateral Export Controls) is a committee of NATO which also has Japanese membership and which monitors and restricts the export of technology to Warsaw Pact countries, China, Viet Nam, North Korea and Mongolia. The banned list includes computers, micro-electronics, robotics, radar and echo-sounding equipment and telecommunications generally. But much gets through, especially from Japan and Norway, to the fury of US Congressmen. (ed.)

Union's accumulated experience in the production of titanium and of the equipment to process it, and in heat-resistant alloys and ceramics, is especially highly regarded. No less well-known are Soviet achievements in other spheres of materials production, including the production of composite materials for building and metallurgical powders. Recently the greatest emphasis has been placed in the Scientific Research Institute (NIOKP) on those branches of information science and technology which are determining economic progress: instrument-making, computer technology, electronics and robotisation, communication and chemical technology. Currently, almost half of the USSR's inventive research and development capacity is taking place in these branches.

In such circumstances the attempt by the American administration to introduce restrictions on the participation of the USSR in international scientific and technological cooperation has a negative effect not only on Soviet science and technology, but also on the allies of the USA who are interested in using Soviet technology in joint programmes and in scientific and technological exchange. Moreover, export restrictions affect the USA itself in a negative way. Specialists have noticed the perceptible fall in many countries in the use of American manufactures as a consequence of the uncertain export policy of the USA in setting ever new restrictions.

For a variety of reasons the USSR entered relatively late into the world of international scientific and technological exchange. To some extent this has assisted the restrictive policy of the USA and of other capitalist countries. Beside this, within the system of management of the Soviet economy itself there was some underestimation of the advantages of international exchange. Many Soviet ministries and departments preferred to limit the fields of the international division of labour and international cooperation to only those traditional forms of exchange of raw materials and industrial goods. However, despite external and internal restrictions the trade in licences is becoming increasingly widespread.

The western press stereotype image of the USSR as a "backward" country is in increasingly clear contradiction to the growing interest of leading US and other manufacturing companies in the acquisition of Soviet licences for the production of advanced materials, machines, tools, and new technological processes. By the mid-1980s about 80,000 discoveries were being registered annually in the USSR, i.e. twice as many as in the USA or Japan. The USSR maintains licensing connections with more than 2000 foreign manufacturing companies from forty countries. These include De Pont de Nemours, Bristol–Myers, MacDermott, Minnesota Mining and Manufacturing, Nippon Steel. By 1990 around three-quarters of the volume of steel in the USA may be smelted by the Soviet technology of continuous casting. Leading companies from the capitalist countries are showing considerable interest in the technology for cooling-systems of domed furnaces developed in the USSR, as well as for the electric smelting of coke, automatic welding of pipelines, extra high pressure electro-transmissions, various medical appliances and biotechnical and chemical processes.

The Soviet Union has much scientific and technological work and advanced research and development in hand, some of which consists of experimental prototypes of new machines, instruments and appliances which meet the highest modern requirements. The major problem lies in their mass production and broad application. To solve this steps are being taken for the priority development of machine building. As a result the proportion of machines, tools and appliances coming from state machine building branches that are up to world standards will grow to between 80% and 90% by 1990. The further acceleration of scientific and technological progress in the Soviet Union is related to the reform of its economic structure. Measures aimed at raising the level of economic independence of enterprises will undoubtedly be helped by the accelerated renewal of their technology, by larger economies of resources, and by the active participation of the workers in the organisation and technological processes of production.

Apart from anything else, the new developments in the economy are enabling the Soviet Union to achieve the targets established for ensuring sufficient defensive power, not through sacrifices and restrictions, but by the acceleration of socio-economic growth. Can the problems arising from the need to make an adequate response to the unleashing by the USA of a new type of arms race bring *perestroika* to a halt? We can with conviction answer this question in the negative. This process assumes the involvement of individual enterprises, regions and whole branches of the economy, but it is simultaneously based on the powerful moral and political enthusiasm which is now being experienced in Soviet society. The further democratisation of our society, associated with a pronounced feeling of social responsibility inherent in all its members, will guarantee that economic pressure from without, and any individual hardships which may arise as a result, will only engender a more active and effective response. Any pressure brought to bear on the Soviet Union can only strengthen the feeling of mutual solidarity of the Soviet peoples and raise the level of discipline and activity among them.

At the same time the fact that the arms race complicates the process of reform and *perestroika* should not be denied. There is the hope that the treaty limiting thermo-nuclear weapons will liberate resources for peaceful construction.

Examples of the Soviet people's civic feeling and ability to mobilise their forces were thoroughly demonstrated not only during World War II but in many stages of post-war development. Witness the breakthrough in the military sphere – the creation of nuclear missiles and the major results attained over a limited period of time in other fields. In the space programme, the opening up of oil and gas fields in Western Siberia, the construction of the Baikal–Amur Railway, the innovations in the aviation and shipbuilding industries, the rapid construction of the gas pipeline and so on. Surprisingly complex technical problems have been rapidly resolved in the elimination of the consequences of the Chernobyl catastrophe.

The process of *perestroika* has only just begun. Its development is being hindered by a variety of factors: by inertia of economic thinking, by the hidden opposition of certain social strata, by the accumulation of problems arising from imbalances in the economy, etc. However, current analysis shows that the Soviet economy and its scientific and technological establishments are gaining a new dynamism. *perestroika* is extending also to the Soviet defence industry and to the armed forces, where the search is on for optimal strategies and improving cost-effectiveness in military spending. This can only assist the successful implementation of the measures needed to guarantee the development of Soviet military potential.

It should also be said that the right-wing circles in the USA, in attempting to start on another round of exhausting military rivalry, should not forget the consequences of such actions for the American economy itself and the world economy in general. Figures for the first half of the 1980s show that far from all American plans have been implemented in the way they were initially proclaimed. Despite numerous measures to increase the military budget, the current administration has not managed to achieve an increase in military power proportional to the investments made. Moreover, the negative consequences of this period of high military spending are increasingly clearly beginning to tell on the American economy.

Military expenditure is the root cause of the enormous US budget deficit. Many prominent specialists in the United States have convincingly shown that the loss of competitiveness of many American goods, especially in the high-technology sector, and the negative trade balance itself are also largely a consequence of the growth in military expenditure. It is no coincidence that the *Washington Post* reminded its readers of the opinion of a US Congressman many years before. "Nothing will hearten a potential opponent more", he emphasised, "than to observe how we are leading the country to bankruptcy and destroying the economy, to ensure our full preparedness for military conflict." Thus the possibilities for the USA to extend its military preparations are far from infinite.

The search is now starting in the USSR for unorthodox and optimal solutions to ensure sufficient defensive capacity for the country, while not overburdening the economy and its technological, strategic and industrial system. The resolutions of the XXVII Party Congress in January 1987 and of the Central Committee Meeting require deep consideration and a creative and daring use of a systematic analytical and integrated approach. The solution in this as in other areas requires a critical rethink of the experience of the past.

The guarantee of the defence capability of the country is the aim of the development of the military potential of the USSR. Rather than taking initiatives to build up its military might, the Soviet Union considers it sufficient to guarantee the overall military strategic balance in response to the military power of the USA. In line with such an approach the build-up, technological perfection and upgrading of weapons is not an end in itself, but for that matter neither will the Soviet Union strive for a "mirror image" of the respective potential of the United States.

The main factor reinforcing international security lies in the initiative of the USSR and other member states of the Warsaw Pact, for the limitation, reduction and finally the elimination of nuclear weapons, for the reduction of conventional weapons and of the military forces of both sides. Furthermore this implies a plan for preventing the arms race in space, and for reducing the military potential of states to reasonable limits, i.e. to those that are purely defensive. This plan meets understanding and acceptance in broad circles of the capitalist countries, among many people of moderate or centrist political persuasion. But there is very strong opposition to such plans on the part of the right-wing political forces and those with a direct interest in the expansion of military production. For them, arms reduction and particularly disarmament mean death. Historically formed stereotypes of the role of the military still unfortunately affect many people, despite the efforts of peace-loving and realistic thinkers. In such conditions the search by the Soviet Union for optimal ways of building their armed forces is very important, since the efforts of reactionary forces in the West to continue the arms race have not been entirely unsuccessful in sabotaging the real progress of arms limitation and reduction.

The presence on both sides of enormous nuclear arms potential, sufficient under any variation of the outbreak of hostilities to inflict an annihilating retaliatory strike, is the major characteristic of the current strategic balance. This is the basic factor of the military-political situation, which must be understood in estimating the prospects for arms limitation and disarmament as well as for a continued arms race. This fact has been repeatedly emphasised by the Soviet leadership, and by its military specialists. In Edward Shervarnadze's words, "...the essence of the strategic balance lies in the fact that each side, even if it becomes the victim of nuclear aggression, will maintain sufficient strategic means to inflict a crippling retaliatory strike against the aggressor. Consequently in conditions of strategic balance there can be no winner in a nuclear war and its outbreak is equivalent to suicide..."[22]

There exists today between the USSR and the USA an overall military strategic balance despite significant differences in the number of each side's nuclear warheads (the USSR 10,000, the USA 14,800) and their carriers (the USSR 1,480, and the USA 2,208) and in the composition and structure of their forces.[23] Chief

---

[22] *Pravda*, 24 October 1985.

[23] *Rejkavik. Dokumenty i fakty*. Moscow, 1987, p.23.

of Staff of the Soviet Armed Forces, M.A. Gareev, writes that "...military theory must gradually address issues such as the most rational use of resources assigned to military requirements within the limits of strict need, so that defence is reliable and at the same time not too burdensome on the state".[24]

The policy selected by the Soviet leadership in response to Reagan's SDI (Strategic Defence Initiative) programme, should the Americans continue to promote its realisation, is therefore important. The Soviet Union has repeatedly underlined that it will respond if the USA unleashes an arms race in space and this fact has major significance for its defence and its economic and international political position. This position guarantees the resources needed for every aspect of building up the armed forces of the USSR in the interests of the security of the Soviet Union and its allies. It once more demonstrates the futility of all hopes for the "economic exhaustion" of the USSR. It also challenges the thesis of equal superpower responsibility for the arms race, which is unfortunately still very widely held by the general public in the developed capitalist countries and in developing countries. Such a position can be compared with the profound restraint in the character of Soviet nuclear arms when at the end of the 1950s and beginning of the 1960s strategic rockets were built, instead of following the American example and creating a large fleet of nuclear armed strategic aircraft.

The Soviet Union will respond to other challenges from reactionaries, employing the same principles of rational sufficiency in developing military potential expressed at the XXVII Party Congress, based on the fact that Soviet military doctrine and strategy are defensive in character in line with the highest political goals of the socialist state.

Like the people of other countries, we are of course deeply interested in seeing an end to the arms race, and disarmament and a lasting peace. The motivation here is two-fold: above all to guarantee security and the preservation of life, but also to liberate the resources currently used for the defence of the country so as to redirect them to improving the well-being of the Soviet people and assisting the peoples of the underdeveloped countries. The arms race is unwanted and detrimental to the implementation of our

[24] M.A. Gareev. *M.V. Frunze – voennyi teoretik*, Moscow, Voenizdat, 1985, p.425.

plans. We need peace, progress and international cooperation. This is why the leaders of the Soviet Union and above all General Secretary Gorbachev are campaigning so actively for disarmament and peace, for security in all regions of the world and for good neighbourliness and friendship among all peoples.

13 IN PLACE OF A CONCLUSION: THE SOVIET ECONOMY IN THE 21st CENTURY

Perestroika, the acceleration of socio-economic development is changing the whole face of the country. The technological base, the economic forms, the system of management – everything is being renewed and transformed. Can we foresee the future? The future cannot be determined exactly. It is hardly possible to imagine it in full. But the shape of the future can be outlined.

At the XXVII Party Congress a new edition of the Party Programme was adopted in which the basic directions of Soviet development for the next 20–30 years are set out. The Party Congress also approved "The Basic Directions of Economic and Social Development in the USSR, for the period 1986–90 and up to the Year 2000". In this document the most important projections are laid down for the development of the national economy up to the year 2000.

In the Soviet Union, as in other countries, research goes on with the aim of forecasting long-term trends. Two years ago an Institute for Economics and for Forecasting Scientific and Technological Progress was created at the Academy of Sciences of the USSR to take overall scientific direction of this work. The Committee for Science and Technology of the Academy of Sciences of the USSR had already prepared a Comprehensive Programme on Scientific and Technological Progress with basic economic and social indicators to precede the research on the next five-year plan, so that this was considered within the context of a longer-term plan for fifteen years ahead. This Comprehensive Programme was thus developed to cover a twenty-year period and work on this Comprehensive Programme for the period up to the year 2010 is under way. This Comprehensive Programme consists of predictions and projections of development of scientific and technological progress in each branch and each sector of the economy. This immense collective work, in which hundreds of research institutes are taking part, has involved all the leading specialists from the ministries, departments and central economic bodies. In the early stages commissions set up to deal with particular problems gave their predictions and projections with the evidence and supporting figures. More than 50 volumes of materials were offered by these commissions during the preparation of the Comprehensive Programme for the period 1986–2000. These materials form the starting point for the synoptic collected document of the Comprehensive Programme, which is then being used by the State Planning Office (Gosplan) of the USSR and other bodies for planning the future development of the country.

Thus we have at our disposal some of the primary materials of the research which should enable us to get a glimpse of the twenty-first century. Since there is always an element of uncertainty as to future development arising from unforeseen changes in internal and international conditions of development, and because of the incomplete knowledge we have about variables, such as the sources and factors of the economic rate of growth, alternative scenarios are generally prepared in order to make predictions. By systematic methods and situational analysis, attempts can be made to create future scenarios employing different variables of development. The first basic scenario is usually the hypothetical continuation of existing tendencies. If this type of scenario is applied to the Soviet Union, taking into account the fundamental socio-economic tendencies of the last fifteen years, then the picture is a depressing one. Negative tendencies which appeared in the economic development of the country during this period imply stagnation, crisis and a fall in the standard of living. The lag in development behind the USA and other capitalist countries would, in this case, widen further. This reinforces the crucial importance, indeed the imperative nature, of the decision to make the radical *perestroika*, i.e. the economic reforms and an about-turn in the whole economic policy of the country.

Rejecting the scenario of a continuation of existing tendencies, we can now start from the most recent acceleration in the development of the country. Of course, this acceleration can appear in several ways, and bring greater or lesser results depending on changing conditions and on the momentum of development. Projecting into the future, we, naturally, proceed from the premise that peace will continue. If the Soviet proposals for disarmament, security and a stable peace are accepted, the means and resources liberated from the military sector could augment the rate of growth of the economy. The future is being created today. So, our future will depend on the extent to which we undertake *perestroika* and manage now to mobilise the country's reserves to achieve their full potential, and on the extent to which we accelerate scientific and technological progress to improve quality and efficiency and create a mechanism for continued growth.

Table 11: *Growth indicators of USSR resources and efficiency over two fifteen-year periods to the year 2000*

Indicators (growth multiples over 15 years)	1971–85 (actual)	1986–2000 (projected)
National income (consumption and accumulation)	1.8	2.0
Resources used		
Composite inputs	1.5	1.2
Basic capital stock	3.0	2.0
Capital investment	2.0	1.9
Fuel and raw material extraction	1.5	1.25
Number of workers engaged in production	1.15	0.85
Efficiency of social production		
Composite indicator of efficiency	1.2	1.65
Capital-output ratio	0.7	stable
Cost-effectiveness of capital investment	0.9	1.05
Cost-effectiveness of use of fuel and raw materials	1.2	1.6
Social labour productivity	1.55	2.3–2.5

The major acceleration of scientific and technological progress makes possible this sharp change in the determinants of economic development. Towards the year 2000, the role of Soviet science both within the country and in the world must grow substantially. While maintaining the growth in the number of people in science, emphasis will be placed on strengthening the material base of science and raising the efficiency of the work of academics. Science will increasingly become a "direct productive force", as Marx foresaw, and a fundamental integration of science with production will take place as large scientific and production associations become the bases of scientific and technological progress. This will be the major change: the creation of the conditions for the broad application to the economy and society of the achievements of the scientific technological revolution.

By employing to the full the achievements of science, the material and technological base of the economy will be rebuilt. By the year 2000, according to the projected figures, the renewal of plant and machinery in existing enterprises in the Soviet Union will be running at 6% or more per year. Virtually no machinery that is now in use will then remain. Almost all will be new. This is to be ensured by trebling the machine-building output over the fifteen years. In the high-tech branches alone the growth will be between five and ten times.

A major programme to intensify the development of the chemical industry and the use of its products in the economy will also be implemented. Production in the chemical industry will increase 2.5 times by the year 2000, while the production of modern types of plastics, synthetic fibres and fine chemicals will get priority treatment. In the development of fuel and energy emphasis will be placed on their more efficient use in the economy. There will only be a very limited growth in oil and coal extraction; but the growth in demand will increasingly be met by the expansion of the use of natural gas and open cast coal mining.

The construction of nuclear power stations will be continued with improvements being made in the safety of nuclear reactors. This will increase their cost, although stations of more moderate size will be built than were earlier proposed. It should be noted that the proportion of electro-energy produced by nuclear power stations in the USSR is currently one of the lowest in the world, one third less than in the USA, only a half that of Japan, not to mention France. Thanks to measures to conserve resources and to scientific and technological progress in the fuel and energy industry, its share of total capital investment in the Soviet Union will reach a plateau. Later, it is possible that it will even fall, while in the previous five-year period from 1981–85 and in the current period 1986–90 the growth of capital investment in this sector has been proceding at preferential rates.

A fundamental technological reconstruction has begun in Soviet metallurgy. The transition will be completed from open-hearth to converter production of steel together with the installation throughout of continuous steel casting. The proportion of cold-rolled sheet in total output will also be raised, the quality of metals will be improved, the range of products produced diversified and further development of the industry ensured.

In the building sector major technical and organisational changes for the better will take place. The most labour intensive jobs will be transferred from building yards to factories, and the finished sections, blocks, and modules, in the form mainly of light-weight fully pre-fabricated constructions, will be assembled directly on the building sites. Building organisations will become mobile. Construction time will fall and quality will increase at least two to three times.

A unified transport system will be set up gradually for the country, to ensure a rapid and dependable freight delivery service from supplier to consumer.

The key technical advance in the development of all branches of production consists in their automation through the broad use of modern electronics. All branches and sectors of society and of the economy will be subject to the application of electronics. It will change the whole nature of production processes which will become more reliable, intensive and flexible as well as less wasteful.

All this will lead to major structural changes for the better in the national economy. The share of high-technology production will treble, the share of machine construction will rise one and a half times and of the chemical industry by one third. At the same time the share of the extraction and raw material producing branches of industry will decline, although the role and importance of the processing of raw materials will increase. The structure of the economy will be adapted for more dynamic, reliable and flexible development in order to meet all of society's needs more fully.

Side by side with changes in the structure of industry and in capital formation, there will be major changes in the territorial division of labour. The regions of Siberia and the Far East will receive preferential development. About two thirds of all Soviet natural resources are concentrated there, but only about 10% of the population lives there. The flow of population eastwards will probably grow as production is developed there and living conditions are improved. Recently a resolution was passed on the future development of the productive resources of the Far East. This envisaged a rate of growth of social production there above the national average. By the year 2000 the population of the Far East is also to have better than average standards of living compared with other regions in housing and other branches of public welfare.

Regional economic and social enhancement is to be evened out through the more rapid development of economic and social indicators in the regions that have fallen behind. At the same time there will be an increase in the mutual dependence, assistance and economic integration of the several regions of the country, within the whole national economy. Friendship between the hundred ethnic peoples living in the Soviet Union will be strengthened on this base of economic development.

The major change expected in the economic structure of the country is to be the preferential development of all those branches of production working for the individual consumer and the priority given to industries concerned with the welfare of the people in the whole social sector. Given the stability in the retail price system, to be established by the price reforms at the end of the 1986–90 period, average wages and salaries will increase roughly one and a half times up to the year 2000. Real incomes will grow even more as a result of the benefits and subsidies received from the funds provided for social consumption.

Currently two thirds of the income of the population comes from direct payment for labour and one third from these benefits and subsidies. These include education, medical assistance, and help with improving qualifications, all of which are provided free. They also cover welfare payments, pensions, and other awards, like additional payments for leave, and free places allotted at sanatoria and rest homes. The upkeep of pre-school establishments and so on is also found from these funds. The state lays out money in addition to these funds on the building of houses, schools, and cultural and medical facilities. If the average wage of workers is taken as 100, then including these benefits it will come to more than 140. If we include expenditure on construction of housing and cultural and other facilities, it comes to more than 155. In the future, state expenditure on education and health-care will grow sharply. A new pension law will be introduced with larger pensions, also paid for by the state. As the standard of living rises so will the size of these direct and indirect benefits.

In the period up to the year 2000 it is intended that the food supply problem will be solved and the diet of the population will reach the scientifically established norms of intake required. In the future we will also arrange for the full supply to the market of all the sought-after consumer goods in order to ensure full satisfaction of demand. Supply of durable consumer goods will grow especially rapidly.

In accordance with the Party Programme and the goals set by the XXVIIth Congress every Soviet family will have a separate and comfortable flat or house by the year 2000. At the same time rent for flats in the USSR will remain the lowest in the developed world. Recently the basic directions were worked out for the development of health-care and for the improvement of the health of the population, involving large-scale measures to improve the situation in this crucially important area. This programme has been published for public consultation, after which legislation will be passed. A major redistribution is foreseen in the resources available for improving the health of the population.

Recently the authorities came to pay increased attention to environmental protection. Important resolutions were passed on the protection of Lake Baikal, the improvement of ecological conditions on Lake Ladoga. Enterprises polluting the environment have begun to be closed down – something that did not occur before. I believe that this is only a beginning. The question of creating a single state authority to head up nature-protection activities is being considered, in place of the various separate bodies that have already been created in some Republics of the Union. Thus a new initiative is needed here to protect and augment the unique natural environment of the Soviet Union and to guarantee the ecological cleanliness of the air, water and soil.

A general educational reform in the schools and a major *perestroika* of the system of higher and secondary education is to be completed. In this way the whole of education will be raised to a qualitatively higher level.

Two contradictory groups of factors will influence the differences in the standard of living of the population: on the one hand some differentiation will be maintained via the principle of distribution according to work, when the size of the payments will depend with increasing consistency on the results of people's activity; and on the other hand with the increase in benefits, pensions and other grants to the population, those differences in the standard of living will be reduced where they are not brought about by difference in work but as a result of the number of dependents (children, elderly people, etc.).

The decisive principle to underlie future distribution policy will be social justice. The current differentiation in incomes and standards of living and lifestyles of different strata of the population is not very large. If one takes the poorest decile of families and the top decile then the current difference between their incomes is about three to one. In the capitalist countries there are super-rich capitalists and in contrast the very poor. The differences between these two poles in capitalist society are incomparably greater. The guaranteed right to work in the USSR, the absence of unemployment and of the large proportion of the population living on low levels of unemployment benefit that occur in capitalist societies, help greatly to reduce the differences. Thanks to this social protection, Soviet working people are already convinced that they can look forward to a secure future. As people's needs are increasingly fully met, this conviction can only be strengthened.

The radical reforms proposed for management will give a qualitatively new impetus to the whole Soviet economy. This will aim at subordinating production to the demands of the consumer, stimulating both high cost-effectiveness and quality, technological innovation and individual worker involvement. Mechanisms are to be created and refined for accelerating the socio-economic development of the country and removing any barriers and impediments which hinder development.

This renewal of the economy will elevate the role and significance of the Soviet Union in the world. Currently, according to the figures of Soviet statistical authorities, the national income of the USSR is about 66% of the US level, while Western economists usually quote figures of 50%–55%. During the last 25 years the national product in the USA has been growing at less than 3% annually. This indicator for the USSR will in future according to our estimate, be about 5% a year. With these differing rates the Soviet national income by the year 2000 will closely approach that of the USA. If per capita income is taken, the Soviet lag will be more marked, insofar as there are less than 240 million people in the USA and more than 280 million in the USSR. At present rates, the population in the USSR is growing one and a half times faster than in the USA (in 1986 the population of the USSR increased by 1.02% and of the USA by 0.7%). Since a larger volume of labour and material resources is used in the USSR the indicator of cost-effectiveness for the Soviet Union will continue to lag behind the USA, although the difference will be reduced sharply. While productivity over the last 25 years rose in the US economy on average by less than 2% a year, and should increase at roughly this rate in the future, the proposed annual growth in labour productivity in the USSR is roughly 6% per annum. The gap will therefore be narrowing. An issue of especial concern for the USSR is the attainment of leading positions in the world in technology and quality of production. The fundamental technological reconstruction which is being implemented in the economy, the programme to advance machine-building, and the economic and administrative measures to improve the quality of production and its competitiveness are all aimed at this goal.

With the growth of social production in the USSR, its international relations will be developed and deepened, in the first place with socialist countries on the basis of economic integration and the implementation of the Comprehensive Programme of Scientific and Technological Progress for the CMEA members. I believe that in the near future the Soviet Union will overcome the decline that has occurred in international trade with capitalist and developing countries (caused by the sharp drop in the prices of oil and of several other raw materials) and that the country will begin to expand dynamically its economic relations with these countries. We hope that joint ventures with foreign companies on the territory of the USSR will become widespread and will develop effectively. In a word, the USSR will increasingly come to be included in the international division of labour.

As we speak about the future development of the USSR, a particularly noteworthy date should be remembered – the Anniversary of the October Socialist Revolution. In 1987 we celebrated the 70th Anniversary of October 1917. The Soviet Union has come a long way and its achievements cannot be denied. There have been miscalculations, errors and wasted opportunites, but despite these the country has accomplished an enormous leap from a backward to an advanced civilisation. The fundamental *perestroika* of Soviet society and first of all of its economy is a continuation of the Great October Socialist Revolution. This is not only because what is occurring under *perestroika* is revolutionary, but because it is aiming to raise the standard of living of Soviet society to a qualitatively new level, in line with its renewal and transformation according to socialist principles. The *perestroika* is a continuation of the October Revolution also in a more profound sense. The October Revolution began the transition to socialism including the setting up of a socialist economy. Socialism was eventually victorious and socialist relations have come to hold sway completely in Soviet society. The October revolution, in this way, established a base for the socialist system which we consider to be better than the capitalist system.

Socialism must, however, demonstrate its higher economic and social efficiency by its evident advantages. The ongoing *perestroika* in the USSR is aimed precisely at disclosing the advantages of socialism. Lenin said that socialism must ensure a higher level of productivity than capitalism. This has still not been achieved. Only now during *perestroika* is this goal put on the agenda as a practical, albeit long-term task. *Perestroika* must carry Soviet society to a qualitatively new state, when thanks to the advantages of socialism we will surpass the capitalist countries in productivity and other indicators of cost-effectiveness, in quality of production and the level of technology. As the most progressive society, in stimulating scientific and technological progress, we must have the best, the most effective material and technological social base and be at the forefront of scientific and technological advance. Under socialism the best achievements of science and technology must be applied more widely than under capitalism, since there are not the same economic barriers for the application of scientific and technological progress.

On the basis of higher cost-effectiveness we aim to achieve the highest standard of living in the world – in all the component parts: diet, consumer goods, housing, social sector services and, of course, by rendering the population healthier and with a higher average life expectancy. Socialist society must be more educated, more intellectual, more spiritually and morally committed. This is to be achieved with *perestroika* and with the wholesale revision of social relationships.

The largest steps that are to be taken towards achieving these historic goals lie in the period up to the year 2000. Their full resolution may possibly be completed, in my view, by the hundredth Anniversary of the October Revolution in the year 2017. The Soviet people naturally consider their socialist society as the most advanced. In many respects we are still behind other developed industrial countries. But we are convinced that our lag is temporary, that the advantages of socialism will be increasingly clearly revealed through the active work of all the Soviet people. It is therefore with high hopes that we look forward to the future.

APPENDIX 1

USE OF DYNAMIC INTER-BRANCH MODELS TO STUDY THE FUTURE GROWTH OF THE SOVIET ECONOMY

For twenty years now dynamic inter-branch models have been used to study the rates and proportions of future economic development of the USSR. The general principle for constructing such models was offered more than thirty years ago by the outstanding American academic of Russian origin, the Nobel laureate Wassily Leontief, in his book *The Structure of the American Economy*. Leontief's work was introduced into the USSR in the mid-1950s. The arrival of Leontief in the Soviet Union and the contacts he made with a broad circle of Soviet economists facilitated the development of mathematical economics in the USSR.

Research in mathematical economics, including the field of inter-branch balances, was based on indigenous Soviet research work on the balance of the economy for the country as a whole, as well as the systems of materials balances covering individual products and branches of production, which were widely applied to Soviet planning. That is why the idea of the dynamic inter-branch balance fell on fertile soil.

In 1964 under my direction one version of a dynamic inter-branch model was implemented at the Institute of-Economics and Organization of Industrial Production in the Siberia Department of the Academy of Sciences of the USSR for 29 aggregated branches covering the development of Soviet industry and the national economy. Thereafter, the breadth (i.e. increased number of branches and products) and the depth (extent of optimization including new variables) of this model were expanded. It is scarcely appropriate to introduce here the lengthy mathematical formulae for this fairly complex model. I would like to refer those readers who are interested to the specialist literature.[25] Here, however, I will describe the model in general terms, while giving special attention to the conclusions to be drawn from using this model for the future development of the Soviet economy.

For every year of the period covered the model contains:

- material balances for the means of production expressed as an input coefficient for the production of one branch per unit of output of another branch (coefficient Aij in an ordinary inter-branch balance);
- balance of fixed productive capital expressed by a coefficient of the capital intensity of production of one branch in terms of a given type of fixed capital (coefficient Bij);
- balances of labour resources expressed in terms of the labour intensity of every branch (coefficient Ci). A constraint is imposed on the overall volume of labour resources used.

The level of consumption is also set in this model. A set of vectors for the volume of consumption of different products is contructed so that the vector with a higher number corresponds to a higher level of consumption. The goal is to achieve the largest vector of consumption in the course of development.

The solution of this problem for each year yields a balanced set of branch levels of production, consumption and accumulation. A recursive relationship in terms of the fixed capital is used to the following year's goal, for which the capital stock is given by the

[25] A.G. Aganbegyan, K.A. Barinovski, A.G. Granberg, *Sistems modelei narodnokhozyaistvennogo planirovaniya*, "Mysl'", Moscow, 1972, pp.197–243.

previous year's capital, plus new investment taking account of when they are introduced into operation.

The calculations of this model have a step-by-step character, beginning from a base year. The model calculates the rates and proportions in the following year for the given 5, 10 or 15 year periods. This model is used mainly for medium-term calculations. It is highly flexible, especially when used for multi-variant calculations. In setting the time path of coefficients A_{ij}, B_{ij} and C_i for the future, a trajectory of development of the economy is determined based on particular conditions. Trends in the intensification of production, and of scientific and technological progress, and the relation between accumulation and consumption are all taken into account by adjustments to the parameters of the models. Results are then obtained which show how changes in these parameters affect the rate and proportions of development. A whole system of mathematical economic analysis of the solutions has been worked out to identify as much as possible about the workings of the model. This means the study of the resistance of economic development indicators to change of various parameters of the model, and the quantitative analysis of direct, indirect and total inputs of materials, capital and labour supply. In addition it is possible to study the effect of changes in the volume and structure of public consumption on the programme of production and accumulation etc. This dynamic inter-branch model has been used now for four five-year periods for the preliminary stages of working out the five-year plan, when the factors affecting and the conditions limiting development for the period ahead are researched. The model is also used for more detailed analyses of retrospective development.

What conclusions have we reached studying the dynamic of the Soviet economy using this dynamic inter-branch model? One conclusion concerns the consequences of a continuation of the past extensive tendency of development. Calculations from the model have clearly shown that with the predominance of extensive methods of development the rate of economic growth will inevitably fall, disproportions in the development of the economy will worsen and consistent shortages will increase. Using this model a fall in the rate of economic and social development was predicted for every five-year period over the last 15–20 years. A continuation of the extensive tendencies of the last 10–15 years would be particularly ruinous, when the potential for growth of productive resources has fallen, given all the objective reasons which have been mentioned before. The retention of former extensive tendencies would lead to a fairly sharp fall in rates of growth and to a worsening of the whole economic situation. Detailed quantitative forecasts have revealed the inadmissibility of a continuation of existing tendencies, the need to turn around certain factors in the structure of economic growth, and to secure the transition of the economy to intensive development.

Structural factors and conditions of intensification have also been 'played out' on this model. Here the close overlapping and mutual influence of individual factors of intensification on each other became clear. Thus the fall in the coefficient of fuel and raw material consumption per unit of production caused a significant growth in productivity and an improvement in the rate of growth of returns to capital investment and the capital-output ratio. This was related to the fact that the fuel and raw material branches are more labour intensive, and by reducing the coefficient of their consumption by, say, 0.1% we can free 0.2%–0.3% of the work force employed in its production.

At the same time these branches are the most capital intensive and therefore a 0.1% saving in fuel and raw materials frees 0.3%–0.4% capital investment. The extra work force freed and capital investment saved from the fuel and raw material branches and directed to other sectors of development of the economy, would make a significant additional impact. Acceleration thus occurs as a result of savings in fuel and raw materials: an additional fall in material input into social product by 0.1% a year and an increase in the average rate of growth of the national income up to 0.4%.

The model also revealed the quantitative effect of the rate of change of the capital-output ratio on the rates and proportions of development of the national economy. The growing cost-effectiveness of development of the Soviet economy through the improvement in the capital-output ratio was explained as a result. This relation is closely linked to the relationship between the fund for consumption and the fund for accumulation, and also to the proportional relations between rates of growth of production of means of production and of the production of goods for consumption.

Differing calculations have shown the possibility for a significant convergence between the rate of growth of means of production and of the production of goods for consumption without a fall in the rates of accumulation if necessary material consumption falls and the capital-output ratio improves. This conclusion has appeared crucial for the present situation, insofar as the profound technological reconstruction of all branches of production which is being undertaken has necessitated keeping rates of productive accumulation at a fairly high level.

In life we are always coming up against objective contradictions: the combination of high rates of growth in living standards for the population on the one hand and the implementation of large capital investments for applying the achievements of the scientific and technological revolution in production on the other. In present circumstances the intensive renewal of the basic capital stock is an imperative. But this requires higher levels of amortization and productive accumulation, which in turn reflects on the rate of growth of the resources available for consumption goods and other sectors.

Calculations using the dynamic inter-branch model have shown the possibility of accelerating Soviet socio-economic development on the basis of increased cost-effectiveness of social production. It is possible and necessary to resolve simultaneously a dual task: to transfer the economy onto the path of intensive development through scientific and technological progress and implement a profound change in direction in the economy towards meeting social needs and improving the well-being of the Soviet people.

It goes without saying that the dynamic inter-branch model is a powerful but only an auxiliary instrument in making forecasts of future development. Moreover, the version of the model described here is fairly limited. It is beyond the range of the model, at the stage of planning its parameters, to include the trends in scientific and technological progress, but the mobilization potential of organizational, economic and social factors can be calculated in relation to expenditure of resources and use of labour. Technical progress is set exogenously. Currently, work is being undertaken principally on new types of dynamic models which contain alternative technologies, so that the models' solutions to problems will simultaneously provide recommendations for the development of more effective uses of technology.

The version of a dynamic inter-branch model described here is aimed above all at the calculation of material proportions in the development of the national economy. Under the old administrative system of management which predominated for many years, this model could possibly have been sufficient. But now a radical reform of management is being undertaken and a transition to economic methods is being implemented under which the role of money, credit, prices and monetary circulation will increase. In such conditions new elements must be built in, the dynamic inter-branch model must be supplemented by financial relationships. The model should determine the size of money-related demand, and balance the volume of production of means of production and the volume of goods consumption with this money-related demand. One variant of this model has been built at the Institute of Economics and Organization of Industrial Production (Siberian Section of the Academy of Sciences). It has made possible the characterisation in quantitative form of the disproportions between monetary circulation and material and economic turnover, and the tracing of the sources of surplus money within the system. Such a model in an expanded form may be an important support and financial basis for discovering the optimal path of development for the economy.

It would be wrong to undertake all work on macro-modelling of the economy on the basis of only a dynamic inter-branch model. The use of special macro-models, including econometric models, can prove more useful for other purposes. Econometric models are especially important in aggregate financial planning. Such models also have already been developed, some of them at the Institute. For more comprehensive long-term calculations of material and economic proportions, a model of optimal inter-branch balances of productive capacities is a useful instrument. Such models have been used by the Institute for 15 years already.

One further observation may be noted in conclusion. Dynamic inter-branch models have been set out here in the form in which they were developed and used in the work of the Institute. They are being set out here because the author used them extensively as head of the Laboratory for Mathematical Economic Research of this Institute (1961–6) and as Director of the Institute (1967–85).

At the same time reference must be made to the fact that dynamic inter-branch models were developed and used by the Scientific

Research and Economic Institute of the State Planning Office (Gosplan) of the USSR, which was the first in the Soviet Union to introduce inter-branch models of planning. Workers at the Central Mathematical Economics Institute of the Academy of Sciences also made a large contribution to the working out of inter-branch models. There are many other models being designed by macro-economists in the Soviet Union.

Our intention here was not to familiarize the reader with the workings and use of macro-economic models in the USSR but to explain, based on the example of just one of these models, the dynamic inter-branch model, how it may be applied to forecasting the future.

APPENDIX 2

MATHEMATICAL ECONOMIC RESEARCH INTO THE PROBLEM OF COMBINING CENTRALISATION IN THE DEVELOPMENT OF THE NATIONAL ECONOMIC SYSTEM WITH INDEPENDENCE OF ITS SEPARATE PRODUCTIVE UNITS

This study starts from the fact that the national economy is a complex system made up of a large number of inter-related economic organisations, each of which can be interpreted as a sub-system of this complex system. As applied to the whole economy this problem can be defined as one of relating local optima, obtained through the attainment of separate goals by each economic organisation, to the overall economic optimum. The main problem in considering local optima is to ensure their consistency with the interest of the national economy as a whole. This is a crucial test for a socialist eonomic system.

Public ownership unites all of society's economic units and directs their development towards a single end. Strictly speaking, the single objective function of the economy rests on the form in which public ownership is realised as the expression of the unity of the socialist economy.

At the same time public ownership is localised and its individual parts are transferred to the possession, use and management of specific economic organisations. Local interests arise in every economic organisation or, more accurately, in each working collective within this organisation.

Therefore the general problem lies in defining the conditions under which every sub-system (i.e. separate economic organisation) – choosing the optimal variables from the numerous ones available to it according to local criteria – will select just the optimal variables that correspond to the needs of the whole system, determined by global criteria.

Each local sub-system is linked to others. Ther interrelation between sub-systems is reflected in the existence of global constraints, common to all or to some groups of the sub-systems. These constraints are primarily balanced-equations, which express the distribution of each sub-system's output in terms of direct inputs, productive accumulation, or non-productive consumption in other sub-systems.

There are also resource constraints, common to all groups of sub-systems, namely restrictions of capital investment, labour supply and natural resources, environmental conservation etc. In addition to global constraints there are, naturally, constraints specific to every individual sub–system.

The condition of the whole system will be viable if it complies with all the constraints, both local and global. There will be numerous permissible variables in any system. From these numerous variables it is possible, with the aid of the objective function of the system, to select the best state which corresponds to the highest value of this programme.

We will set out the mathematical formulation of this problem.

Let the complex system be composed of L sub-systems. The state of each sub-system can be described by the finite – dimensional vector. We will number the sub-systems with the whole numbers: $\ell = 1, 2,...,L$

Then the condition $\ell - u$ of the sub-system can be described by the vector $\bar{x}_\ell$ of the dimension n_ℓ. Let us assume that there is a set L of vectors $\bar{x}_\ell$ describing the state of the sub-systems of the system being considered.

Then their aggregation, vector $\bar{x} = (\bar{x}_1,....,\bar{x}_\ell,...,\bar{x}_L)$, with the dimensions $n = \sum_{\ell=1}^{L} n\ell$ describes the state of the whole system.

We will signify the optimally admissible state of the system by
and write it as the composition $\overset{\Lambda}{x}=\{\overset{\Lambda}{x_1},....,\overset{\Lambda}{x_\ell},...,\overset{\Lambda}{x_L}\}$, where by
$\overset{\Lambda}{x}\left(\ell=1,....,L\right)$ is meant the state $\ell-u$ of the sub-system, corresponding to the optimal state of the whole system.

The task of communicating the optimal state of particular executants, can, as we know, be resolved in various ways. There is the straight directive, administrative method by command, where each sub-system receives a detailed plan from above. Ideally the plan for each sub-system is calculated so that the whole system reaches an optimal state. This form of management in systems theory of automatic regulation is called "hard management". Apart from anything else it is distinguished by its inflexibility in response to systematic or accidental disturbances of the system, which can result in departures from the optimal state.

These deviations can be compensated for by the introduction of a system of negative feedback. This can take the form of local criteria, constructed by reference to the optimal state of the whole system. In this case each sub-system will endeavour to reach its optimal state in accordance with the optimum state of the overall system.

Proceeding further along this road, it is possible to try and formulate the task by "soft management". This means that each sub-system is allowed to develop according to its own internal incentives and is given its local objective function to implement. The problem lies only in formulating this local objective function in such a way that, while taking it into account, each local sub-system moves towards the global optimum, and so that within limits the aggregate states of the sub-systems would be admissible for the whole system and would guarantee the global optimum state of the economy.

The question arises as to whether there are such parameters of local objective functions on the basis of which we can identify local incentives, linked to the global optimum.

The well-known Soviet mathematician, K.A. Bargrinovskii, and the author have studied this problem mainly as applied to the models of linear programming. First, the following relatively simple theorem was demonstrated. If one discovers the optimal state of the whole global system and hence can determine the plan of each local sub-system, then this plan will ensure the local optimum by a local objective function, the parameters of which are composed of optimal evaluations obtained during the optimisation of the global system.

The reverse problem is more complex. If one formulates local objective functions through optimal evaluations of the global system, then it is questionable whether the aggregation of local incentives will give the global optimum. This shows that with linear restrictions there can be plurality in the resolution of local tasks, even within one sub-system. This can result in the aggregate of the sub-systems' optimal states not coinciding with the optimal state of the whole system. This may violate some of the global restrictions and exceed the permissible limits of the system. Therefore in the case of a linear programming model based on "soft management" (i.e. management purely by means of the parameters of local objective functions), the optima cannot be fully achieved. In addition to these parameters of objective functions some additional information must be given from above – from the global system, which would enable each sub-system to select the unique optimal solution, which corresponds to the global optimum. This can be done in a variety of ways.

Firstly, in addition to the basic regulating device in the form of parameters of objective functions, it is possible to give an extra regulator in the form, for example, of individual constraints on targets. Secondly, if a definite method of iterative reconciliation of the individual sub-system's local plans is set up, it may be possible to attain the global optimal plan. In particular, the iterative process can follow the type of iterative method of Dantzig–Woolf for the resolution of multi-level linear programming tasks. Thirdly, a non–linear penalty function can be added to a linear objective function, which will select from the aggregate of optimal states for particular local sub-systems the one solution which corresponds to the global optimum.

It is possible that there are other ways to reconcile the aggregate optima of local sub-systems with the global optimum of the whole system. Indeed we have considered models with linear constraints and come across the problem of the large number of optimal conditions in individual local sub-systems. In certain types of non-linear programming these difficulties cannot arise.

As is evident there seem to be two very different ways of achieving the global optimum and hence the implementation of a single objective function for the whole system (in our case the whole socialist economic system): one is through administrative methods – by allocative plans specifying targets and constraints for every sub-system; and the other by economic regulation and the use of economic methods. This is a way of establishing parameters of objective functions for local sub-systems. With an additional constraint, the aggregation of local optima gives the global optimum for the whole system.

An economic interpretation of these parameters of objective functions of the local sub-systems is contained in terms of prices for products, payment for resources, tax rates etc. – i.e. the use of economic indicators. For this, it is very important that these prices and payments are set in accordance with the global optimum of the whole system. And this means that prices must be formed on the basis of differential costs, as defined by V.V. Novozhilov in his classic work *Problems of measuring expenditure and resutls in optimal planning. (Problemi inzinereniya zatrat i resul'tator pri optimal'nom planirovanii).*

The theory of optimisation also suggest a need to introduce payments for all types of resources used. This form of economic planning ensures the organic interaction of central control in the development of the whole national economy and the independence of its individual economic units and organisations. It is a question of the *system of democratic centralism.* This system, on the one hand, is opposed to an excessively centralised administrative system of management with its institutional and bureaucratic distortions, absence of sufficient freedom for taking economic decisions by the basic productive collectives; and on the other hand has to respond to the conflict of interests of various branches of management, work collectives etc.

The principle of democratic centralism is opposed not only to a rigidly centralised system, but to a system oriented purely towards the market, with the free play of prices etc. Such a system cannot be socialist because there is no place in it for unitary socialist ownership. Everybody's interests conflict.

A theoretical analysis at the level of a model has shown at the same time that a centralised system of management which is not rigid can be introduced, yet under which development will be consistently socialist and socialist ownership can be succesfully realised. This system can be implemented through the centralised setting of economic proportions, finance and credit facilities and prices. It is only important that for basic goods of key significance these proportions, conditions and prices should be set on the basis of national economic interests. Then in conditions of enterprise independence, full self-accounting, self-financing and self-manage- ment – the development of each economic unit of socialist society can be realised in the interest of the whole society. This will be economic management through economic interests.

INDEX